I DON'T
BELIEVE IT,
BUT IT'S TRUE
A YEAR IN BOXING

# BOOKS BY THOMAS HAUSER

### General Non-Fiction
Missing
The Trial of Patrolman Thomas Shea
For Our Children (with Frank Macchiarola)
The Family Legal Companion
Final Warning: The Legacy of Chernobyl (with Dr. Robert Gale)
Arnold Palmer: A Personal Journey
Confronting America's Moral Crisis (with Frank Macchiarola)
Healing: A Journal of Tolerance and Understanding
Miscellaneous
With This Ring (with Frank Macchiarola)
A God To Hope For
Knockout (with Vikki LaMotta)

### About Boxing
The Black Lights: Inside the World of Professional Boxing
Muhammad Ali: His Life and Times
Muhammad Ali: Memories
Muhammad Ali: In Perspective
Muhammad Ali & Company
A Beautiful Sickness
A Year At The Fights
Brutal Artistry
The View From Ringside
Chaos, Corruption, Courage and Glory
The Lost Legacy of Muhammad Ali
I Don't Believe It, But It's True

### Fiction
Ashworth & Palmer
Agatha's Friends
The Beethoven Conspiracy
Hanneman's War
The Fantasy
Dear Hannah
The Hawthorne Group
Martin Bear & Friends
Mark Twain Remembers
Finding The Princess

I DON'T
BELIEVE IT,
BUT IT'S TRUE
A YEAR IN BOXING

THOMAS
HAUSER

SPORT
CLASSIC BOOKS

www.sportclassicbooks.com

Published in the United States of America by Sport Media Publishing
Inc., Wilmington, Delaware, and simultaneously in Canada.

For information about permission to reproduce selections from this
book, please write to:

Permissions
Sport Media Publishing, Inc.,
55 Mill St., Building 5, Suite 240
Toronto, Ontario, Canada, M5A 3C4
www.sportclassicbooks.com

Cover design: Paul Hodgson
Cover photo: Don King, by Holger Keifel
Interior design: Greg Oliver

ISBN: 1-894963-50-4
ISBN-13: 978-1-894963-50-3

Library of Congress Cataloging-in-Publication Data

Hauser, Thomas.
I don't believe it, but it's true : another remarkable year in boxing / by
Thomas Hauser.
p. cm.
ISBN 1-894963-50-4 (pbk.)
1. Boxing. I. Title.

GV1133.H3444 2006
796.83–dc22
2006003068


Printed in Canada

*To Robert Waterman
and the rest of the team at Secondsout
for giving me the opportunity to
write what I want to write*

# AUTHOR'S NOTE

*I Don't Believe It, But It's True* contains the articles about professional boxing that I authored from October 2004 through December 2005. The one exception is a piece entitled "A Holiday Season Fantasy" which is not included but can be found in the recently-published book, *The Lost Legacy of Muhammad Ali*. The articles I wrote about the sweet science prior to October 2004 have been published in *Muhammad Ali & Company*, *A Beautiful Sickness*, *A Year at the Fights*, *The View From Ringside*, and *Chaos, Corruption, Courage, and Glory*.

Special thanks are due to Secondsout.com and the *New York Sun*, under whose aegis most of the articles in this book first appeared.

# TABLE OF CONTENTS

# ROUND 1

# FIGHTS AND FIGHTERS

*In all the years I'd covered boxing, I'd never had the chance to talk at length alone with Oscar De La Hoya. But in 2005, we had two long sessions together. This article was the result.*

# OSCAR DE LA HOYA: A PERSONAL PORTRAIT

One gauge of celebrity status is name recognition. Like Madonna Ciccone and Oprah Winfrey, Oscar De La Hoya is a first-name phenomenon.

"Oscar" has engaged in 27 world championship bouts. He has entered the ring 21 times to face men who held world titles and participated in 16 pay-per-view fights that engendered $439,300,000 in pay-per-view buys.

There are times when Oscar's life has looked easy. It hasn't been, in or out of the ring. Now his days as an active fighter are dwindling down, and it's worth taking another look at this man of contradictions.

De La Hoya is a gentle man in a violent sport. He's more complex than most people imagine, and gives the impression of bruising easily on the inside.

As an adolescent, Oscar's life was built around the sweet science. "There was a time when I was fourteen or fifteen," he acknowledges, "when I realized that someday I could make a living from boxing. At that point, I began to focus more on boxing than on school. But even then, one of my aspirations was to someday become an architect. I enjoyed architectural drafting classes in school. Now, when I go to Europe, the castles and cathedrals are still fascinating to me. I think about the people who built them and how long they took to build. When I was in the Sistine Chapel, I put myself back in time and imagined myself in Michelangelo's situation and asked myself, 'How did he do this? How many people were helping?'"

The most positive influence in Oscar's early life was his mother. "We grew up humble," he says. "We learned to amuse ourselves by being around family, and the heart of our family was my mother. My mother was very outgoing and very energetic. She always had her make-up on and cleaned the home every day. She taught me to be a gentleman and to be polite with everyone. She never sat me down and lectured me on rules for life. She taught by example. It was important to her that everybody else was happy. The last person she thought of was herself. She made sure that each of us got up in the morning and went off to school happy every day."

When Oscar was in his mid-teens, his mother contracted breast cancer. She died at age 39.

"There's one moment with my mother that sticks out in my mind," Oscar recalls. "She was battling cancer. She'd already had chemotherapy and her hair was falling out. I was walking home from high school. My mother was sitting on the front porch with the radio on. She was singing a song called *Noah, Noah* by a Latin singer named Juan Gabriel. I started singing and dancing with her, and I could see that she was happy despite the pain. That was a very special moment for me. That's the best memory I have of my mother."

"I was seventeen when my mother passed away," De La Hoya continues. "I was heartbroken. Nothing mattered to me anymore. I thought seriously about not finishing high school, even of dropping out of boxing. Not one day passes that I don't think about my mother. And to be honest, there are still times when it's a lonely world without her. But I feel that I was blessed to have her in my life, and I believe she's still looking out for me."

Two years after his mother's death, De La Hoya won a gold medal at the 1992 Barcelona Olympics. "That moment will stay with me forever," he says. "It was my most satisfying moment ever in boxing." At that point, he toyed with the idea of retiring from the ring because, in his words, "My mother's dream for me had been fulfilled." But the siren call of professionalism was too great to ignore.

Wealth and greater glory followed. There was also a lot of pain.

"Once, I was at a party," Oscar remembers. "This was at a time when it seemed like I had everything. I was young. I was undefeated. I had money. I'd just moved into my own home. People at the party were laughing and having fun. And I missed my mother. I felt so lonely. I remember asking myself, 'Why isn't my mother here? Why are all these people around me? I don't want these people around me.' I looked out the window and started crying."

Meanwhile, De La Hoya's ring legend was growing.

"Oscar is one of the most naturally-gifted fighters I've ever seen," says trainer Emanuel Steward, who worked with De La Hoya for the David Kamau and Hector Camacho fights. "When Oscar fights on his toes, he reminds me of Sugar Ray Robinson. What they have in common is, Ray punched best from his toes, and Oscar punches best from his toes. It's the opposite of what you'd expect and I don't understand it completely, but it has to do with rhythm. When Oscar stands flat-footed, he loses his punching-power."

De La Hoya's first defeat as a pro was a loss by decision at the hands of Felix Trinidad. "That's still the loss that hurts the most," he says, "because I really feel that I did not lose that fight. Yes, there were those two rounds at the end when I just boxed. But all that means is it hurts for two reasons: because I could have done more and because of the injustice of it."

"After the loss to Trinidad," Oscar continues, "I was angry; I was sad. When you're undefeated, it's really really difficult to lose. Then I decided that life goes on and I just had to deal with it. But what happened in the Trinidad fight started me thinking seriously about someday changing the business of boxing."

Hence, Golden Boy Promotions. De La Hoya has extensive business interests that include endorsement contracts, real estate holdings, and media-entertainment ventures. But his most visible financial under-taking to date has been his boxing promotional company.

Much of the success of Golden Boy Promotions is based on De La Hoya the fighter. But the company has a good infrastructure. Unlike Roy Jones and Lennox Lewis (two other elite fighters who established promotional entities), Oscar devotes an enormous amount of time to promoting fights. And Golden Boy is about more than Oscar. Bernard Hopkins, Marco Antonio Barrera, Shane Mosley, Oscar Larios, and myriad other fighters are under contract.

De La Hoya has also funded numerous charitable initiatives. The Cecilia Gonzalez De la Hoya Cancer Center in East Los Angeles offers free mammograms for low-income women and community programs on health awareness. The Oscar De La Hoya Youth Center provides free boxing instruction for local youths, but a requirement of membership is that participants stay in school and maintain their grades. Another foun-dation funded by De la Hoya hands out college scholarships in amounts as high as $20,000. And recently, De La Hoya donated the land for what will be the first public high school to be built in East Los Angeles in several decades.

"I've said for years," De La Hoya notes, "that my biggest heroes are school teachers. A good school teacher is like another parent."

"Talking is one thing," adds Richard Schaefer (chief executive officer of De La Hoya's business empire). "Action is another. Oscar has made a substantial seven-figure charitable commitment and helped literally thousands of people in a hands-on way."

"The community work is central to who I am," says De La Hoya. "I want to get across the idea in the community that all children have some golden boy or golden girl in them."

Golden Boy. The moniker has been affixed to Oscar for as long as the public has known him. Good looks, charisma, and skill don't necessarily go together. But De La Hoya is the whole package. He's clean-cut with no body-piercings or tattoos. Men admire him; teenage girls adore him. He has always had an understanding of what the public wants. He's conscious of the image he projects. And he delivers.

De La Hoya is a superb ambassador for boxing. He is important to the sweet science precisely because he matters to people who don't care about the sport. He is their window onto boxing and, when they look at him, the view is good.

De La Hoya works a room as well as anyone. Many high-profile athletes arrive late for functions, sit at a table surrounded by body-guards, and talk only with people they already know and feel comfort-able with. Oscar is almost always on time. Once he arrives, he moves from person to person, saying hello to everyone.

In public, De La Hoya talks with fans, poses for pictures, and signs autographs. "It's tiring sometimes," he admits. "I'll be out on the street with my wife. We'll just want to be alone, and people will come over to me constantly. But when it doesn't happen, if I go somewhere and no one comes up to me, I miss it. So I guess you can say that I love it, I hate it, and I can't live without it."

"I would have loved to have met Elvis Presley," Oscar adds, offering a bit more insight into his psyche. "He was the King. It's very interesting to me; the way he grew up, the demons he battled, how he handled the pressure and how, after a while, it became a burden he couldn't carry."

It's hard to make the transition from a golden boyhood to adulthood, but De La Hoya has done it well. He has matured from boxing's version of a child star into a man. And he has done it in the glare of the spot-light with the public watching every move.

"I've grown up," says Oscar. "I'm less naive than before. I stopped the party scene a long time ago and started spending more time with family and real friends. I'm not perfect. Sometimes, I think about what I would say if I could talk to my mother again. First, I'd get off my chest the mistakes and bad decisions I've made. I'm married now with a wonderful wife. We're expecting a baby boy in December. I'm doing LaMaze classes and experiencing morning sickness with her. As a father, I'm going to be there every day I possibly can. But I had two children out-of-wedlock, not with my wife, before I was married. They're beau-tiful children; I adore them. But I grew up with a solid family, and Jacob and Atiana [ages 7 and 6] are entitled to that too. I try to be a good father to them, but it's not the same. And there were other times when my head was turned by fame and fortune. Maybe the best way to say it is that I've made mistakes in my life, but they were innocent mistakes and I've grown from them."

Critics say that De La Hoya is too carefully programmed; that he's too perfect. "There's Oscar the person, Oscar the fighter, Oscar the image, and Oscar the product," they snipe. "Oscar smiles whether he wants to or not."

But it's more complicated than that. De La Hoya takes his craft seriously, whether he's fighting or promoting. And unlike many of today's superstar athletes, he believes that fame brings added responsibilities. He feels that he has a responsibility to boxing, a responsibility to society, and a responsibility to himself to act and project himself in a positive manner. "I understand that I'm a role model," he says. "I accepted that a long time ago and I've embraced it as part of my obligation to the community."

"I've learned to not take media criticism personally," Oscar continues. "Seven or eight years ago, I would have said 'I hate the media; there are people in it who are always bashing me.' Now I understand that, when someone writes something negative about me, it's part of the game. Media criticism will destroy you if you take it personally, so now I play with it. I stay away from politics. Some people criticize me for that, but it's a choice I've made. I have my views, but politics can be very sensitive. I've struggled so hard to get fans and people behind me for what I want to accomplish that it would be a mistake to support one party publicly and have the other party against me."

Still, when a fighter gets in the ring, glitz and glory don't lessen the impact of punches. The key to it all is that the Golden Boy can fight.

"One of the things that bothers me most," Oscar says, "is that very few people really understand what it means to be a fighter. I hate it when I hear someone say, 'That fighter doesn't have guts.' I hate that; it really ticks me off. I don't care if you're a world champion six times over or a four-round fighter who just got knocked out in thirty seconds of your first professional fight. To step inside that ring, you have to have guts."

"But people get these crazy ideas," De La Hoya continues. "I went on my own roller-coaster ride to gain acceptance from Mexican-American fight fans. It was very difficult and frustrating. There were times when I felt like shouting, 'I can be your hero too.' And there were times, like my fights against Ike Quartey and even against Fernando Vargas, when I fought more aggressively and took more risks than I should have to please those fans."

At present, De La Hoya doesn't appear to be living the lifestyle of a man who plans to fight again. He weighs more and exercises less than in the past. He has homes in California and Puerto Rico (his wife's native land), although he complains that, at times, it feels like he lives on a plane. That, of course, leads to the question of whether his fighting days are done.

"I don't know if I'm going to fight again or not," Oscar acknowledges "I have an odd relationship with boxing. Boxing took me to a better life, and I love being in the ring. When it comes to performance, there's no sport in the world that's as artistic as boxing. It takes genius to win a championship fight at the highest level. Boxing is a love I have that will never go away. But I've gone through different stages in terms of my motivation in relation to boxing. At first, I was fighting to please my father. Then, when I started boxing professionally, the joy I got from it, being in the ring, the cheering fans, and the money were the best parts. After that, there was a time when I did it for the belts. Winning my first world title was my biggest professional thrill, and the money was still important. Now I'm doing it for history. The money doesn't matter anymore."

"The only reason I would fight again," De La Hoya continues, "is to erase the memory of losing my last fight. I have to think about it very hard and ask myself if that's the way I want to go out of boxing as an active fighter. My last two fights were at 160 pounds, and I'm not happy with either of them. Fighters are like cars. At some point, the gas tank is empty. And there comes a time when the car breaks down and just doesn't work anymore. I can't be a boxer for my entire life. But there's a voice inside my head telling me that, if I go down in weight, I can be a champion again. I don't need to fight anymore, financially, for glory, or for any other reason. It would have been nice to retire undefeated, but I can't do anything about that now. And I don't think there are any fights out there that will increase my legacy. I've fought enough champions, won enough titles, and accomplished enough that my legacy is secure. And I hate getting hit. Getting hit hurts; it damages you. I have no fear of boxing. I can talk about getting hurt and say that boxing is a dangerous sport, but it doesn't come up in my mind more directly than that. When a fighter trains his body and mind to fight, there's no room for fear. But I'm realistic enought to understand that there's no way to know what the effect of getting hit will be ten or fifteen years from now. I've been asking myself for years, 'How much longer will I box?' And the answer is, I don't know."

Oscar De La Hoya came along at a time when he was desperately needed by boxing. He kept the sport afloat with his skill and charisma, but was unable to bring it to safe harbor. Still, as he himself says, "Boxing is a never-ending story. New fighters keep coming along.

Opponents keep popping up. The next superstar is always on the way."

Then Oscar adds, "Whatever comes next for me, as far as boxing is concerned, I have no regrets. I would never change what I've accomplished and the history I've made."

There are journeys still to come.❏

*For most of 2005, the heavyweight division was dominated by a man who wasn't there.*

# LENNOX LEWIS: 2005

Lennox Lewis is happy. There's a look of joy on his face. The former heavyweight champion is in a conference room at the Trump International Hotel in Manhattan, playing with his nine-month-old son, Landon.

"Fatherhood is everything I thought it would be and more," says Lewis. "One day, I'm watching Landon learn to lift himself up and stand on his own. Then he's walking. And now, the beginnings of language. Every moment is precious to me."

Landon is exuberant and cute. Clearly, he has bonded with his father. His favorite word is "da-da" and one of his favorite pastimes is pulling on his father's dreadlocks.

"I'm looking forward to the responsibilities of fatherhood," Lennox said last summer, shortly after Landon was born. "Landon comes into the world completely vulnerable with no ability to make choices. I'm one of the two people most responsible for shaping his life, and I'm looking forward to protecting him and making the early decisions that guide him. I want to teach Landon how to give. I want to give him a base so he knows the difference between right and wrong because values are the key to life. I want him to understand the human condition. I want him to know about soup kitchens and homeless shelters and to have a social conscience."

Lennox's partner in that endeavor is his fiancee, Violet Chang. "V" was born in Jamaica, but grew up in the Bronx (one of five boroughs in New York City). She's in her late twenties; a college graduate and former beauty-pageant winner; charming, articulate, willing to voice her opinions, and smart. She and Lennox are well-matched and well-suited for the demands of parenthood.

Unlike many world-class athletes, Lennox left religion out of his public dialogue. But fatherhood requires constant examination of the world that Landon is growing up in. And Lewis has given considerable thought to religious values.

"Religion is a touchy subject," he says. "And I try not to throw stones. But I see people who claim to be very religious and talk a great deal about religion but don't seem to live by it. My belief is that God lives. He's part of us and the world around us."

"I think that religion is part of our core," Lennox continues. "I believe in Jesus. But I also believe that, in God's eyes, all people are of the same denomination. I hope for an afterlife, and I have faith in an afterlife. But I believe that our destiny is determined by how we live our lives; not by what religion we are. These thoughts are personal to me. I can't speak for anyone else. But I believe that religion is just a vehicle to get to our spirituality and give us guidance by whatever book we choose to live by."

As Lennox moves from active fighter to elder statesman, he's also giving considerable thought to the twin demons of bigotry and prejudice.

"I don't think it's human nature to be prejudiced," he says. "Look at young children. They play with each other and don't care about class, color, or religion. But too often, people take on the fears and prejudices of the people they grow up with. Instead of thinking for themselves, they follow blindly down the road of misunderstanding and fear."

How can society teach tolerance and understanding?

"One person at a time," Lennox answers. "You start at a young age. Kids are a blank slate; they sponge up everything. So you have dialogue; you communicate. And you teach by modeling the behavior that you want children to learn. My friends are all different. They're black, white, Indian, Chinese. I don't hang around people who are prejudiced. We're all on the same earth, and we have to learn to live together."

"We're all guilty at times of the tendency to assume things that might not be true," Lennox elaborates. "It used to be that I'd hear a white South African accent and immediately think, 'The oppressor.' But when you get to know someone on a personal level, you realize that he or she might not be like that at all. I get stopped sometimes just for driving a nice car. In Brooklyn, not long ago, the police took me out of my car and frisked me. People started gathering around, asking for my autograph, and then one of the cops realized who I was. After that, the police were apologetic. They said, 'Well, your car has Florida license plates and there have been a lot of reports of cars being stolen in Florida and brought up to New York.' But I've heard that one before."

"It's the way things are," Lennox says with a shrug. Then he smiles. "People have preconceptions. Last year, I was waiting at the airport for my limo and a little old lady, she was about eighty, asked me to put her bags in the trunk of her car."

What did he do?

"She was polite," Lennox recalls. "She seemed nice enough. I've gone into stores myself and approached someone for help, and it turned out that the person didn't work in the store. So I put her bags in the car."

Lewis today looks healthy and strong, albeit thirty pounds over his fighting weight. The high point of his career in terms of public esteem was his 2002 demolition of Mike Tyson. Everything he did in boxing after that was simply an end game. He fought once more, stopping Vitali Klitschko on cuts in June 2003. Then he retired from ring combat, in effect folding up his chess board and saying, "Game's over; I won."

Rumors of a comeback have surfaced periodically since then; most recently in a January 2005 article that quoted Lewis as saying he had agreed to a Klitschko rematch.

"That was bizarre," Lennox says. "But you have to know the full story. I was in Jamaica and saw this guy on my land with a camera. So I stopped him and asked what he was doing, and he said he was on vacation and heard I lived there and just wanted some pictures for the fun of it. He showed me the pictures he'd taken. I asked him to erase two and said he could keep the others. Then he asked if I was going to fight again. And I was playing with him. This wasn't an interview. This was some guy I'd found running around my property. So I told him, 'Yeah, they've offered me forty million dollars to fight Klitschko again. We're finishing up some secret negotiations. I still have to get in shape, but we'll fight before the end of the year.' And the next thing I know, it's in the *Sunday Mirror* and people all over the world are writing that I'm making a comeback. How could they write it without anyone contacting me for a confirmation?"

There will be no comeback.

"I fought Vitali Klitschko in real life and Wladimir Klitschko in *Ocean's Eleven*," Lennox notes. "That's enough. I've tried to make responsible decisions in my life, and retirement is one of them. It was time. I felt the winds changing. You spend a life in boxing, trying to make as much money as possible. And then, when you want to leave the game and you're on the way out, they push more money at you than you've seen before. But money isn't what drives me."

"I think Vitali and his brother are great people," Lennox says of the two men who, at various times, have been talked about as his successor. "Obviously, we had that boxing thing going on between us, but I like them both. As for who's the best heavyweight in the world right now, someone will have to prove himself. And that can only be done in the ring. It can't be decreed by HBO or Don King. No one is given greatness in boxing. You have to earn it and prove it again and again and again."

It's an unfortunate fact of life in boxing that too many fighters are beaten in the last round. They end their careers with no money and in declining health. In the final analysis, Lennox Lewis's greatest triumph might be that he retired as heavyweight champion of the world drenched in Vitali Klitschko's blood rather than his own.

Still, the mind plays funny games.

"I had a dream the other night," Lennox confides in closing. "In my dream, I was offered a hundred million dollars to fight Vitali Klitschko. Everyone was saying, 'A hundred million dollars; you've got to take it. A hundred million dollars! No one has ever made anything close to that before.' Finally, I agreed to the fight. There was a huge build-up. The whole world was watching. 'Is Lennox too old? Has he laid off too long?' The drama was incredible."

Lennox's face grows more animated.

"The fight began. I was fighting a good technical fight, but Vitali was strong in the early rounds. He was hard to hit, very awkward. It was a difficult fight. Then, in the sixth or seventh round, Vitali hit the wall, the dreaded stamina problem, and the tables turned."

How did it end?

"I don't remember," Lennox acknowledges. "I know I won, but I'm not sure if it was by decision or a knockout." Then he smiles. "But it was only a dream."❏

*There are few constants in boxing. But for the past thirty years, Don King has been one of them.*

# DON KING, HBO, AND THE HEAVYWEIGHT MUDDLE

Like a traveling salesman displaying his wares, Don King returned to Madison Square Garden on November 13, 2004. The promotion was labeled "Night of the Heavyweights" and offered some competitive heavyweight fights. But as is often the case in boxing, the action outside the ring was as compelling as the action inside it.

The fights took place against the backdrop of heated squabbling between King and HBO.

"I love HBO," King once said. "I helped build it." But at present, DK is upset that HBO is backing Vitali Klitschko as the true heavyweight champion to the detriment of his own heavyweight interests. It aggravates him that HBO rarely interviews him or shows him on camera. He doesn't like Larry Merchant's commentary. And he's troubled by the fact that HBO has more power to rearrange the landscape of boxing than he does. That power was most recently displayed when the cable giant enticed Antonio Tarver and Glencoffe Johnson to give up their light-heavyweight championship belts and fight one another after King had won a purse bid to promote a WBC title defense by Tarver against Paul Briggs.

In the past, King has voiced his frustration with comments like, "HBO thinks it runs the world . . . HBO is the Evil Empire . . . HBO covers its arrogance and its mistakes with money." Then, on the afternoon of the October 2nd fight between Felix Trinidad and Ricardo Mayorga, he exploded.

"I don't give a fuck about HBO," King declaimed, "because HBO doesn't give a fuck about me. I work my ass off for HBO and then I get kicked in the butt every fucking time. They smile to my face and then they manipulate things and stab me in the back. They try to steal my fighters and do everything they can to hurt me. I don't need this shit. I resent this shit. I'm tired of kissing HBO's fucking ass. Fuck HBO. They got me begging like a fucking vagrant, knocking on the fucking door."

King also claimed that HBO had announced inflated pay-per-view numbers for Oscar De La Hoya versus Bernard Hopkins to his detriment. He accused Merchant of "discriminatory remarks and outlandish hatred for everybody." And he closed with the broadside, "HBO wants to control boxing without having any of the responsibility or accountability that come with power. HBO is diminishing boxing in pursuit of its own selfish agenda to control the sport."

In response, HBO Sports president Ross Greenburg said simply, "I'm not going to get into a verbal sparring match with Don. We appreciate his ability as a promoter and hope to buy fights from him in the future. But the things he's saying now are ridiculous." And Merchant added, "Don's problem is that he thinks every fight is about him, and they're not."

But the verbal assaults continued. "The fans at home believe what you tell them if you keep telling them long enough," said Bob Goodman (a DKP vice president and King's point man on boxing). "HBO barrages the public with publicity that they're the heart and soul of boxing and their boxers are the best. The way they work at HBO is, if they can't control a fighter, the fans won't see him. The people at HBO are the ones who will ultimately kill boxing by destroying competition and free enterprise. Someday, when Don and Bob Arum leave the business, we'll all be at the mercy of HBO. And believe me, it will be 'no mercy'."

Then King himself poured more fuel on the fire with talk of creating a television boxing network that would feature live bouts, archival fight footage, martial arts matches, and hip-hop music.

"That's really the only way to go," King declared, "because you don't have to worry about someone sabotaging you or putting a knife in your back when you do it yourself. My channel will be a global channel. I'm looking for international partners. I have the greatest boxing library in the world. I have the press conferences, the up-close-and-personals, the human interest stories that give character to boxing. And I've been on top for thirty years, so I've got the fights. This isn't a dream; it's going to happen. I'm not going to be an indentured servant anymore."

Meanwhile, King's Madison Square Garden card highlighted the gruesome state of the heavyweight division. Give DK credit for taking his best heavyweights and matching them against one another. But the best he has are less than sterling.

The first pay-per-view fight of the night pitted Evander Holyfield against Larry Donald. For two decades, Holyfield has been one of the most compelling figures in boxing. He won his pro debut on a six-round decision over Lional Byarm at the Garden on November 15, 1984, and a glorious career followed. But Evander is now a shot fighter, and everyone except Evander knows it. Hence, the familiar Holyfield mantra:

- "The problems I had the last few years weren't about age. They were about my not doing the things I used to do in training camp and in my other preparation for my fights. You look at a champion and ask what it was that made him great. With me, it was my work ethic. And what happened was, I was with people who didn't believe in me, so they didn't push me hard enough in camp."

● "I'm not in denial about my age. I know how old I am, but I refuse to quit. And because of that, eventually I'll get everything I want. At one time, they said I shouldn't be in the game because I was too small, and then they realized that size don't make a difference. Now, they're looking at my age, and I've got to show them that age don't make a difference as long as one is willing to pay the price necessary to be the best. I still have a passion for the game. I go to sleep and wake up wanting to fight. You're only old when they throw dirt on you."

● "My goal is to retire as the undisputed heavyweight champion of the world. It's just a fact that I have to finish the right way. None of us choose our beginning, but we can choose our end. And at the end, if I retire as undisputed heavyweight champion, I will have had a perfect career."

● "In life, there are always more doubters than people that have faith in you. They say you can't do it, and I understand that they're only telling me that because it's something that they wanted and they didn't do it and they're trying to talk me into being like them. But I'm gonna do it whether they say I can or not."

● "Don't sit here and make people feel sorry for me. The best is yet to come. You ain't seen the best yet."

Still, reality has a way of seeping in. Evander had headlined every fight card he'd been on since 1986. This time, he was in the opening act.

And then there's the matter of money. Evander needs it, despite having made well over $100,000,000 in his ring career. His Atlanta mansion is costly to maintain and will be difficult to sell if and when the time comes. He lost a small fortune investing in a Christian television network and a rap music venture. There have been two divorces. And for a while, there was a serious gambling problem.

Holyfield was paid $8,000,000 for his 1990 victory over James "Buster" Douglas. This was the first time in 24 fights since then that his purse was under $2,000,000. Evander said he was getting $1,500,000 for the Donald fight. Contracts filed with the New York State Athletic Commission put the figure at $1,000,000. There were whispers that the true number was $500,000.

It's hard to imagine Holyfield being in a dull fight, but this one was. Only the fact that Evander was a participant gave it drama.

Larry Donald is a journeyman fighter. He's 37 years old and had won only three fights in the past four-and-a-half years. Moreover, those wins had come against opponents with a combined record of 5 victories and 28 losses in their most recent outings.

Still, Donald dominated from start to finish. Evander knew what to do. He just couldn't do it. His balance was bad and his timing was worse. His trademark aggressiveness was gone, and he got hit with right-hand leads all night. He was weak and unable to manhandle Donald in the clinches as he used to do to opponents. There were times when Larry was wide open for counters, and Evander simply couldn't pull the trigger. All totaled, Donald outlanded Holyfield 260 to 78. Mercifully, he doesn't have a big punch. The judges scored it 119-109, 119-109, and 118-109. The judge who gave two rounds to Evander was being kind to him.

One image from the contest lingers. Midway through round one, Evander threw a punch, stumbled, and fell.

There's a particularly painful memory for baseball fans who grew up watching Willie Mays ply his trade in centerfield for the New York Giants and later in San Francisco. At the end of his career, Mays returned to New York for one last season with the Mets. Except he wasn't Willie Mays anymore. And in the World Series, chasing a routine fly ball, he fell down. Mays was 42 years old at the time; the same age that Holyfield is now.

Next up in the Garden was Hasim Rahman versus Kali Meehan.

Meehan is an immensely likeable, big strong guy without world-class skills or a heavyweight punch. King touted him as the "uncrowned WBO champ" by virtue of his recent disputed-decision loss to Lamon Brewster. But given the fact that Brewster has won only one round convincingly since knocking out 309-pound Joe Lenhart twenty months ago, that credential hardly struck terror into Rahman's heart.

Meehan was brought in on the assumption that he'd lose to Rahman. "It's obvious that he's more experienced," Kali acknowledged. "He has all the advantages in his background and training, but I can't go into the ring thinking like that. Few people gave me a chance against Brewster, and I expected that. Few people give me a chance against Rahman, and I expected that, too. But it doesn't matter what I'm brought in as. It matters how I perform."

"I like Kali Meehan; we're cool," Rahman said in response. "But when the bell rings, I'm going to knock his head off."

That's pretty much what happened. People keep expecting big things from Rahman and not getting them. He'd been 4-3-1 in eight fights since his 2001 victory over Lennox Lewis. Part of the problem is that Hasim tends toward laziness in the gym. He also eats too much and has fought at weights as high as 259 pounds.

This time, Rahman came in at 232 pounds, his second-lowest weight in eight years. He also remembered to bring his jab, which he sometimes forgets. In the second round, he used the jab to bloody Meehan's nose. Then he began the process of chopping his opponent down. Finally, in round four, he trapped Kali in a corner and battered him like a heavy bag. Meehan's seconds stopped the action at the end of the stanza.

Then it was time for the title fights. Chris Byrd and Jameel McCline came first.

Byrd is the IBF champion. But in recent defenses against Fres Oquendo and Andrew Golota, he needed questionable scoring from the judges to keep his crown. "Most boxing fans don't understand the sport," Byrd said of those fights. "I don't worry anymore whether people appreciate me. Maybe I'll be appreciated after my career is over."

But for a guy who "doesn't get hit," Byrd has been getting hit a lot lately. Also, he's 34 years old. And fighters who rely on reflexes and speed, as he does, age more quickly in the ring than punchers.

Byrd said he was looking forward to fighting McCline, who towered above him and outweighed him by 56 pounds (270 to 214). "Muscles don't turn you into a puncher," Chris said. "I know Jameel very well. I've been at a lot of his fights. He has good hand speed, a good jab, and he's a big man with power. But I know how to shut down every opponent's game. I love fighting these big guys. It's exciting; it's a challenge. It's going to be like a piranha against a whale. The piranha is constantly biting away." Then Byrd added a cautionary note. "But the whale could end it all in one big gulp."

On paper, Byrd was a good opponent for McCline. Jameel is huge; but often in the ring, he thinks like a small heavyweight to the point of being intimidated by his opponent. Byrd's size and lack of power were expected to give McCline confidence.

At first, that's the way things unfolded. In round two, Jameel trapped Byrd in a corner and missed badly with a volley of punches, then landed a solid right hand that put Chris down. Around that time, McCline also seemed to realize that Byrd might be able to sting him with punches but would be unable to take him out. Thus, for a while, Jameel got brave and mixed his punches nicely. But he tired in the middle rounds and reverted to fighting like a small heavyweight. Byrd came on late for a 115-112, 114-113, 112-114 split-decision triumph. This observer scored it 115-112 in favor of McCline.

Then came the main event. John Ruiz versus Andrew Golota for the WBA title.

Ruiz has spent years trying to overcame the stigma of his 19-second knockout obliteration at the hands of David Tua. Then, just when he was beginning to gain acceptance, he was dominated by Roy Jones. "I've always been a worker, but my confidence wasn't always there," Ruiz acknowledged earlier this month. "In many fights, I never really had the strength, heart, and balls to fight. I never had the mentality to think, 'I'm the best.' The main thing I lacked, the thing I work on, is a champion knows every fight that he's going to win. I didn't have the mind of a champion."

"This is a perfect fight for me," Ruiz said, shifting his thoughts to Golota. "Is it going to be tough? Yes, every fight is tough. But like you've seen in a lot of other fights, Golota ends up quitting. What better opponent to have than someone who's going to quit as soon as I put the pressure on. Either he quits or I knock him out."

Meanwhile, given the tactics employed by each fighter in the past, the feeling among the boxing intelligentsia was that the Marquis of Queensberry rules were about to be broken. Indeed, there was a school of thought that Ruiz would try to win the fight by provoking Golota to the point where Andrew was disqualified for hitting below the belt. That's quite a fight plan: to go out and encourage an opponent who weighs 240 pounds to smash your testicles.

It's hard to land a good clean punch on Ruiz. But against Golota, John came out hard, throwing overhand rights, going for all the marbles. That left him open to a perfectly-timed right-hand counter in the second round. The blow landed flush on Ruiz's jaw and put him down. He rose but was hurt and went down again before the bell.

Then Ruiz reverted to form: clutching, grappling, holding, and mauling. In round four, referee Randy Neumann deducted a point from the champion for illegal blows to the back of the head. Meanwhile, Golota was responding in kind.

Eventually, the fight settled into a pattern, with Ruiz slipping Golota's jab and lunging forward with his head low like a fullback trying to work his way into the end zone. He also landed some effective body punches and, at one point, came close to head-butting Golota in the groin.

The judges scored it 114-111, 114-111, and 113-112 for Ruiz. That seemed odd, given the fact that he incurred a three-point deficit in the knockdown round, was penalized a point for rabbit-punching, and was outlanded by Golota 152 to 121. This observer scored it even at 113-113.

But there was a second plot-line to Ruiz-Golota. Eight years ago, Golota fought Riddick Bowe at Madison Square Garden and was disqualified for repeated low blows. A riot followed, with Golota's Polish countrymen and Bowe's African-American supporters assaulting one another. This time, both the Ruiz and Golota camps were warned in advance by Ron Scott Stevens (chairman of the New York State Athletic Commission) to be on their best behavior.

As Ruiz-Golota progressed, there were scattered fist-fights throughout the crowd. Meanwhile, after the first round, Norman Stone (Ruiz's manager-trainer) ran across the ring to confront Golota's corner over a perceived slight. Stone also screamed obscenities at referee Randy Neumann throughout the bout. Finally, Neumann advised Stevens, "I might want this guy ejected."

"You're the referee," Stevens told him. "Do what you have to do."

Then, in round eight, Neumann brought Ruiz to his corner to repair some loose tape on his glove. But Stone refused to do the job and berated the referee with another stream of profanity. At that point, Neumann told Stevens, "Ron, this guy's got to go."

Stone was led by security guards from the arena.

It's not uncommon for a manager to be ejected from a baseball game by an umpire. But it's rare for a trainer to be banished in boxing. This time, it was warranted.

"He can scream and curse at me all he wants," Neumann said afterward. "But when he interferes with the flow of fight, something has to be done."

Stone is lucky that he was ejected instead of additional points being taken away from his fighter. Two days after the fight, the NYSAC took further action against him, imposing a $1,000 fine and 60-day suspension.

So, where does it all leave boxing?

For starters, there won't be a war between King and HBO unless King wants one; and DK has nothing to gain by war right now.

King is frustrated by his inability to make money from his three heavyweight belts. In particular, it angers him that HBO has thrown its support behind Vitali Klitschko (the one titleholder he doesn't control) as the most credible of the four heavyweight champions.

"Klitschko is white," King complains. "That's the only credibility he's got. He's white and he's got HBO behind him. That's why he's where he is. Period, end of story."

The last time King left HBO, it was to form KingVision under the protective umbrella of a deal with Showtime for the services of Mike Tyson. But things are different now. The public doesn't care about King's heavyweights. The only real bullet in his gun is Felix Trinidad. So yes, Don would like more money for his fights and more support in selling his product; and he wants to be on camera more often. But HBO still writes the biggest checks in boxing, and no one else comes close.

Next, there's King's plan for the creation of a boxing network.

Certainly, he has the programming. A boxing network could begin like Classic Sports Network did, with an eight-hour cycle repeating three times each day. The core programming would be fights, live and on tape. Start with King-promoted main events. Add on thousand of clubs fights from around the world that are taped each year. Throw in DK's archives. And supplement the package with movies about boxing, documentaries, panel discussions, and interview shows.

But the economics, logistics, and the mechanics of the real world make it almost impossible to create a boxing network. For starters, there's a need for capital. Best estimates are that investors would have to be prepared to lose between $50,000,000 and $70,000,000 during the first five years. That's for a low-end, tape-driven, basic-cable network.

Next, a network needs distribution. And it's unlikely that a multi-system cable operator would give Don King (or anyone else) his own dedicated channel for a scandal-ridden niche sport with an aging fan base that can't draw more than a few commercial sponsors.

Moreover, King might be serious about starting a boxing network. But saying "I'm gonna do boxing, hip-hop, and martial arts" doesn't equal a serious business plan.

Clearly, there are opportunities for King to do business with the giant cable companies for video-on-demand. And somewhere down the road, an Internet boxing network is feasible. But for the moment, the most realistic appraisal of the situation comes from Seth Abraham, who has reigned in the past as president of HBO Sports and chief operating officer of Madison Square Garden.

"Don has two chances of forming a boxing network," says Abraham. "Slim and none, and slim just left town. To launch a cable network, you need ongoing corporate support. And corporate support simply isn't there for boxing at the present time. What Don is doing, really, is putting out a business card to the television community, saying 'I'm at war with HBO; do you have a home for me?' That's all. And if he doesn't find someone who gives him what he wants, he'll stay with HBO."

That, of course, leads to the question of what fight fans might see next in the heavyweight division on HBO. King's November 13th card resolved nothing. No one delivered a dominant performance and no new blood emerged to excite the public. The big winner, assuming he beats Danny Williams when they meet on December 11th, was Vitali Klitschko. Right now, by the process of attrition, Klitschko is probably the best of the bunch. But the truth is, at present, the heavyweight title is vacant. Today's championships are no more real than the faux diamonds and rubies in the various sanctioning-body belts.

King says he wants to promote an elimination tournament in 2005 to crown an undisputed heavyweight champion. But for the tournament to be credible, he needs the winner of Klitschko-Williams to participate. That's not likely to happen. DK doesn't control either fighter and probably wouldn't allow either of them into the tournament unless he had options on future fights. That leaves open the possibility of title-consolidation fights among King's three champions. But no one would pay much for those fights. The only way for a promoter to make big money in the heavyweight division today is to control THE champion or Mike Tyson. So look for King to throw mandatory challengers at Klitschko while he maintains the other three belts (and multiple title fights) for the forseeable future.

And that's it, except for one final note. On November 15th, the New York State Athletic Commission placed Evander Holyfield on indefinite suspension for "poor performance" in his losing effort against Larry Donald. The suspension is for medical reasons, which means that it must be honored by all members of the Association of Boxing Commissions. In order to be taken off suspension, Holyfield must undergo extensive medical testing under the supervision of the NYSAC and satisfy the commission that his recent performances have been an aberration. Alternatively, he could challenge the suspension in court.

"I have enormous respect and admiration for Evander Holyfield," Ron Scott Stevens said in announcing the action. "But as a regulator, my first obligation is to ensure the health and safety of all fighters. It should be apparent to anybody who follows boxing that Mr. Holyfield's skills and reflexes have declined to the point where it is no longer safe for him to continue in the ring."

It's sad when a great fighter loses his greatness. Evander Holyfield has enjoyed a career of legendary proportions. But he has won only two of his last nine fights and three fights in the past seven years.

"I know that I'm good enough not to get hurt," Holyfield said last week.

So did Muhammad Ali.❑

*On April 30, 2005, after an ugly pre-fight build-up, James Toney enjoyed his greatest moment of ring glory.*

# JAMES TONEY SHAKES UP THE HEAVYWEIGHT DIVISION

On March 29th, Don King appeared at the kick-off press conference for the April 30th WBA heavyweight title fight between John Ruiz and James Toney with Bello Nock at his side.

Nock is a clown with a pompadour of strawberry-blond hair that rises eight inches into the air. He's also star of this year's Ringling Brothers, Barnum & Bailey Circus, which had just opened at Madison Square Garden. That led to some uncharitable whispers regarding two clowns standing side-by-side with their hair reaching toward the heavens. But the overriding theme of the moment was, "Get the microphones ready. Don King, James Toney, and Norman Stone are coming to town."

Toney is a trash-talker. At the kick-off press conference, he told the assembled media, "The heavyweight division is garbage now. I'm coming in to clean up the garbage. Playtime is over with. Just let the bell ring, and I'll take care of him. We can do it the easy way or we can do it the hard way. And trust me; Ruiz don't want to do it the hard way. I got knockouts all the way from middleweight to heavyweight. I'm so powerful, I'm like a goddamn elephant. As soon as I hit him flush, he goes."

Asked for more, the bombastic Mr. T declared, "Fans come to see blood and guts, and that's what I give them. I'm a fighter. I hunt people down and destroy them. Trust me; when the bell rings, John Ruiz's last day as champion will come to a screeching halt. He's boring, so he's gotta go. I'm gonna knock Ruiz out; I promise. You'll never see this guy again, and you can all consider it a personal favor from James Toney."

There was a time when Toney seemed destined for greatness. He knocked out Michael Nunn for the IBF middleweight title in 1991 and successfully defended it six times. Next, he moved up in weight and KO'd Iran Barkley for the IBF super-middleweight crown. By late 1994, James was undefeated in 46 fights and near the top of most "pound-for-pound" lists. Then he fought Roy Jones and lost in a bout that Jones dominated from beginning to end.

Ruiz-Toney was James's chance to return to center stage. In the past decade, he'd had only one fight that the public cared about—an October 2003 demolition of Evander Holyfield. Injuries had kept him on the shelf for all but one fight (a desultory 12-round decision over Rydell Booker) since then.

Toney fights like a pit bull. He's tough, skilled, and takes a good punch. He's at his best on the inside, which was where everyone except Jones had wound up fighting Ruiz. And he's a counter-puncher who, like Bernard Hopkins, breaks people down and beats them up.

"I don't care about styles," Toney said when asked about Ruiz's grab-and-hold modus operandi. "Styles mean nothing to me. I've had 74 pro fights. I've seen every style in the world. Whatever he wants to do, I don't care. But I don't see him fighting me any different from the way he fights everyone else. He fights like he's retarded; hug and hold. And for me, it will be uppercut city. He'll have a bad case of whiplash when I'm done. I'll eat him up like Pac-Man all night."

The oddsmakers made Toney an 8-to-5 favorite. But Ruiz supporters noted that their man had been the underdog in five of seven previous title fights and lost only two of them. As far as they were concerned, Toney's victory over Holyfield was unimpressive in light of Evander's deterioration in recent years. And James's other signature triumph (his 2003 "Fight of the Year" struggle with Vassiliy Jirov) had lost its shine in the wake of Jirov's one-punch demolition at the hands of Michael Moorer. In other words, Toney had never beaten a quality fighter in his prime at more than 168 pounds.

Moreover, Toney is 36 years old (three years older than Ruiz) and had been through surgeries accompanied by long layoffs for a torn biceps and torn Achilles tendon during the previous year. Ruiz's style of holding, grabbing, wrestling, and mauling was expected to test James's fragile limbs. And while Toney is hard to hit cleanly, Ruiz doesn't hit cleanly. That's not his style. Every now and then, he might land a sneaky right hand flush, but that's about all. He does his damage by attrition, slowly wearing opponents down.

Then there was the matter of weight. Toney's suits are generously cut. But as the fight approached, he looked the way a boxer is supposed to look on the first day of training camp, not the last. Freddie Roach (James's trainer) said that his 5-foot-10-inch charge reported to camp at 260 pounds. Toney himself acknowledged, "I only had five weeks to prepare for this fight. I'm not in my best shape."

Ultimately, Toney weighed in at 233 pounds (to Ruiz's 241). Discount three pounds for the sweatsuit that James was wearing and he weighed 73 pounds more than the 157 he registered when he knocked out

Michael Nunn fourteen years ago. And James hasn't gotten any taller since then.

Thus, the general view prior to the fight was, Ruiz does more with less, and Toney does less with more. James knew exactly what to expect from Ruiz. If he hadn't prepared properly and went on to lose, he'd have only himself to blame.

But another thought was circulating as well.

Ruiz is the Rodney Dangerfield of boxing. He don't get no respect. The criticism starts with his personality. John plods onward through life with the appearance of total calm. That's disconcerting to some, who see dollars in fighters with a more Tysonesque persona.

"Everyone has a little crazy in them," Ruiz once said. "Boxing is one way to express it." But when asked about the meanness that a boxer is required to summon up in a fight, there was no reference to making opponents cry like a woman or pushing the bone of their nose into their brain. Instead, Ruiz said simply, "You can't be thinking about butterflies and rainbows when some guy is coming to kill you."

Then there's the matter of the way Ruiz fights; what Larry Merchant calls "the Greco-Roman style of boxing."

"It's not the prettiest style in the world," Ruiz acknowledged. "My main thing is to go out there and win. That's what boxing is. It's not about looking pretty."

Regardless, Ruiz's style makes for boring fights.

And most significantly, each time in the past that Ruiz neared public acceptance, he'd lost big. The first disaster came on a 1996 HBO card styled "Night of the Young Heavyweights" when he was obliterated by David Tua in nineteen seconds. Over the next seven years, he fought his way back to take the WBA title from Evander Holyfield and successfully defend it against Kirk Johnson. Then, just when Ruiz was gaining credibility with the public, he was totally outclassed by Roy Jones.

Subsequent to the Jones debacle, Ruiz defeated Hasim Rahman, Fres Oquendo, and Andrew Golota. "I'm fighting top fighters and having tough fights and coming out winning, but they don't want to give me credit for it," he complained before the Toney fight. "I'm fighting guys that they predicted to be the next heavyweight champion. I beat them, and then they just change their whole outlook on what they were thinking about the other guy."

Now, there was a feeling among the boxing establishment to the effect of, "Well, if John wins this one, we'll give him his due."

"The more I watch John Ruiz, the more impressed I am," IBF heavyweight champion Chris Byrd noted. "He finds ways to make you fight his fight. I have no idea how that happens, but he draws these guys in.

Just about the time you think he's going to start beating on you, he'll take a step back and start boxing. Then when you start boxing he says, 'Okay, time to get rough again.' You're off balance and uncomfortable and, next thing you know, he's hurt the guy."

"He's better than people think," Freddie Roach acknowledged. "It's weird, the way people look at him. All these other guys—Holyfield, Rahman, Golota, Johnson—they were supposed to beat him, but none of them did. Don't you think he had something to do with that? He's beaten some quality guys and he hasn't made the mistake of changing his style to please the public. I don't go by style. I go by whether you win your fights."

And Robert Cassidy Jr. wrote, "Here's the positive spin. Ruiz doesn't have Mao Zedong tattooed on his body. He has his children's names embroidered across his boxing trunks. His name hasn't shown up in the police blotter. Instead, he has started a charity that benefits the homeless. If you can't appreciate what he does in the ring, appreciate who he is outside of it. Do that and you just might start rooting for him."

And there was one more subplot. Ruiz is trained and managed by Norman Stone. A lot of people in boxing feel ambivalent about "Stoney." On the one hand, it would be nice if more managers were as loyal and fought as hard for their fighters as he does. But on the other hand, Norman can be a pain in the ass; and that's putting it politely.

Stone got into a fist-fight with Alton Merkerson (Roy Jones's trainer) at the weigh-in for their 2003 fight in Las Vegas. He was ejected from the corner midway through Ruiz's most recent bout (against Andrew Golota at Madison Square Garden). From time to time, his name appears on police blotters in his home state of Massachusetts. Stone sees demons and conspiracy theories everywhere.

James Toney carries a lot of turmoil inside. It's always bubbling near the surface, sometimes shooting out of him in machine-gun-like bursts. The difference between Toney and Stoney is that James can control himself but at times chooses not to. Norman, on the other hand, can't always control himself.

Their first confrontation came at the March 29th kick-off press conference.

"Toney's a phony," Stone shouted.

"So's your mother," James countered.

"Shut the fuck up."

"I don't play," Toney warned.

"Go play with yourself."

"Like with your mom last night?"

At that point, the two men had to be separated. It wouldn't be the last time. And the bottom line was, on top of everything else that the New York State Athletic Commission and Madison Square Garden had to worry about on fight night, they were concerned with potentially incendiary behavior by Toney and Stone.

At five o'clock on the night of the fight, Ron Scott Stevens (chairman of the New York State Athletic Commission) met, as is his custom, with the NYSAC personnel who would be working that evening. The inspectors assigned to the Toney and Ruiz corners had been carefully chosen. George Ward (a prison guard at Rikers Island for 21 years) would be with Toney. Felix Figueroa (a manager for the United States Postal Service at the Ansonia Station in Manhattan) got the nod for Ruiz. That seemed appropriate, given Stone's tendency to "go postal" under certain circumstances.

Ward and Figueroa would shadow their charges from the moment they entered Madison Square Garden until they left the arena. "You're not security," Stevens told them. "I don't want you getting in the middle of a fight. But by your presence, the way you position yourself and carry yourself, you can forestall a bad situation. Boxing should be conducted in a sportsmanlike manner. Let's try to maintain that standard tonight."

Four hours later, Stevens revisited the issue when he went to the fighters' respective dressing rooms with referee Steve Smoger. In the past, Smoger had worked four Toney bouts and two Ruiz fights, so he knew what to expect from the combatants.

There was a brief discussion in Ruiz's quarters about whether or not John should be required to trim his beard. Stone objected, and it was agreed that it was too late in the day to fairly impose that requirement.

"All right; let's move on," Stevens said. "Mr. Smoger will be the referee for the fight. He'll give you the pre-fight instructions."

The pro forma instructions followed. Then Smoger turned to Stone. "The facts indicate," he began, "that in your last time in New York, you were ejected from ringside, fined, and suspended. And the language you used was atrocious. I don't —"

"You're prejudiced," Stone interrupted.

"Norman —"

"You're picking on me," Stone snapped. "You're prejudiced. The fight's off. We're not fighting."

"I'm not picking on you. What I saw and heard that night —"

"You heard shit," Stone shouted. "You couldn't have heard what I said because you weren't the referee. You're fucking prejudiced."

Tony Cardinale (Ruiz's lawyer) reached out and put a steadying hand on Stone's shoulder.

"Norman, this is preventative," Smoger said. "I'm asking you to not jeopardize the evening by a repeat of last time. We don't want the fight to end on a disqualification. This is not a pick on. This is preventative. I have to state the facts. Maintain yourself."

"Fuck you. I'm suing."

Next, Stevens and Smoger went to Toney's dressing room. After the ritual instructions, Smoger gave Toney a similar warning. "I want you to behave. Don't ignite. Don't incite."

"There won't be a problem," Toney promised. "I give you my word, man-to-man."

There was no music in Toney's dressing room. James chatted amiably with the people around him. He seemed calm and relaxed, like a man who was looking forward to the hour to come. As the moment of truth drew closer, he gloved up, shadow-boxed, and hit the pads with Freddie Roach. Finally, Roach told him, "You're ready, son."

It was an interesting fight. Toney was the aggressor for most of the night, moving forward and getting off first. Both men fought cleanly, although Ruiz skirted the rules with rabbit punches from time to time. Toney's money punch was an overhand right that landed all evening. And his elusiveness on the inside was particularly frustrating for Ruiz. At times, John looked like a man trying to punch sand in a hurricane.

Toney won the fight on the inside with basic geometry and physics. His arms were shorter than his opponent's and his hands were faster. Each time Ruiz landed a clean shot, he seemed to wait for a receipt, and James gave him one.

John's best round was the sixth, when he backed Toney up and landed some significant blows. At that point, James appeared to be tiring and the Ruiz blueprint for the next six rounds was obvious. Press the action and make Toney fight three minutes of every round. But that plan, if it existed, went out the window in the opening seconds of round seven. Toney came out with a left-right-shove combination, the shove coming while he was standing on Ruiz's foot, and John went down. Smoger, who otherwise did an outstanding job, mistakenly called the incident a knockdown.

At that point, Ruiz's spirit seemed broken. Thereafter, Toney was able to fight when he wanted to fight. And when he wanted to rest, he let Ruiz hold him. The judges scored it 116-111, 116-111, 115-112 in James's favor. This observer had it 116-112. Overall, Toney outlanded Ruiz 195 to 139.

After the fight, Ruiz announced in his locker room that he was retiring. "I did all I could to lift up the sport of boxing," he said. "I extended my hand to everybody. I didn't say anything bad about anybody. And all they did was say bad about me. I'm a nice guy. They

want assholes up there. Now they got one. All the criticism and negativity in the last few fights have taken their toll. My heart isn't in it
anymore. I always treated everybody with respect, but they didn't treat
me the same way. It hurts me to walk away like this. I grew up in boxing;
I've been fighting since I was seven. It's sad for me to put it this way, but
boxing was the sport I loved. Now it's the sport I hate. It's time for me
to move on with the rest of my life."

Ruiz may, or may not, stand by that pledge. But it's not in the best
economic interests of boxing's powers-that-be for him to win a title
again. Thus, it's unlikely that John will be the challenger for anyone's
optional defense, and the sanctioning bodies won't make him a "mandatory" without Don King pushing for him (which is unlikely since King
now has more marketable commodities). Moreover, contenders like
Calvin Brock won't want to fight Ruiz because he might beat them. So
what's left for him to do? Fight guys like Ray Austin and Larry Donald?
After his loss to David Tua, Ruiz had reason to take the long road back.
He was only 24 years old. He's not young anymore.

Meanwhile, James Toney isn't exactly a breath of fresh air for boxing.
A gust of wind is more like it. But he's a provocateur and a compelling
presence whose victory injects some life into the moribund heavyweight
division.

"I'm a violent person," Toney said last week. "The best thing about
being a fighter is knocking somebody straight on his ass, out cold, blood
everywhere, Fans come to see a fight, blood and guts, and that's what I
give them."

This from a man who once approached the seven-year-old son of one
of his sparring partners in the gym and announced, "Watch this; I'm
going to kill your daddy." Of course, in the next breath, James might say
(as he did minutes after trading insults with Norman Stone), "I love
Jackie Gleason. He's one of my favorites."

Toney, Vitali Klitschko. Chris Byrd, and Lamon Brewster are now
boxing's "Fab Four." The problem is, with each of them wearing a
different belt, they're not so fabulous. Boxing should get its act together
and hold a tournament to crown a legitimate heavyweight king. If it
does, the most marketable heavyweight will be the one who emerges
from the process. But as HBO Sports president Ross Greenburg
acknowledged last month, "It's going to be up to the promoters, fighters,
and managers to huddle and determine if identifying a unified champion is in their interests. It's in the public's interest and obviously it
would be in our interest. But whether they can put aside all of their
separate interests and come together to get it done is a different story.
We just don't know."

Meanwhile, in the dressing room immediately after Toney's victory over Ruiz, Freddie Roach shared his thoughts regarding James's most likely future opponents.

On Chris Byrd: "James and Chris used to spar together. James always seemed to have his number; and since then, Chris has slowed down a bit."

On Lamon Brewster: "Lamon is one of my favorite people in boxing. I like Lamon a lot. But James and Lamon used to spar together, and James always dominated. James walks through Lamon."

On Hasim Rahman: "Rock runs hot and cold. If the real Rock showed up, that would be a good fight."

On Vitali Klitschko: "Vitali would pose problems because of his size. But at the end of the day, James would probably be a bit too slick for him."

And then there's Mike Tyson, who Roach trained for two fights: "James knocks Mike out in four or five rounds. Mike is still dangerous early. But James is a good defensive fighter, and he has the greatest chin I've ever seen. Businesswise, that would probably be the best fight for James."

Then Roach smiled. "Middleweights are better fighters than heavyweights," he said.

James Toney is no longer a middleweight. But if he got in shape, he could be cruiserweight champion of the world.

Probably, he figures that being heavyweight champion is better.❑

*Trainer Brendan Ingle once said, "Boxing is a theatre of life."*
*That was evident during in nine-day stretch in May 2005.*

# NINE DAYS IN LAS VEGAS

Sanitized vice is always on display in Las Vegas. The unsanitized kind takes place behind closed doors. The city works hard to create an environment in which each of its 37,000,000 annual visitors feels welcome. But there's a world beyond what the common tourist sees, where rank and privilege are defined by how much money a player risks and sheer power.

Within a span of nine days earlier this month, the biggest players and power brokers in boxing came together in Las Vegas. The festivities began on May 6th with the eightieth annual Boxing Writers Association of America awards banquet. The BWAA is a once-moribund organization that is showing signs of life under the leadership of Bernard Fernandez. For the first time ever, it had moved its showcase event away from the east coast. Mandalay Bay (the host site) did what it did does best. The dinner sold out. Power brokers mingled with high rollers and champions. Excitement was in the air.

One night later, the scene shifed to the Mandalay Bay Events Center for the lightweight title-unification fight between Jose Luis Castillo and Diego Corrales.

Castillo and Corrales came into the bout as the two best lightweights in the world. Castillo is a skilled durable fighter who, outside of two defeats at the hands of Floyd Mayweather Jr., hadn't lost since 1998. Corrales was stopped on cuts by Joel Casamayor in 2003. Since then, he'd won a return bout against Casamayor and knocked out the previously-undefeated Acelino Freitas. His only other loss was a tenth-round stoppage at the hands of Mayweather in 2001.

The consensus belief was that Corrales hit harder than Castillo but Castillo took a better punch. That was based on the fact that Corrales had been down eight times in his career (five of them against Mayweather) while Castillo had never been on the canvas.

Corrales is likeable and articulate. "I'm a happy guy, a free spirit," he noted shortly before the fight. "The best thing about being a fighter is the people you meet." Showing a sensitive side, Corrales talked about not bringing his four children to his fights. "I don't want them to be afraid for me," he explained. "And I don't want them to see that very aggressive hurting side of me either."

Still, there's an ugly incident on Corrales's resume that he can't fully shake. In 2001, he pled guilty to felony spousal abuse and spent fourteen months in prison for beating his pregnant wife. Now divorced and remarried, he says simply, "It wasn't all my fault. Two people have to play a part in that. But I played my part and I bear my responsibility."

In the days leading up to the fight, Corrales was respectful of Castillo. "Everything about Castillo impresses me," he said. "He's a consistent true champion who always finds a way to win." But Diego was unfazed by the fact that many people were picking Castillo to win because they thought that Jose Luis had a better chin.

"If they believe that, then that's okay," Corrales said. "My chin has stood up against some of the best. I respect his power, but I'm not concerned about getting knocked down because I know I'll get up. We'll see exactly what happens in a week."

What happened was emblazoned into boxing lore before either man left the ring.

This observer's notes from ringside tell the tale of the first nine rounds.

Round 1: Trench warfare; a good action round.

Round 2: Both fighters landing to the head and body with vicious hooks. Corrales chosing to fight on the inside rather than use his longer reach.

Round 3: Non-stop action. Tony Weeks doing a good job of letting the fighters fight.

Round 4: Corrales's punches seem to have the greater impact, but Castillo is landing more consistently with solid blows. This is a "Fight of the Year" candidate.

Round 5: A breathtaking fight; brutal pace, round after round. Whatever these guys are getting paid, it isn't enough.

Round 6: Castillo still more consistent; Corrales beginning to show signs of being broken down.

Round 7: Corrales's left eye is hideously swollen. He's fighting a wonderfully courageous fight; both men are. Castillo wobbled by a left hook at the bell ending the round. This type of fight can ruin both fighters.

Round 8: Corrales can no longer see the right hands coming. They're trading hooks with abandon. Horrific head blows.

Round 9: Rocking each other with right hands. This has turned into a historic fight.

Then came round ten. Twenty-five seconds into the stanza, Castillo decked Corrales with a left hook. "That's the one that really hurt me," Diego said afterward. "That's the one that did the damage. I went low because I thought he was going to throw a left hook up high, but he came low and caught me. It was a shot I never saw. I rolled right into it."

Corrales's mouthpiece was knocked out by the blow. Twenty-three seconds after he hit the canvas, it was back in and the action resumed. Another left hook put him down again.

At that point, Corrales looked like a thoroughly beaten fighter. He also looked like a man who was thinking about quitting and just didn't want to do it on the canvas. He removed his mouthpiece and got to his feet very slowly. "The first time it came out, it came out by itself," he later acknowledged. "The second time, I took it out to breathe but I didn't drop it on purpose."

Referee Tony Weeks deducted a point from Corrales for intentionally spitting out the mouthpiece and led him to his corner. If Diego expected sympathy from trainer Joe Goossen while Goossen reinserted the mouthpiece, he didn't get it.

"You gotta fucking get inside on him now," Goossen ordered.

The action resumed 28 seconds after the knockdown.

Then everything changed.

"Castillo dropped his left hand to throw a right," Corrales said later, "and my right hand got there first. That set the whole thing off."

Corrales's right was followed by a left hook . . . Another right . . . And suddenly, Castillo was back against the ropes, taking punches, glassy-eyed, his head wobbling like it was on a bobble-head doll.

At 2:06 of the round, Weeks leapt between the fighters and stopped the carnage. Judges Lou Moret (87-84) and Daniel Van De Weile (86-85) had Corrales ahead after nine rounds. Paul Smith and this observer had Castillo leading 87-84. It was a great fight, but two controversies were spawned by the final round.

Both controversies related to Weeks. The lesser dispute concerned his stoppage of the fight. He could have called a knockdown against Castillo (the ropes were holding him up), given him an eight-count, and then decided whether or not the fighter was fit to continue.

Weeks explained his action, saying, "Castillo was naked. He was being hit with bombs. He went limp. He was unable to defend himself. He was out on his feet."

Certainly, the stoppage was within the bounds of discretion; and there's no doubt that Weeks intervened at the right time. Also, had he given Castillo an eight-count to assess the fighter's condition, he might have reached the same conclusion. Were that the case, it would have been a more satisfying and equitable process. Castillo said as much when he declared, "The referee gave him a lot of chances. He didn't give as many to me. I'm not saying I wasn't hurt, but I still had a chance. I don't know why the referee didn't let me continue. He let him get up from two knockdowns. He didn't let me get up from one."

The second controversy, of course, concerns Corrales's mouthpiece. As noted, Diego conceded that he removed it on purpose after the second knockdown (to catch his breath). Without the extra time that gave him to recover, he might not have survived.

In boxing, a fighter who loses his mouthpiece, intentionally or otherwise, is required to fight without it until there's a lull in the action. A knockdown is not a lull in the action. Nor is there a rule that reads, "A fighter who has been knocked down may signal the referee by spitting out his mouthpiece that he would like an extra fifteen seconds to recover in exchange for a one or two-point deduction."

There are no optional time-outs in boxing, but Weeks let Corrales call one.

In the aftermath of the fight, Bob Arum (Castillo's promoter) was an almost-sympathetic figure at ringside. "The stoppage was at the referee's discretion," said Arum. "I can't argue with that. But I never heard of a rule that, when you're knocked down and throw your mouthpiece away, the action stops. That's crazy. You make him fight without the mouthpiece. He pulled it out and threw it away to get more time. Either you disqualify him or you make him fight without the mouthpiece. But this is boxing, so they'll find a way to rationalize it."

Arum was right. Clearly, a fighter who deliberately removes his mouthpiece should be penalized one or two points. But more important, whether or not the action is intentional, the flow of a fight should not be interrupted at a crucial time. Yes, fighters are at greater risk of injury without a mouthpiece. But it's dangerous to fight, period, and a foul should not be allowed to benefit the transgressor.

The loophole in the rules has to be closed. One solution would be for the referee himself to reinsert the mouthpiece. There was a time when it was considered essential to rinse a fighter's mouthpiece because resin was sprinked on the ring canvas. But resin is no longer used. As for the objection that the referee might not know how to insert a particular kind of mouthpiece, that can be covered during the instructions in the dressing room prior each fight.

Meanwhile, no rules interpretation could ease Castillo's pain in losing. After the fight, Margaret Goodman (chief ringside physician for the Nevada State Athletic Commission) examined the fighter in his dressing room.

"Does your head hurt?" she asked.

"No," Castillo told her. "But my heart hurts a lot."

After Castillo-Corrales, the drama moved up the strip from Mandalay Bay to the MGM Grand. There, as everyone awaited Felix Trinidad versus Winky Wright, boxing's players jostled for position like NBA power forwards.

Castillo-Corrales had been promoted by Top Rank in association with Gary Shaw Productions and was televised by Showtime. Trinidad-Wright was primarily a Don King venture backed by HBO. But the timing of Castillo-Corrales worked to Showtime's advantage. Because it took place one day after the BWAA dinner, more writers were on hand to witness it than would otherwise have been the case. Also, most of these writers were staying in Las Vegas for Trinidad-Wright. They had a lot of free time early in the week; and much of it was spent talking among themselves, with other boxing aficionados who had seen the fight, and with Corrales (who was readily accessible in the media center).

"After the fight, I slept a lot," Corrales said. "It took a while to realize what a big deal it was."

"Have you watched the tape?" he was asked.

"Yes."

"What did you think?"

"Ow! It was hard to watch because I knew what I was feeling. I kept saying to myself, 'Yeah, I remember that shot; that one really hurt.' When I watched the tape, I was reliving each punch as if I was getting hit all over again. Emotionally, I feel so good," Diego continued. "Emotionally, I could go back to the gym tomorrow. Physically is something else. But I've been waiting for this. I always wanted to match my personal will against someone else's and see how far I could will myself, how far I could go."

Meanwhile, boxing's heavyweights had come into play. On Monday, May 9th, it was announced that the WBC had authorized an "interim heavyweight championship" fight between Hasim Rahman and Monte Barrett. The following day, word circulated through the media center than James Toney had tested positive for Nandrolone (an illegal steroid) after beating John Ruiz for the WBA title in New York. The outcome of Ruiz-Toney was changed to "no decision" and James was suspended for ninety days. More significantly, he was stripped of his WBA belt and Ruiz was reinstated as champion.

This is the third time that Ruiz has claimed the WBA crown and the second time in a row that he has done so without winning a title fight. His prior ascension came by virtue of winning a "title elimination bout" before Roy Jones relinquished the throne.

"To all of the assholes who want me out of the game," Ruiz said graciously, "I'm back."

The Toney debacle showed once again the arbitrary and capricious nature of regulating boxing state-by-state instead of having one national standard. If Ruiz-Toney had been contested in one of the dozens of states that don't require steroid testing, James would still be champion.

The WBC's ruling with regard to Rahman-Barrett was equally significant. Don King has spent millions of dollars in an effort to lock up the heavyweight division, and the WBC edict was part of his plan. Vitali Klitschko (the WBC champion) is promoted by K2 Promotions. Rahman is promoted by King, who controls the other three belts. As the mandatory challenger for Klitschko's crown, Hasim was entitled to 25 percent of any purse bid for the fight. But the Klitschko camp gave him a 65-35 split in exchange for a rematch clause. Then Klitschko was injured and Klitschko-Rahman was postponed. Under WBC rules, an "interim champion" is entitled to 45 percent of any purse bid, and no rematch clause is required.

"And the new interim WBC heavyweight champion" doesn't have much of a ring to it. But the bottom line is, boxing will soon have six heavyweight champions: Vitali Klitschko (WBC), Hasim Rahman or Monte Barrett (interim WBC), John Ruiz (WBA), Chris Byrd (IBF), Lamon Brewster (WBO), and James Toney (champion in exile).

The folks at HBO aren't happy campers right now as far as the heavyweight division is concerned. Indeed, last week, HBO Sports president Ross Greenburg bemoaned the ongoing heavyweight muddle with the observation, "When you have an elimination tournament, fans want to see the semi-finals and finals. But it feels like we're stuck in a never-ending quarter-final void."

Meanwhile, as May 14th approached, Don King was concerned with middleweights; and more specifically, with Felix "Tito" Trinidad.

Some fighters are simply more exciting than others by virtue of personality and the way they fight. Trinidad is one of them. His good looks and smile light up an arena.

After losing to Bernard Hopkins in 2001, Trinidad fought once more before going into a 29-month "retirement." Last October, he returned and faced Ricardo Mayorga at Madison Square Garden. "It was one of the most exciting times of my life," Tito recalled at the kick-off press conference for Trinidad-Wright. "Just to hear the fans chanting 'Tito, Tito,' when I stepped into the ring. The only way I knew how to pay them back was to give them every single round and give the best performance that I could ever put together."

He did just that, knocking out Mayorga in the eighth round of a brutal fight.

Trinidad is one of the few elite fighters in the world who gives the impression that boxing is still a game to him. He's an exciting fighter and he goes in tough. His mantra is, "I want to fight the best guys out there that are willing to fight me." His roster of opponents includes Pernell Whitaker, Oscar De La Hoya, David Reid, Fernando Vargas, and Hopkins.

Wright is a 33-year-old southpaw who made his way to the top as a blue-collar fighter with no glitz and no big-name promoter behind him. Like Hopkins, he wanted to make his mark against Trinidad.

"A lot of people get to this point and then they get scared," Wright said in the days leading up to the fight. "Get scared for what? This is exactly what I've been fighting for all these years; to have all the writers asking me questions instead of De La Hoya. It's so sweet, it's ridiculous. They couldn't write a movie script better than this. This is exactly what I want."

"I don't care who he is," Wright continued. "When we step into the ring, he's just another opponent. I'm not good at staredowns, but I can fight. I know what Tito can do. Tito's got a lot of punches; he punches hard; and he always comes in shape. Against Mayorga, he looked marvelous, but Mayorga was tailor-made for Tito. Mayorga can't box; he was just a blown-up welterweight. I'm not worried about Tito. Look what happened when he fought Hopkins. Tito may be stronger than me, but he's one-dimensional. I have better skills. Styles make fights, and I'm the wrong style for Tito."

Asked to elaborate, Wright declared, "I can move, slide, box, jab, fight inside, fight outside. I have a lot of different weapons and styles and can adapt to the situation. The only thing Tito can do is punch, but boxing isn't about one big shot. A big punch doesn't help if you can't land it. I may not have a knockout punch, but I punch hard and Tito's going to feel it. When he throws punches, I'll be throwing punches back. I hit hard enough to hurt you, and that chin of his ain't the greatest. I'll mess up his rhythm and take him out of what he wants to do. I'll beat him with my jab. I'll beat him with my defense. I'll hurt him to the body and go upside his head. And when he realizes that he can't do what he wants to do, frustration will set in. I don't have to knock out Tito to win the fight. My strategy is simple: to win the fight round by round. I'm a better fighter than he is, and I'm going to beat him up for twelve rounds. I'm definitely thinking it will go the distance, but I'm winning this fight. I close my eyes and I can see so many ways this fight may go, but every one of them ends with me winning."

"I've watched and broken down tapes of many of Tito's fights," added Dan Birmingham (Wright's trainer). "All you have to do is study the first six rounds of De La Hoya-Trinidad and the last six rounds of Hopkins-Trinidad to get a blueprint on how to defeat Tito. Winky handles pressure well. He thinks this is all fun and games. And he's unlike any fighter Trinidad has ever faced. Winky times you; he boxes you; he makes you miss. He's not a knockout puncher, but he hits hard enough that you're not going to walk right in on him without worrying. The jab and straight left will be his bread and butter all night."

The fighters weighed in one day before the fight. Each man tipped the scales at 160 pounds. Trinidad was a 5-to-3 favorite. Wright looked stronger and more muscular.

Then came the moment of truth.

Trinidad has two weaknesses as a fighter. His aggressive puncher's stance makes it difficult for him to implement quick defensive adjustments. And on the inside, he sometimes waits too long before punching. Wright took advantage of both flaws.

Winky began the fight as the aggressor behind a stiff right jab and occasional straight lefts. For the most part, he caught Trinidad's punches on his arms and gloves. And for twelve rounds, that's the way it was.

Wright put on a clinic, getting off first consistently and never letting Tito set himself to punch. The only blow that Trinidad was able to land with regularity was a hook to the hip that finally cost him a one-point deduction in round nine. Meanwhile, Wright was masterful. His jab was a stinging punch in the face (*bang! bang!* rather than *pop-pop*). His straight left remained on target. In the late rounds, he mixed in some hard hooks to the body.

Trinidad never did anything differently to change the flow of the fight because he couldn't. Wright never did anything differently because he didn't have to. Winky landed 262 punches to Tito's 58. Those are staggering numbers and accurately reflect Wright's total dominance.

The judges' scores were 120-107, 119-108, and 119-108. This observer gave Trinidad the twelfth round. Wright could have won that one too, but he didn't bother to throw enough punches.

Don King tried to put a positive spin on things at the post-fight press conference. He praised Wright's "masterful virtuoso performance" (which he likened to Beethoven, Brahms, and Mozart) and said that fight fans everywhere were clamoring "Encore! Encore!"

For the uninitiated, that means King wants to exercise the rematch clause in the Trinidad-Wright contracts. But the fight was so one-sided that a rematch would be unlikely to generate big dollars. And worse, unlike Trinidad's previous fights, this one was largely lacking in passion.

Moreover, the current word out of Puerto Rico is that Tito will retire.

Trinidad was King's flagship fighter. And Wright is promoted by Gary Shaw. Hence, King was smiling his trademark smile for the media late Saturday night. But it was the saddest smile that most of the onlookers had ever seen.

And that was Trinidad-Wright, with one more twist worthy of mention.

Wright appeared at the final pre-fight press conference on Wednesday, May 11th, with a bandage on his neck. When asked about it, he said that he had nicked himself shaving.

Nicks from shaving don't require bandages. In truth, an ingrown hair had led to an infected abscess on Winky's neck. That evening, according to Keith Kizer (chief deputy attorney general for the state of Nevada), Wright went to the emergency room at Valley Hospital, where Dr. Jeff Davidson drained the abscess and put the fighter on an antibiotic. The following day, Wright returned to the hospital and Davidson performed further work.

The problem with these visits was, among his many duties, Davidson is a ringside physician for the Nevada State Athletic Commission. Moreover, he had been assigned to work Trinidad-Wright. And Nevada law states that, absent special circumstances, a ringside physician may not treat or examine a fighter. "The regulation is pretty clear," said Kizer. "It's black and white."

Two members of the Nevada commission knew about the treatment, one of them in advance. However, commission chairman Raymond "Skip" Avansino didn't learn about it until Friday afternoon. Avansino was unhappy. This isn't the first time that events of importance have transpired behind his back. There's no reason to believe that Wright gained a competitive advantage from Davidson's treatment or that Davidson had ill intent. Still, as a first step, Avansino removed Davidson from the fight.

The incident brought to mind several comments regarding the Nevada State Athletic Commission that were made on recent HBO telecasts. Last September, when Oscar De La Hoya fought Bernard Hopkins, Jim Lampley spoke of "unusual issues" and Larry Merchant referenced "the appearance of a cave-in to business interests" by the Nevada commission. Then, on March 26th of this year at the close of HBO's telecast of Fernando Vargas versus Raymond Joval and a delayed tape of Manny Pacquiao against Erik Morales, Merchant chastised the NSAC more directly for the manner in which it was appointing officials for fights.

"Once again," Merchant told a national audience, "the chief medical officer of the Nevada commission, Margaret Goodman, was missing in action and missed in action. Once again, her back-up over or underreacted in the heat of battle. This is happening because business and political interests in Las Vegas think she is overprotective of fighters, which can at times be costly. Once you have business and political interests calling the shots, whether it's picking judges or ring physicians, trouble lies ahead. We'll be watching."

Three days later, at a March 29th press conference to promote Castillo-Corrales, Gary Shaw and Bob Arum assailed Merchant. "I thought HBO took an unfair shot at Marc [Ratner] and the commission," Shaw said. "I think it stinks."

"I join Gary in deploring what another network did," Arum added. "A know-it-all analyst for HBO claimed that, through political influence, the person he claimed was the best doctor was banned from working the fight. That's the most yellow journalism I've ever heard. For him to have said that to the nation is absolute demagoguery, a falsehood. Somebody has to bring somebody like that to account. This nonsense has to stop. There is no place in this sport for that type of behavior."

Shaw, fight fans will recall, is the man who told a national television audience that Jay Nady should apologize to Zab Judah after Judah assaulted the referee and threw a stool at him in response to Nady stopping his 2001 fight against Kostya Tszyu.

Twenty months ago, Bob Arum implied that Ratner and Flip Homansky were involved in fixing a fight after Shane Mosley won a unanimous decision over Oscar De La Hoya. More specifically, Arum claimed that Homansky had a vendetta against him and accused Homansky of improperly influencing the selection of Stanley Christodoulou as one of the judges for the bout. Then, for good measure, Arum called Ratner a "tool" of Homansky.

Thereafter, the Nevada commission demanded that Arum appear at a hearing to present evidence supporting his allegation. In response, Arum sent a letter to the NSAC stating that he had no evidence and asked to be excused from appearing at the hearing. "My comments," he wrote, "were made in the heat of passion, without thinking about how such comments would be interpreted as both impugning the integrity of the commission and discrediting the sport I love so much."

But let's look at Merchant's comments.

Bob Arum is believed to have been at odds with Dr. Goodman for her role in spearheading mandatory MRIs for fighters (which cost promoters money) and her efforts to place Jorge Paez (formerly a Top Rank fighter) on medical suspension.

According to information made available by the Nevada State

Athletic Commission, from the start of 2004 through March 26, 2005 (when Merchant made his comment), there were seventeen major fight cards in Nevada. A "major" fight card is defined by the commission as a card that is on HBO, Showtime, or pay-per-view. Seven of these major cards were promoted by Top Rank. Ten of them involved other promoters. Dr. Goodman was the lead physician for two of the seven major Top Rank fights (29%). She was the lead physician for seven of the ten other major fights (70%).

It's also worth noting that, in April of this year, Paez applied for permanent Social Security disability benefits on grounds that he was unable to perform normal tasks as a consequence of brain damage suffered while boxing.

Shaw's criticism of Dr. Goodman stems in part from her stoppage of the October 4, 2003, fight between Diego Corrales and Joel Casamayor, which made Casamayor a sixth-round TKO victor. But there's a school of thought that Corrales owes his career and more to Goodman. He had suffered a deep laceration on his lower lip, another laceration that went almost completely through his right cheek, and more cuts inside his mouth. Swallowing blood was the least of his problems. Most likely, that would have resulted in nothing more serious than vomiting. Inhaling the blood could have caused temporary choking. But more ominously, if the laceration on Corrales's lip had worsened, it might have resulted in a permanent deformity.

Thus, Corrales himself now says, "I was upset when she stopped the fight. But after seeing it on tape, I've let it go. It was a freakish cut, and Dr. Goodman did her job. She really cares about the fighters, and she was looking after me. What she did was for the best."

As for Merchant's comments regarding judges, on September 13, 2003, Duane Ford, Anek Hongtongkam, and Stanley Christodoulou each scored the rematch between Oscar De La Hoya and Shane Mosley 115-113 in favor of Mosley. Bob Arum's reaction to that decision has been noted above.

Since then, Hongtongkam and Christodoulou have not judged a Top Rank championship fight in Las Vegas. That's understandable. They're from Thailand and South Africa respectively. Ford is another matter. He's a Las Vegas resident and one of the most respected judges in the world. However, according to Fight Fax and boxrec.com, Ford has worked only two of the twenty Top Rank championship fights held in Las Vegas since then. And those two (Jose Luis Castillo versus Juan Lazcano and Juan Manuel Marquez against Orlando Salido) were under-card bouts on the same card as more important championship fights.

By contrast, on June 5, 2004, Paul Smith was one of three judges who scored De La Hoya a 115-113 winner over Felix Sturm. Since then, Smith has been given the lucrative judging assignment in four major Top Rank championship bouts: De La Hoya-Hopkins, Morales-Barrera III, Morales-Pacquiao, and Castillo-Corrales. Dave Moretti (the other Nevada judge who scored De La Hoya-Sturm 115-113 in favor of Oscar) has also been assigned to four Top Rank championship bouts since then including De La Hoya-Hopkins and Morales-Pacquiao.

Coincidence?

I think not. And keep in mind, Ford is obviously still capable of judging big fights. Last year, he was assigned to Jones-Tarver II, Wright-Mosley II, and Vitali Klitschko versus Danny Williams. Last weekend, he judged Trinidad-Wright.

Bob Arum is a promoter. He can, and should, lobby to protect his interests. But the Nevada State Athletic Commission has a responsibility to stand its ground. It also has a responsibility to enforce the law, and that's not always being done. Let another example suffice.

On September 18, 2004, Oscar De La Hoya and Bernard Hopkins fought in Las Vegas for the undisputed middleweight championship in a bout promoted by Top Rank. Hopkins and his attorney have testified under oath in litigation between Hopkins and Don King that Bernard's purse for the De La Hoya fight was $8,000,000 plus seven dollars for each pay-per-view buy above 800,000. De La Hoya-Hopkins engendered one million pay-per-view buys.

Here's the rub. Last September, Top Rank filed an official bout agreement between Top Rank and Hopkins and an official bout agreement between Top Rank and De La Hoya with the Nevada State Athletic Commission.

The Hopkins bout agreement was signed by a representative of Top Rank and Hopkins himself. In relevant part, it read, "The Promoter will pay the Contestant for the Bout and the Contestant agrees to accept in full of all claims and demands for his services and performance by him of the Bout, the sum of $4,000,000."

The De La Hoya contract submitted to the commission was similarly flawed. It stated that De La Hoya's purse was $8,000,000, which was less than half of Oscar's actual minimum guarantee.

It's possible that Top Rank filed the contracts with the Nevada commission to help Hopkins and De La Hoya avoid paying the full sanctioning fees that would otherwise have been due to the world sanctioning organizations that sanctioned the bout. This view is bolstered by a September 8, 2004, letter from Todd duBoef (Arum's son-in-law and now Top Rank's president) to the World Boxing Association and International Boxing Federation. That letter states, "Top Rank has been directed by the representatives of the above-referenced fighters that the purses filed with the Nevada State Athletic Commission for their September 18, 2004, bout will be the following: Oscar De La Hoya $8,000,000; Bernard Hopkins $4,000,000."

The IBF subsequently sued Hopkins and De La Hoya, claiming breach of contract and fraud with regard to the underpayment of sanctioning fees.

One can construct a strong legal and ethical argument for minimizing the fees that are paid to world sanctioning organizations in conjunction with championship bouts. The "alphabet-soup" organizations often engage in the bogus rating of fighters in violation of federal law. It's not uncommon for skilled fighters to be denied championship opportunities, while less-talented (but better-connected) boxers fight for belts. However, filing false documents with a government agency is an improper remedy.

Under Nevada law, a person who knowingly procures or offers a false document for filing in any public office is guilty of a category C felony punishable by a minimum of one year and a maximum of five years in prison.

If the Nevada State Athletic Commission condones the submission of inaccurate bout agreements, where on the slippery slope does other misconduct lie? Will the NSAC look the other way if a fighter gets less than his officially-reported purse rather than more? Will it condone the submission of false medical documents that endanger fighters' lives?

Ignoring the facts doesn't change the facts. In boxing, as with other government-regulated activity, the integrity of public records should be preserved. That isn't being done now in Nevada. Rather, too often when an issue of wrongdoing is brought before the commission, its reaction is to make excuses and paper things over rather address the problem. Laws are in place for a reason, and they should be followed.

Las Vegas has an ad campaign that shows people behaving unwisely in different situations followed by the slogan, "Las Vegas: What happens here stays here." It would be unfortunate if the Nevada State Athletic Commission chose as a matter of policy to emulate that slogan. When boxing reaches breathtaking heights, as it did earlier this month with the heart shown by Diego Corrales and Jose Luis Castillo and the sublime artistry of Winky Wright, it's a shame to spoil things with "politics."

Castillo-Corrales and Trinidad-Wright showcased boxing at its best. They reminded everyone of what the sport is all about. Wright's performance exemplified the sweet science: to hit and not get hit. And Castillo-Corrales was a post-graduate course in courage.

Corrales was getting beaten up badly and came back to turn the tide. "I didn't even know what round it was," he said afterward. "It was just one round after another. There were so many times when either one of us could have said, 'That's it; I'm done,' and no one in the arena could have complained. But our job is to keep fighting."

Corrales paused for a moment before continuing. "It took two of us to make the fight what it was," he said. "Both of us did our job. It takes a great athlete to play basketball, baseball, or some other professional sport. You have to be more than an athlete to be a fighter."❑

*Bernard Hopkins began 2005 on a roll.*

# GOOD TIMES FOR BERNARD HOPKINS

These are heady times for Bernard Hopkins. Last September, he was paid $10,000,000 for knocking out Oscar De La Hoya. He's the undisputed middleweight champion of the world. On May 6th, he will be honored by the Boxing Writers Association of America as the "Manager of the Year." And most remarkably, at age forty, he's considered "pound-for-pound" the best fighter in the world.

When is the last time a fighter was rated number-one pound-for-pound at age forty? Never! Roy Jones lost the designation at age thirty-five. Pernell Whitaker (Jones's predecessor) relinquished it at age thirty. Sugar Ray Robinson had one win in the five fights just prior to his fortieth birthday.

"But I'm still here," Hopkins says proudly. "I'm forty, but I'm a young forty. I'm on that Jerry Rice level; that Barry Bonds level."

In recent years, Hopkins has assumed an aura of invincibility. He gives the impression that he's made of granite; a bit worn from erosion at the edges, but still granite. Last Saturday night (February 19th), he made the twentieth defense of his championship reign against Howard Eastman, a 34-year-old Guyanan now living in England.

Eastman talked a good fight before the fact, saying he'd knock Hopkins out in five rounds. But few people took him seriously. Bernard has never been knocked out. And as Patrick Kehoe noted, "Even British boxing insiders admit that Eastman will have to fight the perfect fight to have a chance. Not a happy prospect, having to fight your absolute best fight just to make a contest out of it."

Meanwhile, Hopkins had his own take on things. "He's a B-minus fighter," Bernard said of his opponent. "Eastman says he'll knock me out in round five, but that's just the hype talking. What happens in rounds six, seven, and eight? It's a twelve-round fight. I look at him and see a guy who has scar tissue and cuts around his eyes. That tells me he doesn't move too good up top, and it's too late for him to learn now. I'm the better fighter, the better thinker, the better puncher, the sharper puncher, and the quicker fighter. I'm going to go in there and remove any thoughts from Eastman's mind that he can win the fight, so that in his mind he's only trying to survive. I will force my will and demeanor upon him. I plan to counter him mentally and physically. I'm a good predictor of fights, and I predict I'll be sending him back to England with ice packs on his eyes."

Hopkins also spent a lot of time talking about the fact that this would be his twentieth defense in a middleweight championship reign that has lasted for ten years.

"Twenty title defenses," Bernard proclaimed at the final pre-fight press conference. "I just want you all to spend ten seconds thinking about this. Twenty defenses in today's world, when all the distractions are at your beck and call. Twenty defenses. That's very rare, unique, and extraordinary. This is very very special to me because history can never be forgotten. This will follow me to my grave. It will be a trivia question in fifty years. 'Who made twenty successful defenses of the middleweight title?'"

The fight took place at the Staples Center and was the first middleweight championship contest in Los Angeles since a fifteen-round draw between Sugar Ray Robinson and Gene Fullmer 44 years ago. Both men started slowly. Through three rounds, Hopkins landed only 17 punches and Eastman 15. That led to boos from the crowd. But as the bout wore on, the judges' scorecards took on the look of a typical Hopkins fight, with Bernard dominating the middle and late stanzas and controlling the pace of the action. Most significantly, Hopkins took away Eastman's jab. The challenger connected on only 16 of 260 attempts, a meager six percent. All totalled, Bernard outlanded his foe 148 to 82. And that's not counting illegal blows to the hips and thighs that escaped the notice of referee Raul Caiz Jr.

The judges' scores were 119-110, 117-111, and 116-112. This observer favored Hopkins 117-112. As for the boos, Bernard said afterward, "They want to see a Gatti-Ward sort of thing, but I don't fight like that." Then he added, "But I can turn it on when I want to."

That's Hopkins. He does things for himself and no one else. He doesn't suffer from stress. He's a carrier. Bernard has made a lot of enemies over the years by standing up for what's right. And he has made some enemies by standing up for what's wrong too; most notably by discarding old allies in an ugly way once they'd outlived their usefulness to him. Some observers liken him to Old Man River for the way he just keeps rolling along. But Old Man River "don't say nuthin'," and Hopkins speaks his mind.

"There are a lot of people that wish Bernard Hopkins would get on a plane and that plane don't land safely," Bernard said recently. That followed other bon mots like, "The boxing business is just as bad as the drug business. There's a lot of people in boxing who act worse than drug dealers, and I'll name them for you."

Given Hopkins's warm cuddly personality, some detractors say that the reason he's up and doing roadwork at 5:30 each morning is that all the bad things he's done keep him from sleeping anyway. But not even his most severe critics question Bernard's consummate professionalism as a fighter.

Hopkins always pays the price in training. "I can't afford at this stage in my career to cut corners," he says. "It's something I've never done. I approach each fight like it's my last fight and I have to make a statement."

Also, in the ring, Hopkins does what has to be done to win fights. He's hard to hit cleanly. He's a patient fighter, who bides his time and takes a little piece here and a little piece there, until his opponent can't see the right hand coming anymore because his left eye is swollen and it's hard to keep his hands up because his ribs ache.

For a guy who doesn't take many risks inside the squared circle, Hopkins dishes out a lot of punishment. And he's a smart fighter. "Bernard is like a computer," says his longtime trainer Bouie Fisher. "Everything is in his brain. When he has to alter his game plan, he Google-searches his computer, which is his knowledge of boxing, to find the solution he needs to be successful."

Everyone has an occasional bad day at the office. If a world champion has one, he loses his job. Hopkins has now joined Joe Louis (25), Dariusz Michalczewski (23), Ricardo Lopez (21), and Sven Ottke (21) as one of only five fighters in history to defend the same title twenty times or more. He's also one of four fighters to successfully defend a legitimate world championship at age forty or older. Bob Fitzsimmons, Archie Moore, and George Foreman were the others.

Hopkins envisions having two big-money pay-per-view fights this year; one in late-summer and one in late-autumn. Realistically, that leaves him with three viable opponents.

First, Bernard has stated a desire to fight Glencoffe Johnson for the 175-pound throne. "I'm a boxing history fanatic," Hopkins said last week. "I want boxing history to follow me to my grave. I want to do what Ray Robinson couldn't do and go right from middleweight and win the light-heavyweight title."

Hopkins would be a clear favorite over the 36-year-old Johnson, who he knocked out eight years ago. But Johnson has said that his first order of business is a rematch against Antonio Tarver. Let's see how anxious Bernard is to fight Tarver should Antonio beat Johnson the second time around.

Alternatively, Hopkins could make a title defense against the winner of the May 14th bout between Felix Trinidad and Winky Wright. But Don King controls Trinidad and is expected to have options on Wright should Winky emerge victorious. King and Hopkins are currently engaged in an ugly legal arbitration. Their battle could be settled by making a fight between Hopkins and the winner of Trinidad-Wright with appropriate financial incentives thrown in. But that's speculative and contingent right now.

The third possibility, of course, is Hopkins versus Jermain Taylor. Taylor has been touted as the heir apparent to the middleweight throne. That and two dollars will get you on the subway in New York. But Jermain has the physical tools to make things interesting against Hopkins.

To beat Bernard, a fighter has to press the action, set a fast pace, and tire him out. That's easier said than done, but it has to be done. Taylor is tall with a good jab and power in both hands. He's also young, which would work for him in terms of stamina and against him when Hopkins starts playing with his mind. Unlike the other potential big-money opponents, Taylor is available without strings now.

Hopkins rarely goes in tougher than he has to. So of the three, most likely he'll opt for the opponent he regards as the most beatable foe. But when the chips are down, Bernard will be a formidable adversary for whomever is standing across the ring. At his core, he's a great fighter. And his essence is best described in words written by William Ernest Henley more than a century ago:

## Invictus

Out of the night that covers me,
Black as the Pit from pole to pole,
I thank whatever gods may be
For my unconquerable soul.

In the fell clutch of circumstance
I have not winced nor cried aloud.
Under the bludgeonings of chance,
My head is bloody but unbowed.

Beyond this place of wrath and tears,
Looms but the horror of the shade.
And yet the menace of the years
Finds, and shall find me, unafraid.

It matters not how strait the gate,
How charged with punishments the scroll.
I am the master of my fate;
I am the captain of my soul.❏

*The "Fighter of the Year" doesn't have to be a great fighter. Sometimes, a good one will do. Shortly after this article was written, the votes were counted and Glencoffe Johnson got the nod.*

# GLENCOFFE JOHNSON: FIGHTER OF THE YEAR

Five candidates were on the ballot distributed last month [January 2005] by the Boxing Writers Association of America for designation as 2004's "Fighter of the Year":

- Marco Antonio Barrera for victories over Erik Morales and Paulie Ayala
- Bernard Hopkins for triumphs over Oscar De La Hoya and Robert Allen
- Winky Wright for defeating Shane Mosley twice
- Diego Corrales for besting Joel Casamayor and Acelino Freitas
- Glencoffe Johnson for toppling Clinton Woods, Roy Jones Jr., and Antonio Tarver

It's hard to find a sport with as many underdogs as boxing. One of those underdogs, Glencoffe Johnson, got my vote. Coming into 2004, the 35-year-old Jamaican now living in Miami had a record of 7 wins, 9 losses, and 2 draws in his most recent 18 fights. Then, in the course of ten remarkable months, he won three title bouts, toppled two fighters who were on everyone's "pound-for-pound" list, and moved from journeyman boxer to stardom.

Johnson is a soft-spoken man without the bravado often associated with his sport. "Talk is talk," he says. "Anyone with a mouth can talk."

Last spring, things were so rough financially that Johnson took a parttime job as a construction worker to make ends meet. Still, in an age when too many fighters enter the ring looking like Elvis in his last concert, Glencoffe always stays in shape. And yes, he's a one-dimensional fighter; but opponents don't beat him by just showing up. He makes them earn it.

In February 2004, Johnson won a decision over Clinton Woods to capture the International Boxing Federation 175-pound crown. But virtually no one took notice. All eyes were on Roy Jones and Antonio Tarver.

Then, in May, Tarver dethroned Jones on a second-round knockout to became The Man in the light-heavyweight division. Four months later, Johnson and Jones met in the ring. Their confrontation was widely regarded as a tune-up for Jones prior to a rematch against Tarver. Except Johnson dominated from start-to-finish en route to a devastating ninth-round knockout.

It didn't mean much, the critics said. Jones was shot.

On December 18, Johnson challenged Tarver for the right to be called the number one light-heavyweight in the world.

Tarver was a 7-to-2 favorite. And just as important, he had become a favorite of the boxing establishment. He was one of the few potential superstars who the public might take note of and latch onto to boost the sport. He was personable, good-looking, verbally gifted; and he could fight.

"No one has approached us about a television contract," Henry Foster (Johnson's manager) said before the fight. "HBO, Showtime, they're not interested in Glen, just Tarver. That's the way things are and we have to live with it, but I expect Glen to win the fight."

"I know that Tarver is the favorite," Johnson added. "But I don't think about that. I never allow myself to adopt a journeyman mentality."

Fighters and their managers always say things like that.

But against Tarver, Johnson fought aggressively and proved that a good chin is as important as a good punch; maybe more so. Two judges scored the contest 115-113 in Glencoffe's favor. The holdout judge had it 116-112 for Tarver. This observer scored it 115-114 in favor of Tarver, who outlanded Johnson 296 to 217. But two out of three judges on your side means you win the fight.

Now people are paying attention to Glencoffe Johnson. They're acknowledging that the scoring in several of his losses against home-town opponents was suspect. And they're taking note of the fact that the last fifteen opponents he faced had a composite record of 380 wins against 22 losses with 5 draws at the time he fought them. That's known as "going in tough."

With victories over two of boxing's best, Glencoffe Johnson deserves recognition as Fighter of the Year.❏

*Floyd Mayweather Jr. versus Arturo Gatti was a mismatch from the day it was signed.*

# GATTI-MAYWEATHER: WHAT DID YOU EXPECT?

Cus D'Amato once said, "When two fighters meet in the ring, the fighter with the greater will prevails every time unless the other man's skills are so superior that his will is never tested."

That adage was central to the marketing of last Saturday's fight at the Atlantic City Convention Center between Floyd Mayweather Jr. and Arturo Gatti.

Gatti is a warrior who excites the crowd every time out. Witness the words of Roy Jones ("Arturo Gatti has given boxing better fights than the ones they make up in movies"); promoter Lou DiBella ("Arturo Gatti is the most made-for-TV fighter I've ever seen"); and sportswriter Tim Graham ("Arturo Gatti is a breathtaking attraction who gives new meaning to the term 'plasma television'").

Gatti himself reinforces that view with comments like, "People only recognize me when I'm beat up. If my face isn't puffy, they don't believe it's me . . . The only problem I have is, when the phone rings, I start shadow-boxing . . . It's a victory for me just not to be going to the hospital after a fight . . . I came back from the dead; I dug myself out of the grave."

But talk is cheap. More often than not, Gatti backs up his words with deeds. Micky Ward, whose "club-fight trilogy" with Arturo has become part of boxing lore, looks back on their final encounter and says, "It takes a lot out of you to go through something like that. In the seventh round, I had nothing left in me. Then he caught me in the head so hard that my brain shifted in my skull and banged the back of my head so hard my eyes didn't see straight. But we both had that will and desire to not stop and go through anything. I think it's bred in you; you can't learn it. Either you have it or you don't."

Gatti's response?

"I'll fight like that anytime I have to."

But as the build-up to Gatti-Mayweather continued, it became clear that the fight was being marketed, not just as a test of toughness, but also as a confrontation between good and evil.

Mayweather styles himself as "the guy who brought mink and chinchilla to boxing." He also has a collection of chains, pendants, watches, bracelets, and rings (most of them gold and platinum with large-carat diamonds) that rivals Don King's bling. But beyond that, as Ron Borges has written, "The only things pretty about 'Pretty Boy' Floyd are his smile and his boxing skills. He's worked overtime to make himself about as repulsive a human being as possible. He can't act even remotely like he understands the meaning of the word 'class' except when he's in the ring."

Outside the ring, Mayweather, like Mike Tyson, has become a poster boy for bad behavior. In 2002, he plead guilty to two counts of domestic violence in Nevada. Last June, he was found guilty on two counts of misdemeanor battery for beating two women in a Las Vegas night-club. In that case, Mayweather took the stand and acknowledged he was at the club but claimed that he never saw or touched the women. At the close of the trial, which was conducted without a jury, Justice Deborah Lippis found the fighter "guilty" and told him, "Mr. Mayweather, I've seen some incredible stories in my life on this bench. But when you testified here, I was pretty shocked at some of the things you said." Lippis gave Mayweather a one-year suspended sentence, fined him $1,000, and ordered him to undergo counseling.

Another criminal charge is pending against Mayweather in Las Vegas; this one a felony indictment for allegedly beating Josie Harris, the mother of one of his four children. Harris, who initially filed a complaint, is currently refusing to cooperate with prosecutors. If convicted, Mayweather could be sentenced to five years in prison and fined $10,000. Also, last December, an arrest warrant was issued for Mayweather in Michigan after he failed to show up for trial on charges that he assaulted a bouncer in a bar. He subsequently appeared in count, pled nolo contendere, and received a suspended sentence.

In the days leading up to Gatti-Mayweather, Floyd bristled at references to his criminal record. "I don't want nobody to judge me on what I do outside the ring," he said. He also demanded to know why the media hadn't paid equal attention to Gatti's substance-abuse days, which included several drunk-driving incidents, threats against a police officer in Miami, and a charge (later dropped when the woman recanted) that Arturo sexually assaulted his girlfriend.

As for the fight itself, Gatti versus Mayweather shaped up as a mismatch. Mayweather is a complete fighter. He's techically proficient, can box and punch with blinding speed, and (when it comes to boxing) has a Spartan work ethic. Gatti was thought of as the "naturally bigger man." But Floyd is an inch taller than Arturo and made his professional debut at 130 pounds, whereas Gatti turned pro at 126. Also, in the days before the fight, Arturo's face looked weak and drawn, and he acknowledged that he was having trouble making weight.

Gatti's partisans talked about their hero's newly-developed boxing skills under trainer Buddy McGirt. But it's one thing to outbox Micky Ward, and quite another to outbox Floyd Mayweather Jr. Gatti had lost to King Solomon, Ivan Robinson (twice), Angel Manfredy, and Micky Ward. He'd been in life-and-death struggles with the likes of Wilson Rodriguez. As Roy Jones noted, "When guys like Ivan Robinson give you a problem, you know Floyd Mayweather is going to be too much."

Roger Mayweather (Floyd's trainer and uncle) summed up his camp's view when he was asked about Floyd's strategy for fighting Gatti. "He don't need no strategy to fight Gatti," Roger answered. "Close your eyes and throw your hands, and you'll hit him in the fucking face."

That left Gatti's fans relying again on their fighter's toughness and mouthing platitudes like, "Arturo is a live underdog" and "Floyd will have to earn his victory; Arturo won't just give it to him." But the bottom line was, in boxing, the better fighter beats the more exciting fighter almost every time. And Gatti-Mayweather was the most over-matched that Arturo had been since he fought Oscar De La Hoya in 2001. Conventional wisdom was that Mayweather would carve him up and that, sometime in the middle-to-late rounds, the referee would intervene to stop the carnage. To have any chance at all of winning, Gatti would have to turn the match into a brawl.

"No point talking about boxing," said Emanuel Steward. "Floyd is too quick, too slick, and much more skilled than Arturo. Think Rocky Marciano and Jersey Joe Walcott. Marciano would have had no chance at all if he'd boxed him, so he banged away from the opening bell. If Arturo is unable to get inside and bang, the fight is over very early."

The oddsmakers were in accord, making Mayweather a 7-to-2 favorite. Floyd, who has no bigger fan than himself, thought that wasn't one-sided enough. "You can call me the bad guy; you can call me the good guy," he told the media. "But no matter what anyone says, I'm dedicated to boxing. There's no way to beat me."

If Mayweather had ended his remarks on that note, there would have been little notice. But he then went on to demean Gatti:

- "The truth is, he's not a good fighter and he's not on my level. He shouldn't even be in the ring with me."
- "Arturo Gatti is a heavy bag with legs. He's so slow it's ridiculous. When he punches, I can turn, say 'hi' to my mom, talk to the TV people, turn back, and still beat him to the punch."

● "He's a C-plus fighter. He's a street bum. I'll walk right through him. I don't have any respect for him."

● "I'm not going to let some guy beat my brains out. The name of the game is to hit and not get hit. The less you get hit, the longer you last in this sport. I'm not in this sport to see how many big punches I can take. That's what he does."

● "Gatti will go and say how much he did for the sport. All he did for the sport was make the ring mat bloody. You can tell this guy's taken a lot of punishment. He's had so much plastic surgery, he's starting to look Japanese."

As for the fight, Mayweather envisioned an easy victory. "It's a walk in the park, a piece of cake," he said. "I'm going to be a technician. Then I'm going to mix it up. I'm going to box circles around him. Then I'm going to go in the pocket and punish him. I'm going to take him out. Then I'll say, 'I told ya'll so.' This fight won't go past six rounds. It might not even go three. If you want to get rich, bet the house on this one. I'll destroy Arturo Gatti."

Gatti, needless to say, was offended by Mayweather's mouth. "I've been in a lot of fights," he said prior to the bout. "But I've never been in a fight where my opponent was talking like he is. He has no class, to speak about another fighter like he does."

"He has ability," Gatti continued. "But I don't know how tough he is. He's never had to dig deep. I don't know what size his heart is, but I'm gonna shrink it. He thinks I'm a C-plus fighter. We'll see what he thinks after he's been in the ring with me. It runs in the family, that big mouth; but it also runs in the family, a glass chin. Floyd talks a big game, but he's never fought anyone who hits as hard as me. When I punch my opponents, I hurt them. People fall down when I hit them, and he's going to walk into it. The only thing he has over me is speed. We'll see what happens when speed and power go against each other."

Then Gatti sounded an almost plaintive note. "I don't know what people are watching if they don't think I'm talented," he said. "I'm recognized as a tough fighter and a gutsy fighter and a warrior. You're not going to see for a long time someone like me. But I have skills; I'm talented. I want to be recognized as a great fighter, and winning this fight will do it. Everything I've learned about boxing will come out that night. A lot of people are going to have to apologize to me after this fight."

It was an ugly fight. It's hard for people to watch a fighter they care about lose, and harder still to watch him get beaten up. When both happen, it's worse.

Mayweather was exponentially faster that Gatti. He was also younger, stronger, a better boxer, and hit harder. From the opening bell, he exposed his opponent's shortcomings and fired hard clean sharp punches through every chink in Arturo's armor.

Gatti absorbed a brutal beating. In round one, he was dropped by a left hook when he inadvisedly turned to complain to referee Earl Morton about Mayweather hitting on the break. Then things got worse. Almost every round could have been scored 10-8 for Mayweather, although there were no knockdowns after the first.

By round three, Gatti's right eye was badly swollen. Two rounds later, the left one joined it. Arturo has an inordinately high threshhold of pain, but this was too much to endure. Mayweather outlanded him 168 to 41, and most of those blows were genuine "power punches". It was total domination, target practice all night. Finally, after six rounds, the slaughter was stopped.

The fight took place ten years and a day after Roy Jones massacred Vinny Pazienza at the same site. In that bout, Pazienza set a CompuBox record that will never be broken by failing to land a punch in the fourth round. Like Gatti, Pazienza was stopped in six. The two fights were equally one-sided. This time, Gatti was on the business end of exactly the kind of beating he used to dish out to mismatched opponents like Joey Gamache and Eric Jakubowski.

Gatti is 33 years old now and carrying the accumulated weight of thousands of blows to his head. After losing to Mayweather, he said he planned to fight again at 147 pounds. Perhaps he should talk first with Jesse James Leija.

Leija retired earlier this year after being knocked out by Gatti in five rounds. Like Arturo, he was a warrior, who went in tough against Oscar De La Hoya, Shane Mosley, Azumah Nelson, and Kostya Tszyu in their prime.

"When I saw Arturo Gatti and Micky Ward," Leija noted earlier this year, "I said they were crazy. They have huge hearts to take that type of punishment. You look and you're awed by it. But those types of fights come back to haunt you. They slow you down and you're not as sharp as you once were. You take punishment to give punishment. Once you get hit a lot, you get used to it and that's never good. And it's not good for your health. Micky is still having trouble from those wars with Gatti and it will probably affect him for the rest of his life."

Pay attention, Arturo.❏

*Jermain Taylor and his camp gave me full access prior to his first fight against Bernard Hopkins. The result was one of the most emotionally-draining weeks I've experienced in boxing.*

# HOPKINS-TAYLOR: THE CHANGING OF THE GUARD

On August 26, 2000, Jermain Taylor witnessed a professional boxing match in person for the first time. "I had just qualified for the 2000 Olympics," he recalls. "Some guy took the entire U.S. Olympic boxing team to Las Vegas on his private jet to see Fernando Vargas fight Ross Thompson. Vargas knocked him out. Dominick Guinn was on the undercard and knocked his opponent out too. That was special to me because Dominick and I are both from Arkansas."

"You could count the number of people in the stands when Dominick fought," Jermain continues. "The arena was almost empty. But I still remember the excitement I felt, seeing fighters with no headgear and no shirts. The whole thing was amazing to me. I asked myself, 'Am I gonna be here someday?'"

Taylor now knows the answer to that question. On July 16th, he won a split-decision victory over Bernard Hopkins at the MGM Grand in Las Vegas to capture the undisputed middleweight championship of the world.

Hopkins is one of the most forceful personalities to ever step into a boxing ring. He was born in 1965, the year that Sugar Ray Robinson retired from the sweet science. He likes to hear himself talk, and his favorite subject is Bernard Hopkins.

Boxing fans are familiar with the Hopkins saga. At age seventeen, he was sentenced to five-to-twelve years in prison for multiple street crimes. Fifty-six months later, he was released and his life began anew.

"When I got home from Graterford State Penitentiary," Hopkins reminisced earlier this year, "it wasn't like I knew I was going to be middleweight champion of the world some day. It was, I got eight years of parole and I don't ever want to go back there again."

On October 11, 1988, Hopkins weighed in at 177 pounds for his first professional fight and lost a four-round decision to Clinton Mitchell, who was also making his pro debut. "I wanted that fight to keep my mind off being on the streets," Bernard says. "I got my ass kicked, but I didn't get knocked out. After that, I took fifteen months off. I stopped training, never went to the gym, and blew up to 185 pounds. The only jobs I could get were off the books. I worked as a roofer for two hundred dollars a week. I got a job in the kitchen of the Penn Tower, polishing brass, scrubbing the floor, doing everything I was asked to do. Then new management came in and decided to do things by the book, and I got fired because they found out I was a convicted felon. And the whole time, I'm seeing a parole officer and pissing in a bottle to make sure I'm clean. I could have said, 'Fuck everything; I can't win; I'm going back to the streets.' I had a lot of options to do wrong, but I didn't want to be Y4145 [his prison number] again. And then I met a guy who knew a guy named Bouie Fisher."

When Hopkins met Fisher, to use his own words, "My record was zero and one; I was a loser." With Fisher as his trainer, he would become boxing's reigning pound-for-pound champion; a man with twenty consecutive successful title defenses, undefeated over a span of twelve years.

Hopkins is a fighter with no visible weaknesses. In the ring, he gives the impression of being as inexorable as a force of nature. At age forty, he challenges the proverb that time and tide wait for no man. He has a credo: Never get soft, mentally or physically. Not for a moment; and certainly not for a day.

Often, the public hears a fighter say, "I'm in the best shape of my life," and then watches as the fighter comes into the ring physically unprepared for battle. That never happens with Hopkins. Over the years, he has maintained his body through a mix of extraordinary discipline and hard work. He knows anatomy; his own and that of his opponent. He has turned himself into a finely-honed precision weapon.

Hopkins breaks his opponents down physically and mentally. "I'm in the fight business," he says. "While the fight's going on, the fight business is not about, 'Are you okay? Are you all right? Did I hit you too hard? Oh, I'm sorry I hit you in the ribs.' It's legal to hit a guy in the Adam's apple. A shoulder can be hit. Trust me; whatever limb you give me, I'm punching it."

Hopkins carries an aura of menace into the ring with him like an impregnable shield. By his conduct, he says, "I'm going to fight you for twelve rounds. If you beat me, it won't be by luck. You'll have to prove that you're a better fighter than I am, and I'll do anything to win."

But a mean streak only helps a fighter if he has the skills to go with it. Mind games only work if a fighter can back them up with his fists. Hopkins has the tools of a great fighter.

No boxer's defense is "impenetrable" but Bernard's comes close. One shouldn't confuse his ring style with his aggressive "executioner" persona. Hopkins is a smart conservative boxer who adheres to the view that, in boxing, every fight, every move, everything is a gamble.

"I'm not a guy who comes to blast you out of there," Hopkins says. "I've never considered myself a one-punch knockout artist. I'm more of a technician. I take my time. I dissect. Eventually, I'll get rid of you or beat you up."

Hopkins's superb defensive skills allow him to dictate the pace of his fights. He's often out of punching range; and any fighter who forces him to engage is skating on thin ice. Yes, Bernard might get tired if required to exchange punches for three minutes of every round, but so will his opponent. And his opponent will get hit a lot.

Bernard doesn't "execute" each of his foes; but almost always, he methodically tortures them. Thus it was that, earlier this year, Patrick Kehoe wrote, "No one has been able to stand up to Hopkins. Bending only leads to breaking. Toughing it out has been a prescription for a beating. Attempt to wage an insurgent strike and you are overwhelmed. Fight the smart fight and you are mastered. Rough up Hopkins and you are mugged. Speed is met with deception; strength with nimble endurance. In the face of passionate desire, he delivers waves of rage."

Nor is that rage limited to physical combat. The paradox of Bernard Hopkins is that there are times when he's articulate and charming. But too often, those times give way to something ugly.

Hopkins appears to approach all of his dealings in boxing as though they were street confrontations. He is vicious in and out of the ring. "Hopkins has made war upon us all," Kehoe continues. "He has no other persona. We don't suspect there's another personality lurking, something more tempered, reasonable, or mature."

Fighters leave promoters all the time. But on numerous occasions, Hopkins has left more bitterness than the norm in his wake. "Bernard Hopkins is a master villain," says Don King. "His villainy exceeds anything good in him. How do you spell 'difficult'?" King proclaims. "B-E-R-N-A-R-D. How do you spell 'problem'? H-O-P-K-I-N-S."

King, of course, carries his own baggage. But the truth is, a lot of people who have done business with Hopkins despise him. At one point, even Bouie Fisher (with whom Bernard has now reconciled) sued him. Hopkins, in turn, wants people to respect him. Whether they like him or not is of secondary importance. He seems to adhere to the view that no one's needs and desires matter except for his own. "I am who I am," he says. "If you forget the personal stuff and just look at me as an athlete, you'd be a fool not to respect me."

Jermain Taylor is the antithesis of Hopkins. The 26-year-old native of

Little Rock, Arkansas, is immensely likeable with a wholesome gentle quality about him. He's down-to-earth, unfailingly polite, and good looking. "Jermain Taylor has charisma," says HBO's Larry Merchant. "There's something about his look and bearing that gets your attention."

Taylor's father abandoned the family when Jermain was five, leaving Jermain, his mother, and three younger sisters behind. The children were raised in large part by their maternal grandmother, who was murdered by her own son (Jermain's uncle) seven years ago.

"He had a bad drug problem," Jermain says. "He wanted money and she wouldn't give it to him, so he cut her throat and then killed himself. I was at the Goodwill Games when it happened. They told me about it when I got home. I heard what they were saying, but it wasn't real. Then I went into her bedroom. There was blood all over the sheets, all over the floor, and I realized that what they were saying was true. I'd won a bronze medal at the games and, at the funeral, I put it in her casket. I wish I could see my grandmother now and share with her all the good things that have happened since then."

"Jermain grew up in a neighborhood where there was violence all the time," says police detective Dennis Moore, who has known Taylor since Jermain was in sixth grade and now travels to fights with him. "He needed someone to show him a better side of life from what he was seeing."

The man who stepped into the breach to do that was Ozell Nelson.

"I had a cousin who boxed," Jermain remembers. "One day, he took me to the gym with him. It was a while before my mother would let me box; but once she did, nothing deterred me. Ozell was my coach. The first time I sparred, it was with his son and he beat the crap out of me. But six months later, I was beating him with one hand."

Nelson became a stabilizing force and father figure in Taylor's life. "He was a scraggly little kid the first time I saw him," Ozell recalls. "He didn't look any different from any other kid who comes in. But when he started sparring, you could see that he had a lot of heart. When you meet a young man at that age, you never know how he'll turn out. But Jermain turned out just fine; better than fine."

Fighting as an amateur, Taylor won National Golden Gloves championships at 156 pounds in 1998 and 1999 and was a 156-pound bronze-medalist at the 2000 Olympics. Looking back on those days, he says, "In the amateurs, I was ignored most of the time because I come from Arkansas. I was skipped over a lot when boxers were chosen for teams that went to tournaments because Arkansas is small and doesn't have much boxing. Then I started winning national tournaments and it was like, 'Wow! Look at Jermain.'"

Taylor today is happily married to Erica Smith-Taylor. Like her husband, Erica is an accomplished athlete, having starred for the Louisiana Tech basketball team. Recently, she was drafted in the second round of the WNBA draft by the Washington Mystics. Rather than play pro ball, she is staying home to care for the couple's seven-month-old daughter, Nia Jay.

"My wife changed my whole view of women's sports," Jermain acknowledges. "We play one-on-one, and I can't stop her. The first time, she wanted this outfit and I said, 'I'll play you for it.' She beat me 10-6. Then we played again and she beat me again. I still haven't beaten her. And I'm walking around, saying, 'Damn! I can't beat my own wife in basketball.'"

"Family is very important to me," Jermain continues. "I'm not a flashy guy. I think I'm a nice person. A fighter has to have meanness, killer instinct. It has to be born in you. It can't be taught. If you don't have it, you're in the wrong sport. But I'll beat the hell out of you in the ring and then take you out for dinner. People say I've had a hard life that could have made me ugly, but who hasn't had problems. Everybody's been through something."

Enter Bernard Hopkins.

Hopkins and Taylor had been on each other's radar screen for several years. Bernard was the undisputed middleweight champion, and Jermain was seen by many as his heir apparent. In spring 2004, Hopkins appeared as a studio co-host on ESPN2 *Friday Night Fights* and dismissed Taylor's boxing skills. More specifically, he said that Jermain cocks his right hand when throwing his jab, leaving himself vulnerable to left-hook counterpunches.

"I don't worry about what Bernard says," Jermain stated afterward. "I know what I do. And when I do it, I'm in a safety zone. In fact, when I heard Bernard talking, I was like, 'Wow! He's talking about me; he's thinking about me.' That made me feel good."

Then Taylor had added. "It's important to me to fight Bernard Hopkins. Bernard is a great fighter and a real champion. I take nothing away from him. He earned what he has the hard way, and I honor him for that. But if I don't fight him, it will always be in people's minds, 'Well, he didn't beat Bernard Hopkins, so he's not a real champion.' So I see Bernard as my opportunity to make a name for myself. Someday, I'm gonna beat him. I won't put a timetable on it, but my time will come. I'll be disappointed if Bernard isn't there when I'm ready for that level of competition, but I got a feeling he'll still be on top."

Hopkins-Taylor was a hard fight to make. There were other opponents Bernard could have fought for just as much money as Jermain.

The negotiations were long and acrimonious. In the end, though, a deal was struck. One can speculate regarding Hopkins's motivation. But most likely, two factors were involved. First, Bernard wanted to wipe out Taylor as a cloud on his legacy. Had he ducked Jermain, each time their paths crossed in the future, Taylor would have known that Hopkins was afraid to fight him. And second, many people feel that Bernard took the fight to hurt Taylor's promoter, Lou DiBella, whom he despises. If so, it was Hopkins's hatred for DiBella that brought him down.

The early odds were 2-to-1 in the champion's favor, reflecting both Bernard's greatness and doubts regarding Jermain's seasoning as a fighter. Yes, Taylor was undefeated, but he had yet to step into the ring against an elite opponent. The best he had faced was a faded William Joppy. And Hopkins was in the habit of administering first-time defeats to the likes of Felix Trinidad and Glencoffe Johnson.

As for Bernard's age, trainer Bouie Fisher opined, "When it comes to boxing, Bernard isn't old; he's old school. There's a difference. You can see a lot of things with old eyes if you've been around boxing a while. Young eyes aren't always as good."

And Hopkins declared, ""Experience is more important than youth in all walks of life. Any young guy can get his driver's license, but that doesn't make him a good driver. My thing is, whatever Jermain Taylor will do, I can do better. I'm the better fighter; I'm the better athlete; and I'm the more experienced athlete. Come July 16th, I'm going to show that Bernard Hopkins is not here by any accident. Bernard Hopkins is not here by any fluke or any favors from the industry of boxing. I've been here twenty times. I know the sound of, 'This is for the undisputed middleweight championship of the world.' There's fifteen thousand people in the arena screaming. You're not in Little Rock, Arkansas; you're not in your hometown. You're not fighting a five-eight, five-nine small guy who you can bully. This is a different ballgame, dude. In forty-nine fights, I've never been cut. Bruises, yes; and my nose don't look the same. But I've never been cut. I know Jermain had to grow up quick and become a man before he was one. I respect Jermain for what he had to do to get where he is. He has the talent to take my place one day. One day. But not now; not against me. When he loses to Bernard Hopkins, twenty other guys will say, 'Hey, don't feel bad. We got beat too.'"

But Taylor's partisans were equally optimistic. They felt that, in recent years, Hopkins had been relying heavily on intimidation and bravado against fighters who were either too small (like Oscar De La Hoya) or simply not very good (e.g. Carl Daniels, Morrade Hakkar, and Robert Allen). The Trinidad fight, they noted, took place four years ago. And they believed in Jermain.

Taylor shared their confidence. "I'm ready," he proclaimed. "Hard work pays off, and it's paying off for me now. I put my time in. I've been boxing since I was twelve years old. I've got some good boxing experience myself. I fought the guys I needed to fight. I'm right on schedule. It's time for me to put up or shut up. I love a good challenge. Either I'm good or I'm not. It's my time now."

As for his opponent, Jermain declared, "I have to give respect where it's due, and Bernard deserves it. He does have a lot of professional experience, and I respect that. If you let him set the pace of a fight, he'll pick you apart; but I'm not gonna let him do it. Whatever he does, I can adapt. If he wants to box, I'll box. If he wants to brawl, I'll brawl. I won't do anything fancy; just go in the ring and take care of business. I wish he was thirty, because I'd beat him then too."

Still, one thing was very clear. Talk of Taylor as the successor to Bernard Hopkins was theory, not fact. And after the fight, win or lose, Jermain would no longer be a rising star. Either he would be the undisputed middleweight champion of the world or just another name on Bernard Hopkins's ring record.

Meanwhile, as July 16th approached, Hopkins-Taylor was catching on within the boxing community. In the ring, Bernard is an all-time great, but he has never been an all-time attraction. It aggravates him to hear people say that Philadelphia hasn't had a champion in a major sport since the Philadelphia 76ers won the NBA title in 1983. "What about me?" he asks.

But Hopkins-Taylor was selling well. Advance pay-per-view buys were ahead of expectations. Ultimately, HBO would report 350,000 purchases. And after a slow start, tickets were moving. A lot of that was attributable to Taylor. Best estimates were that 4,000 fans were making their way across the continent from Arkansas to Las Vegas. But Hopkins deserved credit as half of a great match-up between two distinct personalities at the highest level of the sport. This was boxing at its best.

There's something special about the week of a big fight, and this one was no exception. The final pre-fight press conference was held on Wednesday, July 13th. Hopkins seemed to be looking past Taylor as he talked about moving up in weight to fight Antonio Tarver or Roy Jones next.

"I'm forty, but I'm the youngest forty you've ever seen," he said. "In the last ten years, I haven't even had a fight that was considered close. I've been in the ring with Roy Jones, Oscar De La Hoya, Glencoffe Johnson, Felix Trinidad. Who has Jermain Taylor been in with? Jermain Taylor says I'm not going to show him anything he hasn't seen before. But Jermain Taylor doesn't know what he's getting into. Seeing and experiencing are two different things. I had fifteen world championship fights before Jermain Taylor turned pro. When you got twenty championship defenses and you've been undefeated since 1993 and you've heard twenty fighters, trainers, and managers say the same thing, it's hard to convince me at a press conference that I got a problem."

Hopkins also chose to comment on Taylor's persona, saying, "Jermain Taylor and I are both African-Americans but that's where the similarity ends." A mocking appraisal followed, highlighted by, "Jermain uses words like 'golly gee.' That's not my style."

"As a child, I had a real bad speech problem," Taylor said when it was his turn to talk. "I stuttered a lot. I still do it some, so it's hard enough for me to talk without trying to talk trash. Bernard Hopkins might outtalk me, but I'm gonna outfight him. I want to be number one; and now that I got that chance, I'm gonna take it. I'm a lot faster than Bernard; faster and stronger. However he brings it, I'm going to take it to him. I know how Bernard fights. If he wants to make it a dirty fight, then it's going to be a dirty fight because I ain't backing down from nobody. My time is now, and Bernard is ready for the taking. There's been a lot of ups and downs in my life, a lot of hurt. I've had to step up to the plate when it wasn't my time. All that has prepared me for this moment. This is what I've wanted since I first started boxing. I'm not just coming to fight. I'm coming to win."

Still, anyone can say anything in boxing. Fighters have to prove the truth of their words with their fists. Taylor was relaxed all week, confident and looking forward to Saturday night. But there are things that a fighter can't prepare for in his head or in the gym. He has to experience them in fights. Jermain had never encountered real trouble in the ring as a pro. And at some point during the fight, no matter how it went, he could expect real trouble from Hopkins.

Knowing how Bernard fights and being able to deal with it are two vastly different things. The man who was primarily responsible for giving Jermain the necessary tools and preparing him for battle was his trainer, Pat Burns.

Burns was born and raised in Miami, where he has lived for virtually all of his 55 years. A self-described "family man" who goes to mass every Sunday, he served from 1972 through 1995 as a detective, an undercover officer, and with special units of the Miami police department. "You name it, I did it," he says.

After the 1980 riots, Burns was asked by the department to start a Police Athletic League boxing program for inner-city youths. Soon, he was accompanying fighters to international matches. In 1992 and 1996, he was one of the coaches for the United States Olympic boxing team.

There's one experience in his life that he doesn't talk about much. In 1968, he was a marine in Vietnam and "got blown up pretty good; shrapnel and gunfire; spent a year in the hospital."

Thus, Burns said of Hopkins-Taylor, "This isn't Vietnam or being a police officer. It's a prizefight. No one is getting killed here."

Burns has guided Taylor from his first day as a professional fighter. "At the beginning, my relationship with Jermain was very autocratic," he recalls. "When I first saw him, he was fast and strong but his technique wasn't what it could have been. The potential for growth was there. But it was clear that, to be a great professional, he was going to have to channel his wildness. Now Jermain is in his fifth year as a professional and he's earned my full respect for his views. A lot of guys are determined on the night of a fight, but Jermain has the everyday work ethic to back up his determination. He has a determination to win and also the willingness to do what it takes to achieve his goals."

But the relationship between teacher and student got off to an unusual start. "When a fighter turns pro," Burns says, "you sit him down and tell him, 'Okay, everything they told you that you couldn't do as an amateur—hold, bump, push, spin, use your shoulders—you have to do now as a pro. And there were some other issues."

Such as?

"When I first met Pat," Jermain offers, "I thought he was crazy."

Because?

"One day, I was tired and slacked off in the gym. There was this lizard on the ground, about six inches long. Pat picked it up and . . . Ugh!"

"Jermain was training for his first pro fight," Burns recalls, picking up the story. "He was showing some fatigue, and I wanted him to understand that he was expected to maintain a new level of intensity if he was going to be a professional fighter. So I told him, 'When a lizard gets in a fight, there's no quit in it.'"

Then Burns bit the head off the lizard.

Jermain's eyes grew wide.

Burns spit the lizard's head out of his mouth and held out the still-squirming body.

"Oh, my God," Jermain blurted out.

Burns came closer, waving the decapitated lizard.

Jermain took several steps back. "Oh, my God," he said again.

Then the man, who five years later would challenge Bernard Hopkins for the undisputed middleweight championship of the world, turned and ran out of the gym. He returned several minutes later, but only to look in through the door.

"It's safe," someone told him. "The lizard is in the garbage."

The lesson had been learned. Professional boxing is a cold hard brutal world where only the strong survive. Right and wrong don't matter. Your opponent will do anything and everything to win. You will have to be prepared to do the same. If you can't be like this in the ring, get out now.

Burns readied Taylor for the Hopkins fight the same way he'd prepared him twenty-three times before. "If we started doing things differently now," the trainer explained, "Jermain would question everything we've done in the past. Besides, if it ain't broke, don't fix it."

"We expect Bernard to fight this fight like every other fight because he thinks Jermain is just another young kid," Burns continued. "Bernard fights one minute a round and cons you the other two. If you let him come out of the gate with a lead, playing catch-up is a problem. To beat him, you have to press the action, set a fast pace, and tire him out. That's easier said than done, but it has to be done."

"I expect Jermain to control the pace of the fight with his jab," the trainer elaborated. "Every fighter who ever lived had trouble with an opponent who has a good jab. Yes, Jermain drags his right hand when he throws a jab. So let Bernard eat that jab and try to counter. Jermain's jab is too fast and too strong for Bernard. Let them each throw five jabs, and we'll see who takes a step back."

"I've never seen a fighter who makes adjustments during a fight as well as Bernard," Burns acknowledged. "That means Jermain is going to get hit. But we'll see who gets hit more often and harder. Think of a man who walks down the street every day past a fence with a pit bull behind it. If the man just walks on by, he's fine. But if he kicks the fence every day, one day the pit bull is going to come over the fence and bite him hard. Bernard is kicking the fence with Jermain. Jermain has nothing personal against Bernard and he respects him as a fighter. But Jermain is going to hurt Bernard. Jermain matches up well against Bernard, physically and mentally, and he can go down in the basement and get nasty if he has to."

Burns's face turned deadly serious.

"And one thing more. Listen to me. Look at me, because what I'm about to tell you is very important. Jermain will not be intimidated by Bernard Hopkins. There is no intimidation factor here at all. Zero. None."

That proposition had its first test on Friday. The day began with HBO conducting its usual meeting with each of the fighters who would be on the pay-per-view telecast. At 11:00 a.m., Jim Lampley, Larry Merchant, Emanuel Steward, and the other major players on the HBO production team met with Hopkins in Studio 3 adjacent to the arena. Hopkins began by complaining that he didn't get proper respect from HBO and criticizing Merchant for on-air comments about Mike Tyson that the analyst had made the previous month. Then Bernard aimed his venom at Emanuel Steward, who had predicted earlier in the week that Taylor would beat him. That tirade, according to several persons present, began with the declaration that Hopkins would have beaten any of Steward's past middleweights and quickly turned personal with Bernard likening Emanuel to Sammy Davis Jr. and calling him an Uncle Tom.

Then the unexpected happened.

Merchant stood up, glared across the table at Hopkins, and said, "Fuck you. I'm not going to sit here and let you insult my colleague."

That led to a louder "fuck you" in return, at which point Merchant, Steward, Lampley, producer Tom Odelfelt, and director Marc Payton walked out of the room.

"Bernard wants to sit there and say anything he wants about anybody without anything coming back at him," Lampley said later. "But the world doesn't work that way."

"I came to Las Vegas to see a fight, not to be in one," Merchant added.

Then came an uglier, more serious confrontation. Hopkins, as previously noted, despises Lou DiBella, and the feeling is mutual. Two years ago, DiBella won a $610,000 libel judgment against Bernard that was affirmed on appeal. Fight fans don't care who promotes or manages a fighter. They're interested in what goes on in the ring. But Bernard had made his hatred for DiBella a subplot to Hopkins-Taylor.

Two months before the fight, Pat Burns acknowledged, "Jermain and I have already discussed the fact that Bernard will try to get at him through Lou in a way that creates doubt in his mind and causes distractions. Jermain is ready for that. In fact, he's looking forward to it. It will break the monotony."

Taylor, for his part, had said simply, "It's not between Bernard and Lou. He's not fighting Lou. He's fighting me."

Still, the Hopkins assault continued unabated. "I take all fights personal," Bernard said in the days leading up to the fight. "But this one's extremely personal. It's a fight that motivates me more than any fight I ever fought. This ain't no lawyer stuff. In this fight, there's no objections; there ain't no overruling. I am the judge, the jury, and the executioner. I'm not going to act like Jermain's even in there. It's not even important that he's in there, because it won't be his face I'm seeing. I will win, must win, and there's no other way that I'm looking at it. I cannot and will not lose this fight. I'd rather be carried out on a stretcher than lose this fight to [Lou DiBella] and give him a day in the sun. Everybody in their lifetime has the experience where they want to get revenge. That's my motivation. I can't hit [DiBella]. He would love for me to do that. He would love for me to lose my temper and clock him upside the head in front of thirty, forty reporters. I'm too smart for that. But how fortunate Bernard Hopkins is that God gave me somebody who just happens to be the only bankroll that [DiBella] has in his portfolio. This is a great country, where I can go in a ring and do something I love to do and actually assault somebody and got a personal reason why I want to clock this guy. Jermain Taylor is going to pay the price for what I feel in my heart. Jermain Taylor is gonna be the whupping boy of my controlled frustrations. Jermain Taylor is the closest guy I can go ahead and physically hurt and physically beat up without going to jail."

At the final pre-fight press conference, for good measure, Hopkins proclaimed that beating DiBella's fighter would be "like a second erection."

By this time, Hopkins and DiBella were adversaries whose hatred for one another was bubbling over. But while one man seemed to be thriving on the confrontation, the other was sickened by it. DiBella was sinking into depression. Hopkins-Taylor had become an agonizing experience. Bernard had gotten inside him like some kind of food poisoning that he couldn't expurgate from his system.

One day before the fight, at the fighter weigh-in, the ugliness burgeoned uncontrollably over the line. Outside, the heat was blistering with the temperature topping 110 degrees. Taylor entered the MGM Grand Garden Arena and stepped on the scale. The crowd roared. Perfect weight, 160 pounds. Hopkins followed to a chorus of boos, while DiBella stood near the back of the platform, gesturing with both thumbs down.

"Bernard Hopkins, 160 pounds."

"Face off the fighters," someone instructed.

But instead of moving to a staredown with Jermain, Bernard approached DiBella. Hopkins knows how to place his punches in and out of the ring. In both venues, he has been known to go low. Twelve years ago, after being disabled in a skiing accident, DiBella's brother had committed suicide. DiBella had shared that information with Hopkins in earlier years when the fighter and promoter had been friends. Now—

"You're going to kill yourself tomorrow night," DiBella says Hopkins told him. "It's the end of your life tomorrow night. You know about people killing themselves. You'll slit your throat or take pills and not wake up on Sunday morning."

Then Hopkins moved toward Taylor, who was tying his shoes, and stood over him. "You're a puppet," Bernard sneered.

Taylor stood up and the two men were nose-to-nose with perhaps two inches between them.

"I ain't no one's puppet, you ugly motherfucker."

They stood that way, jawing at one another, until calmer heads separated them.

Afterward, Jermain was pleased with the confrontation. "There was a whole lot of motherfucking going on," he said on the way back to his hotel room. "Bernard got in my face, and my first reaction was to step back and throw an uppercut. I got two sides. I'll beat him in a street fight too. Man, we were so close, our lips were almost kissing. I said to myself, 'This won't look good to my wife.'"

"Bernard is trying to get his courage up; that's all," Pat Burns offered. "Some guys drink to get that liquid courage. Some guys do it like this."

"Some people need anger management," Jermain responded. "I don't mind smack-talking, but this went too far. I like Lou, and I don't like what that ugly motherfucker is doing to him."

On Saturday morning (the day of the fight), Jermain rose at 5:30 and went downstairs with Burns for a second weigh-in. Under the rules of the International Boxing Federation (one of the organizations sanctioning the fight), neither fighter could exceed 170 pounds the morning after the official weigh-in.

The IBF weigh-in was scheduled for 6:00 a.m. With a representative of the Hopkins camp already present, Jermain got on the scale ten minutes early. 168 pounds. Burns and Taylor didn't bother to wait for Hopkins. "He'll be on weight," Pat explained later. "And we wanted to send a message. It doesn't matter what he weighs. Jermain will beat him." Then Burns and Taylor ate breakfast. At 6:40, Jermain went back to sleep and Pat turned his attention to credentials, tickets, and other details.

Burns is meticulously organized. "Hard work is crucial for a trainer too," he explains. "If the trainer is lazy, it rubs off on the fighter. A lot of my work takes place outside the gym. I break down hours of tape, but that's just the start of it. I know the rules. I'm always running different scenarios through my mind, from the ring collapsing to some guy flying in on a parachute. I make sure that everything is done right, from medical tests to plane and hotel reservations. I'm very organized. It's important to me that every 'i' is dotted and every 't' is crossed. Jermain is not going to lose a fight because of some little thing that I didn't do during the fight, the day of the fight, or a month before the fight. Attention to every detail is crucial."

At 1:15 p.m., Burns went to the arena with his brother Joey to check out the ring. Carefully, he examined the canvas, ropes, turnbuckles, and view from the corner. He even stood on the Nevada State Athletic

Commission table set against the ring apron to see if it would support
his weight should it be necessary to stand on it. Then he went to the
dressing room to determine how much space would be available for
Jermain's preparation in the two hours before the fight. The heating was
of particular concern to him. Las Vegas is heavily air-conditioned. Burns
wanted the dressing room at 85 degrees. Seventy-two degrees was the
norm.

"We can do eighty," a maintenance supervisor told him. "I'm not sure
about the other five."

Five hours later, Burns had a heater in the dressing room to make up
the difference.

Meanwhile, Jermain slept until 12:30. Then he showered and
dressed. Most fighters spend the afternoon of a big fight in their room.
At 2:15, Jermain went downstairs for a boisterous pre-fight meal. Two
dozen family members and friends from Little Rock had gathered at
Wolfgang Puck.

"Why are you eating here instead of in Jermain's room?" Burns was
asked.

"Look at him," Burns answered, nodding toward Jermain, who was
laughing and talking animatedly. "We've done it this way twenty-three
times before. You do what works."

The mood was akin to a holiday family dinner. Jermain and Erica
began talking about their most recent confrontation on the basketball
court.

"Tell the truth," Jermain prodded. "It was close."

"It wasn't close."

"Yes, it was."

"Ten-six isn't close," Erica countered.

"It was ten-eight. And the only reason you won was because, when I
was ahead, you started trash-talking and fouling and throwing elbows,
and I was too much of a gentleman to hit you back."

"You did too foul me."

"No, I didn't. I touch you once and it's 'Jermain, why are you
fouling?'"

Then the conversation turned to the fight.

"Hopkins thinks he can scare me with that look," Jermain
proclaimed. "But he ain't never been looked at by my mother." There
were gales of laughter. Jermain blew a kiss toward his mother, who was
seated at the far end of the table. "When I was little, if I did wrong, that
look was scary. Bernard's look ain't nothing compared to that."

People talk about a big fight atmosphere and how it can freeze a
fighter. But the spotlight had been on Jermain since his Olympic days,

so that was old news to him. The pressure would come from getting in the ring with a great fighter who was favored to beat him.

"This reminds me of my first pro fight, against Chris Walsh at Madison Square Garden," Jermain said. "It's something new, stepping things up to the next level."

"Every time you hit Bernard," he was told, "there's going to be four thousand people from Arkansas in the stands who holler 'golly gee!'"

Evander Holyfield, who had travelled to Las Vegas for the fight, came by to say hello and was asked about the match-up. "Jermain is ready," Evander said. "This reminds me of my first fight against Dwight Muhammad Qawi. Bernard has the same mindset as Qawi, but I don't think Jermain will be intimidated. No one can intimidate anyone else. It's all about how a person feels about himself."

"I'm tired of Hopkins getting in my face and talking bad about Arkansas," Jermain added. "But I don't worry about all the hoopla and trash-talking. I'm just here to get a job done. All my life, I've had this in me, and tonight it's gonna come out."

Shortly after 6:00 p.m., wearing a gray T-shirt and black warm-up pants with a gray stripe down either side, Jermain Taylor arrived at his dressing room at the MGM Grand Garden Arena. The arena was beginning to fill up. At the sports book, Hopkins was still favored but the odds had dropped to 3-to-2. That reflected the view that Jermain was as good as anyone Bernard had ever fought with the exception of Roy Jones and, possibly, Felix Trinidad.

Jermain sat quietly beside Pat Burns on a sofa and watched as Vernon Forrest dismantled Sergio Rios on a large television screen in front of him. Dennis Moore stood guard by the dressing room door. Cutman Ray Rodgers was readying the tools of his trade. Ozell Nelson, Dan Lowry (who ran the gym in Little Rock where Ozell first trained Jermain), and Joey Burns joined them. So did Pat's 12-year-old son, Ryan. Well-wishers came and went.

At 6:30, Burns closed the door to all but essential personnel. Five minutes later, referee Jay Nady came in to give the pre-fight instructions. The Taylor camp was happy with the choice of Nady as the referee. He was a big no-nonsense guy who ran a tight ship and, it was hoped, would keep fouling to a minimum. "This is for every belt that I know of," Nady began. The pro forma instructions followed.

At 6:55, Ozell Nelson went to Hopkins's dressing room to oversee the champion's hands being wrapped. While he was gone, Naazim Richardson (a Hopkins second) watched Pat Burns do the same with Jermain. At 7:20, the taping was done. "Except for the commission inspector," Burns said, "all cell phones off, please."

Everything in the dressing room was relaxed, business-like, and low-key according to plan. There was no music. The temperature was 85 degrees.

Jermain put on his University of Arkansas red trunks. Lou DiBella came in and sat on a chair in the corner. "I don't know that Jermain is going to win," DiBella had said earlier in the day. "I do know that Bernard is in for a long hard night." DiBella looked relatively calm, but his words belied that belief. "It feels like my whole life is bet on this fight," he said.

Jermain went into an ante-room the size of a small boxing ring with a carpeted floor and cinderblock walls. Under the watchful eye of Burns and training assistant Edgardo Martinez, he began to shadow-box, work the pads, and break a sweat.

At 7:45, Naazim Richardson returned and Jermain gloved up. Once a fighter has his gloves on, he can punch but he can't do much else.

Taylor, Burns, and Martinez went back into the ante-room. Work resumed on an intensified level, with Burns giving advice in a reassuring yet authoritative voice.

"Make sure your feet and hands work together . . . He won't be able to stop the jab. The moment you sense he's trying to counter the jab with a jab, double up . . . The last fifteen seconds of each round, you'll have already won it and he'll try to steal it. Don't give up anything cheap . . . Punch him anywhere you can . . . Speed kills. If he's doing forty, you do sixty. If he's doing sixty, you do eighty . . . Don't let the crowd influence you . . . If he gets in a rhythm, go in with a forearm and push him out of it . . . I'm looking for at least twenty-five jabs a round. Pick him apart. That's how you dominate."

At 8:12, the final preliminary fight ended. Jermain started hitting the pads with greater intensity. "He's sharp," Burns said. "We're bringing back a world champion."

Everyone in a fighter's camp believes, particularly when the fighter is young and undefeated. But Jermain would be facing a man who hadn't lost a fight in twelve years.

"Two minutes thirty seconds and then you walk," HBO production coordinator Tami Cotel instructed.

"Everybody do their job," Burns said.

And so it would be. Two men in the ring. One filled with hate and anger; the other with a joy for life. Urban versus country, enforcer versus protector, nasty versus nice. But in the coming hour, none of that would matter. In real life, sometimes the bad guy wins, the good guy loses the girl, and the hero dies of cancer.

It was a pro-Taylor crowd. That was evident from the roar of approval that resounded when Jermain entered the arena. There were 11,992 fans in attendance. One-third of them had come from Arkansas. Two minutes later, Hopkins made his way to the ring. Michael Buffer introduced the fighters. The bell for round one sounded. One could imagine the voice in Jermain's head: "I'm in the ring with a great fighter. Now is the time to find out if I'm a great fighter too."

The early rounds belonged to Taylor. Hopkins goes through the early stages of a fight cautiously. Jermain advanced behind his jab, while Bernard slowed the pace by retreating and keeping his right hand cocked to discourage forays by the challenger. Forty seconds into round two, a chopping overhand right followed by a left hook caused the champion to fall back and downward against the ropes. Some thought it should have been called a knockdown. Jay Nady let the moment pass.

Taylor was faster. Hopkins minimized the number of encounters by moving around the ring and did his best work while punching out of clinches with sharp punishing blows. Bernard is supreme on the inside. That was where he was expected to do the most damage.

Fifty seconds into round five, the fighters clashed heads and an ugly wound pierced Taylor's scalp just above the hairline to the bone. Blood flowed freely and would for much of the night. Jermain had only been cut once before in a professional fight. Blood can undermine a fighter's confidence, and some ring judges score blood more than they should.

Bernard Hopkins, it has been said, takes away his opponent's fight plan. Then he implements his own. Jermain expended a lot of energy chasing Hopkins around the ring and throwing sometimes-wild punches. In round nine, the challenger seemed to tire and the roles of predator and prey were reversed. The champion began his assault. A right hand hurt Taylor in round ten. More punishing blows followed. Round eleven was the same. Now Hopkins's fists were doing his talking for him. That one hurt, didn't it, Jermain?

Then came a moment that will forever define the career of each fighter. There was a minute left in round eleven. The momentum was all with Hopkins. Taylor was backed against the ropes, in trouble. Hopkins landed a big right hand. And in his darkest moment, Jermain summoned the strength to fire three hard shots with lightning speed into Bernard's body. Rather than continue the exchange, Hopkins stepped back. No one knew it at the time, but that was when Jermain Taylor established himself as a champion.

"We have a split decision," ring announcer Michael Buffer told the crowd when the fight was over.

Twelve thousand people held their breath as the final moments of the drama unfolded.

116-112 for Hopkins.

115-113 for Taylor

And 115-113 "for the NEW undisputed middleweight champion of the world, the pride of Little Rock, Arkansas, Jermain Taylor."

In the aftermath of the fight, Hopkins showed a conspicuous lack of grace. "This is a situation where I won and they gave it to the other guy," he said.

Hopkins partisans focused on two issues. First, they claimed, this was an extremely close fight and close fights should go to the champion. But that school of thought was debunked years ago by veteran trainer Gil Clancy who declared, "Once the bell for round one rings, both guys are equal. The only edge the champion should get is, he keeps his championship if the fight is a draw."

That, of course, was where Hopkins moved next. More specifically, he complained about ring judge Duane Ford scoring the last round for Taylor. Had Ford marked his card differently, Bernard would have retained his title on a draw.

For the record, this observer had the fight even at 114-114. But Hopkins has only himself to blame for the result. Rather than focus on one round, let's look at the fight as a whole.

Over the first eight rounds, Bernard threw an average of nineteen punches per round and landed an average of only five. Fighters don't win many fights that way. Most great fighters land more than five punches a round over the first eight rounds of a championship fight. Taylor challenged Hopkins to fight, and Bernard backpedaled.

After eight rounds, Taylor had outlanded Hopkins 63 to 40. In other words, during the first two-thirds of the fight, he landed 57 percent more punches than Bernard. Overall, he outlanded Hopkins in six of the twelve rounds, while Hopkins outlanded Jermain in five (including the final four rounds of the fight). In the fourth round, each man landed seven punches. Bernard pulled ahead in the punch-stat totals over the final four stanzas, but four rounds are less than eight.

Hopkins gives the impression that he's impervious to pain, and he says that Jermain never hurt him. But something kept Bernard at bay for the first eight rounds. Maybe he knows something about his limitations that the rest of us don't.

It should also be noted with regard to the scoring that Duane Ford gave round four to Hopkins, which many observers felt was the wrong choice. Bernard saved a point in the second round when Jay Nady didn't call his being punched into the ring ropes a knockdown. And Nady could easily have taken points from Hopkins for hitting and holding, low blows, hitting behind the head, using his elbows, and leading with his head. Indeed, the referee came close to doing just that when he visited Bernard's corner after round eight and warned, "One more time and I'll take a point away."

And let's not forget, after an accidental clash of heads, Taylor fought the last seven-and-a-half rounds with a gash in his scalp that required six stitches to close.

"I won the fight," Jermain said afterward. "Bernard needs to stop crying, but that's the type of person he is. When he was champion, I gave him respect. Now I'm champion. Give me the respect I deserve."

It's unlikely that Hopkins will do that. But as Jermain's cutman, Ray Rodgers, noted, "Bernard can say what he wants. The belts are going to Little Rock." And one Arkansas traveller queried, "If that Hopkins feller is smarter than everyone else, how come Jermain figured him out in round one and it took him eight rounds to figure out Jermain?"

At the very least, Jermain Taylor fought boxing's reigning pound-for-pound champion even over twelve rounds. On July 16th, Jermain Taylor was every bit as good as Bernard Hopkins. And that requires a tip of the hat to Pat Burns.

Bouie Fisher recently declared, "Becoming a great trainer takes years of knowledge and experience. Some of the trainers who people call 'great' today aren't even good. They were just placed in great situations."

Taylor was a prospect coming out of the 2000 Olympics, but no one said that he was a can't-miss proposition. The big-money contracts that year went to Ricardo Williams and Rocky Juarez. Burns has guided Jermain from his first professional fight to victory over Bernard Hopkins. That deserves attention.

Arkansas hasn't had a lot of individual sports heroes. Dizzy Dean, Brooks Robinson, Bill Dickey, Don Hutson, and Scottie Pippen were hall-of-fame athletes who earned their laurels in the north. Sonny Liston's Arkansas roots hardly made the state proud. That leaves John Daly and Sidney Moncrief. Jermain Taylor might be the biggest thing to come out of Arkansas since Bill Clinton. His victory has been mentioned in the same breath as the Razorbacks' 1994 triumph over Duke for the NCAA basketball championship and the football team's 1965 defeat of Nebraska for a share of the national crown. That could place Pat Burns in the same ledger (albeit not on the same page) as coaches Nolan Richardson and Frank Broyles in Arkansas lore.

As for the big picture in boxing, Taylor might be the new star that the sweet science has been waiting for. The past twelve months have seen the devaluation of the sport's flagship fighters. Oscar De La Hoya, Roy Jones, Mike Tyson, Evander Holyfield, Felix Trinidad, Shane Mosley, Arturo Gatti, and Kostya Tszyu all met with adversity; and there hasn't been much to fill the void. Floyd Mayweather has extraordinary talent but limited drawing power. Zab Judah has shown flashes of both, but sometimes comes up short. Miguel Cotto might not live up to the hype. Ricky Hatton could be the "next Arturo Gatti" but that's different from being a great fighter. As good as Winky Wright, Antonio Tarver, Marco Antonio Barrera, Erik Morales, Manny Pacquiao, Juan Manuel Medina, and Diego Corrales are, their crossover appeal is limited. As for today's heavyweights, the less said the better.

Taylor could be "the man." But first, he'll have to get by Hopkins again in a contractually-mandated rematch. That bout is now expected to take place in December. Everyone acknowledges that Hopkins makes adjustments brilliantly. What does that presage for next time?

"I learned from this fight," Jermain said afterward. "Bernard's not a big puncher, but he's an accurate puncher. He picks his punches well. And he's a dirty fighter, who's very good at what he does. He took me to places where I'd never been before, but all that will make me stronger. I should have cut the ring off more and thrown more body shots. I should have come out of the clinches differently and kept my left hand high. I'll be working on those things in the future."

"I've talked to Jermain until I'm blue in the face about dropping his left hand," Pat Burns said after the fight. "I've told him again and again. There's nothing more I can do on that one. He'll just have to watch the tape and learn for himself, which I think he'll do. I fully expect Bernard to be better next time, but Jermain will be better too."

He'd better be. Hopkins is a masterful fighter. In the ring, he's a work of art. To perform the way he does at age forty is extraordinary. Bernard came into the Taylor fight with a 20-1-1 record in world championship contests and the third-longest championship reign in boxing history (ten years, 82 days). He won't go quietly.

"There was Holyfield-Bowe and Ali-Frazier," Hopkins said shortly after his defeat. "Now maybe we can have Bernard Hopkins against Jermain Taylor."

Perhaps. But before there's a trilogy, Bernard will have to win the rematch. A lot of people said that Jermain Taylor was one tough fight away from beating Bernard Hopkins. When they meet again, Jermain will have that one tough fight under his championship belts.❏

*As Jermain Taylor was reaching for glory, Mike Tyson's career was coming to an end, as noted in the following article written for the* Observer Sports Monthly.

# THE END OF MIKE TYSON

On the night of June 11, 2005, Mike Tyson stepped into the ring at the MCI Center in Washington, D.C. to face Kevin McBride.

McBride is a club fighter with a record of 33 wins, 4 losses, and 1 draw. Prior to meeting Tyson, he had been knocked out four times, most ignominiously by English journeyman Michael Murray. To put that defeat in context, Murray lost 17 of his final 18 fights before retiring in 2001. His sole victory during that stretch was his knockout of McBride.

The "Clones Colossus" (as McBride is known) seemed pleasantly surprised to find himself on his feet when the first round against Tyson ended. Then the sacrificial lamb rose up and slaughtered the butcher. Of course, McBride was helped by the fact that Iron Mike looked worse than he ever had before. Tyson's punches lacked power. His timing was off. In round six, after five lumbering stanzas, he tried to hyper-extend McBride's elbow in a clinch. Then he was penalized two points for an intentional head butt, repeated both fouls, and fell to the canvas in exhaustion. He quit on his stool before the start of the seventh round.

"I don't have the guts to be in this sport anymore," Tyson acknowledged afterward. "I'd liked to have continued, but I saw that I was getting beat on. I just don't have this in my heart anymore. I'm not going to disrespect the sport by losing to this caliber of fighter. This is my ending. I'm not interested in fighting anymore. I hate the smell of a gym. I hate the boxing game. That guy [I used to be] in 1985, 1986, I don't know that guy anymore. I don't have a connection with him anymore. I'm just not that person anymore. I believed that I was still a fighter, but I'm not. I'm washed up."

When Mike Tyson was young, he was a great fighter. It's difficult to gauge how great because he never had the ring inquisitors that most great fighters have. Nonetheless, he began his career with 19 consecutive knockouts, won his first 37 fights, and was heavyweight champion of the world at age 20.

But the last big fight that Tyson won was in 1988 when he knocked out Michael Spinks. After that, he stopped training properly. On February 11, 1990, he was dethroned by James "Buster" Douglas and his aura of invincibility was gone.

In 1992, Tyson went to prison for rape. Three years later, he emerged from incarceration as the ugly face of boxing. Thereafter, he fought fifteen times. But as he admitted following his loss to McBride, "My career has been over since 1990. After I got out of jail, I beat guys because they were scared."

Once Tyson was finished as an elite fighter, there was always someone with deep pockets who was willing to put up big money to get him in a boxing ring. The last twelve fights of his career (of which he won six) damaged his legacy because they obscured the memory of how good he was when he was young. When boxing fans think of Muhammad Ali, they think of his historic victories over Sonny Liston, Joe Frazier, and George Foreman. With Joe Louis, it's his knockout triumphs over Max Schmeling and Billy Conn. Rocky Marciano conjures up images of his devastating thirteenth-round stoppage of Joe Walcott.

When boxing fans think of Tyson, they think of his confrontations with Evander Holyfield and Lennox Lewis. Iron Mike is defined by his losses, not his wins.

Like Princess Diana, Michael Jackson, and a handful of other media superstars, Tyson became part of the world psyche. Everyone knew who he was and everyone had an opinion about him. Tyson, in turn, fed the media frenzy simply by being Tyson. "When I say something," he once observed, "it goes all over the world in thirty seconds. I'm an icon; I'm an international superstar. If they don't know my name, they're from another planet."

However, in addition to his crossover appeal, Tyson engendered crossover revulsion. And there came a time when the magnitude of it all weighed heavily upon him.

"My intentions were not to fascinate the world with my personality," Tyson said recently. "I just wanted the boxing world to bear witness to my existence. I didn't know that I was going to be some big worldwide motherfucker, when I walk the streets of Paris the whole block shuts down." And then he added, "As you get older, all that fun, fame, and fortune isn't what you think it's going to be."

One week before his fight against McBride, Tyson summed up his state of mind when he told reporters at an open workout, "I'll never be happy. I believe I'll die alone. I would want it that way. I've been a loner all my life with my secrets and my pain. I'm really a sad pathetic case. My whole life has been a waste. I've been a failure. I just want to escape.

I'm really embarrassed with myself and my life."

Then came the ultimate irony. It was Tyson who had the dignity to call a halt to it all. Not his advisor Shelly Finkel, who continued to arrange fights pursuant to a plan that called for Iron Mike to fight seven times over a three-year period until he was 41 years old. Not the media, which continued to glorify him. Not the state athletic commissions, most of which showed little concern for his physical and mental well-being. Had Tyson chosen to do so, he could have fought on for a great deal of money by simply sinking to an even lower level of opponent. But in the end, he said "no".

Tyson's decision to retire from boxing offers a glimmer of hope for his future. Let's hope he stands by it. Then, maybe someday, history will focus on how good Mike Tyson was in the ring when he was young.❏

*Boxing, more than any other sport, thrives on ethnic confronta-tion. Hence the marketability of Dmitriy Salita, who I profiled for the* New York Sun.

# DMITRIY SALITA

Fight fans who attend Thursday night's installment of Broadway Boxing in the Grand Ballroom of the Manhattan Center are in for a surprise. As one of the fighters walks to the ring for the main event, *Hava Nagila* will echo through the air.

Dmitriy Salita is a 22-year-old Orthodox Jew with pale skin and soft brown eyes. He was born in Odessa and moved to Brooklyn with his family in 1991. His father works as an inspector for the MTA. His older brother is a librarian at the Brooklyn Public Library.

Salita is articulate, soft-spoken, and polite. He graduated from James Madison High School in Brooklyn and is now a part-time student at Turo College. He's also an undefeated professional fighter.

Salita's journey in the sweet science began when he was 13 years old and weighed 90 pounds. After being targeted by bullies once too often, he made his way to the Starrett City Boxing Club. There, an elderly black man named Jimmy O'Pharrow taught him to box.

"I seen every kind of kid come through the doors," the 78-year-old O'Pharrow says today. "But I ain't never seen one like Dmitriy. Kid looks Russian, prays Jewish, and fights black. Most of the places he went, he fought black and Hispanic kids. They'd look at this white boy and say, 'Hell, I'll kick his ass.' Then, after the first round, they'd go back to their corner, thinking, 'Damn, this ain't going to be as easy as I thought.'"

Salita compiled an amateur record of 59 wins against 5 losses. Meanwhile, fighting at 139 pounds, he won the 2000 U.S. National Under-19 title and the 2001 New York Golden Gloves. Then he turned pro. His professional record stands at 19-0 with 11 knockouts.

Oscar Suarez, who oversees most of Salita's training today, says, "Dmitriy is a kid that's hungry. He's technically sound and very strong for his weight. He'll develop more power as he matures, and he keeps improving."

"I'm a boxer first," Salita notes. "But as I've gotten physically stronger, I've become more aggressive and I'm fighting better now on the inside than I was before."

As for his religion, Salita takes it very seriously. It might make for good marketing, but it's not an act. He embraced Judaism after his mother was diagnosed with breast cancer in 1997. During one of her stays in the hospital, she shared a room with a woman whose husband was an active member of the Chabad Lubavitch congregation. The man gave Dmitriy the telephone number of the local Chabad center. Then, in January 1999 when Dmitriy's mother died, he began going to the Chabad center to pray for her. Next, he sought to learn everything he could about the religion and adopted its rituals.

"Jews in the Soviet Union didn't know much about Judaism because of the repression," he says. "Here, it's open and I gravitated toward it."

In terms of Salita's career, foremost among the rituals he practices is his decision to not fight on Shabbos, the Jewish Sabbath, which runs from sundown on Friday until sundown on Saturday. There are also 70 other days each calendar year on which he will not fight for religious reasons.

"Promoters are aware of my situation," he says. "If they want me, there are six other nights of the week for me to fight."

When Dmitriy has a fight scheduled for a Saturday night, he spends much of the day praying. But life can get complicated when he's on the road, since he's forbidden to use electricity during Shabbos. Thus, by way of example, he can walk the halls or go to other parts of his hotel, but someone else has to press the elevator buttons for him.

Also, as Salita notes, "Many of my early fights were in Las Vegas. And Las Vegas is not an ideal environment for Shabbos."

Salita's first pro fight in New York was an eight-round decision over Ruben Galvan in Brighton Beach on September 14, 2004. This week, he faces Paul Delgado (12-4-1, 2 KOs) in an eight round junior-welterweight bout. The question now is whether he can move from being a curiosity to a world-class boxer.

"I've been waiting for a main-event fight in New York for a long time," says Salita. "It's important to me because I'm from Brooklyn. And if you want to build a fan base in New York, you have to fight in New York. There's a certain star quality for fighters who can make it here. You know what they say. If you can make it here, you can make it anywhere."◻

*I continued to profile young New York fighters with this piece on Curtis Stevens.*

# CURTIS STEVENS: THE PUNCHER

Yuri Foreman fights Jesus Soto in the main event at the Manhattan Center on February 24, 2005. But earlier in the evening, all eyes will be on 19-year-old Curtis Stevens when he enters the ring to face Darin Johnson.

One-punch knockout power is the biggest draw in boxing, and Stevens has it. He's a crippling puncher with an aggressive attacking style that says, "I'm going to knock your head off." Despite his height (he's only 5-feet-7-inches tall), his early fights have been as a light-heavyweight. Fans watch closely when he's in the ring because at any moment—BOOM—something might happen. He has the same aura of ferocious charisma that Mike Tyson had when he was young.

"I put on a show," says Stevens. "I knock people out; I demolish them. I'm fast; I have power. My hook is like a meteorite. You know how, if a giant meteorite hits the earth, we'd all be gone. Well, if I hit you with my hook, you're gone. I can hit you one time, and the fight's over. And I can finish. Once I hurt you, I'm gonna take you out. Outside the ring, I'm a nice person," Stevens continues. "In the ring, I'm a different man. In the ring, I'm someone you don't want to mess with. I get angry; I get violent and crazy. In the ring, I'm the most dangerous person in the world."

Stevens was born in the Brownsville section of Brooklyn, where he still lives with his mother (a counselor at the Department of Juvenile Justice) and 11-year-old sister. "My mother raised me to respect people," he says. "She makes sure I eat right. She taught me to cook, so I wouldn't have to depend on a woman to cook for me. When I do my roadwork in the morning, my mother rides her bike behind me."

The streets where Stevens runs each day are embodied in words and images tattooed all over his body:

- On his back—"Brownsville"
- On his neck—"Don of Dons"
- On his right biceps—"Showtime" ("That's my street name," Stevens says)
- On his left forearm—The image of a heart and crucifix with the

82

words "Pain Is Love" and "Tanya" (his mother's name)
- On his right hand—"Brother", "Hood", and "D.B.D ("Death before dishonor," he explains. "That's the code I live by.")
- On his left hand—"R.I.P. Lo Bloccs" ("'Lo Bloccs' is what we called Anthony Reid. He was a friend of mine. He died on New Years Day 2003. A cop shot him. Wrong place, wrong time.")

"I know the streets," Stevens acknowledges. "But I know the boundaries of life too. Don't be out there selling drugs because, sooner or later, you're gonna get locked up. Don't get in a fight that will land you in trouble. With every option, there's a repercussion; so think before you make a move."

In the ring so far, Stevens has made the right moves. His fistic education began at age five, when an uncle (Andre Rozier) took him to the Starrett City Gym in Brooklyn. At age 8, he had his first amateur fight. The high point of his amateur career were twin championships at 178 pounds in the 2002 United States Amateur Championships and National Golden Gloves.

"God gave me this talent," says Stevens, "and my uncle taught me how to use it. I had maybe 250 amateur fights. There were eleven losses, but I was never knocked down and never stopped. The worst I was hurt was my last year in the amateurs. I was fighting at heavyweight and, in the first round of a fight, I got hit with a hook-uppercut so hard. Damn! My legs wobbled; I got an eight-count. But I survived and knocked the other guy's ass out in the second round."

"Anyone can be hurt," Stevens observes. "Even me. But I have drills for it in the gym. Sometimes, I'll spin around as fast as I can for two minutes without stopping, just to get dizzy so I'll know how it feels, and then I fight through the dizziness."

Stevens turned pro last September and, since then, has four knockout victories in four fights. He plans on going down to 160 pounds on the theory that fighting lighter opponents will maximize his power.

That makes sense. The knock on Stevens in the amateurs was that he wasn't in the best of shape and tended to fade as fights wore on. The question now is, what happens when he gets in the ring with a guy who can take a punch and stick and move and bang a bit, and Curtis is getting stung with jabs, and the round cards are reading, "Round 4 . . . Round 5 . . ." Will he do what has to be done to win or will he just try to survive?

"You know the answer to that," Stevens says in response. "Anyone can be good, but it's hard to be great. I'm gonna be great. Mike Tyson, when he was young, was a great champion. I want to be like him except for the crazy stuff."❑

*In the beginning, there's hope.*

# DERRIC ROSSY: THE PROSPECT

There are hundreds of young fighters whose handlers believe that they've found a future world champion or the next great heavyweight or another Sugar Ray Robinson. The young men who inspire these beliefs are known as "prospects."

Derric Rossy is a prospect. He was born in Manhattan and raised on Long Island, where he still lives with his parents. His father is Italian-American and his mother is Hispanic. He's 24 years old, 6-feet-3-inches tall, and weighs 238 pounds.

Rossy is articulate and likeable. At Patchogue-Medford High School, he was a star linebacker and earned All-American honors from *SuperPrep Magazine* and *USA Today*. At Boston College, he started at linebacker as a sophomore and then moved to defensive end. He graduated in 2002 and took post-graduate courses in education while trying to find a way into the National Football League. He had tryouts as a free agent with the Jets, Steelers, and Bears, but nothing came of it. Meanwhile, to stay in shape, he began working out at the Academy of Boxing Gym in Huntington, where legendary cornerman Al Gavin was training fighters.

"After a while," Rossy remembers, "Al asked me, 'Do you want to try this? I'm not saying you should, but you might be good.' And I was like, 'Wow! Al Gavin is saying I should try boxing.'"

That was in September 2003.

"I was at 270 pounds," Rossy says. "Football weight. In three months, Al had me at 240. I liked the way I felt; I was in great shape. Then Al got me in the ring, and I was dying after one round. I was nervous and, because of the fear, I was fighting myself and another person. In boxing, fear tires you out. But I loved the experience."

"I thought boxing would be similar to football," Rossy continues. "But it's not. Football is about emotion and getting in the trenches. Being in shape means quick bursts and then you stop. You're on the field and then you're off and then you're on again. Boxing is more of a thinking game. It's not just about using your muscle, and it's always your turn to punch."

Rossy first amateur fight was a second-round knockout in

January 2004. Then he entered the New York City Golden Gloves tournament and won four fights to capture the heavyweight novice title. Overall, he had ten victories and no losses as an amateur.

Then tragedy struck. In July 2004, Al Gavin died of a stroke.

"Al was everything to me," Derric says. "He was a great teacher. He was a friend. And because he was so relaxed and confident, it made me confident that things would always work out for the best. Bob Jackson [Gavin's partner for decades] took over after that. Thank God for Bob. It's like Al is still with me."

Last autumn, Rossy decided to continue his ring education as a professional with Sal Musumeci as his promoter. Derric's first fight was a one-round knockout of Jose Luis Gomez at the Orange County Fairgrounds in Middletown, New York. A four-round decision over Rubin Bracero in Brighton Beach followed. Rossy has never been knocked down as an amateur or pro, although he acknowledges, "In sparring, I've been buzzed pretty good."

Jackson believes that his charge has the makings of a world-class fighter. "Derric has the physical tools," the trainer says. "There's a lot of raw material to work with. He's strong with good hand-speed and reflexes. He's got good power and takes a good punch. He's relaxed in the ring and doesn't back down against anyone. He loves to learn. He hustles. He listens. He's mature. He's a good kid. The way the heavyweight division is now and the way Derric has been progressing, he should be ready to fight the best within three years."

Still, Rossy remains a work in progress and the obstacles he faces are formidable. Athletes who migrate to boxing from other sports in their twenties have met with limited success. And more significantly, Derric has other options in life. Right now, he's working as a carpenter for his father's construction company because it fits with his training regimen. But a career in teaching is a possibility. And sooner or later, most young men who have options other than being a fighter opt out of boxing. Getting punched in the face is hard.

Last week (January 2005), Rossy faced a test of sorts when he sparred four rounds with heavyweight contender Monte Barrett at Gleasons Gym. "He has some potential," Barrett said afterward. "But I couldn't tell you how much because I hadn't sparred since my last fight [on March 27, 2004] and I was just going through the motions. Starting late like he's doing is a disadvantage. But I didn't turn pro until I was 25, so it can be done. A lot depends on how much drive he has."

Meanwhile, Rossy is determined and confident. "It's not an easy road," he says. "I don't see how it ever could be in boxing. But so far, so good."□

*As 2005 progressed, many observers thought that Jaidon Codrington was the best young fighter in New York.*

# JAIDON CODRINGTON: THE COMPLETE FIGHTER

Boxing's big guns will be at Madison Square Garden on Saturday night, when John Ruiz defends his World Boxing Association heavyweight crown against James "Lights Out" Toney. But two nights earlier, the eyes of New York will be on The Manhattan Center, where fighters from all five boroughs will see action on the same card.

Thursday night's main event is a rematch between junior-welterweights Jeffrey Resto of the Bronx and Maryland's Michael Warrick. Last June, they fought a pitched battle with Warrick winning a close decision. Their second encounter should be just as good. But the most promising prospect on the card will be super-middleweight Jaidon Codrington.

Codrington, 20, has the look of a champion. He's the youngest of five children. His mother runs a non-profit corporation that shelters battered women. His father is the foreman in an industrial plant. One of Jaidon's brothers graduated from Colgate and teaches school in Bridgeport, where Jaidon was born. Another brother owns a barber shop in Atlanta. Jaidon's sister, who's married and lives in Texas, graduated from Clark Atlanta University. Jaidon's third brother will graduate from Brown University next month.

So what is Codrington doing in boxing?

"I'm a fighter," he says. "I always have been. My uncle Bandy fought as an amateur and got as far as the 1984 Olympic Trials. He took me to the gym when I was twelve, and I liked it. Boxing is the hardest sport there is, and there are times when people have preconceptions because you're a fighter. They categorize you as violent or stupid or in some other ignorant demeaning way. But boxing makes me happy."

Codrington compiled an amateur record of 62 wins against 7 losses and won the 2002 National Golden Gloves. He moved to Queens four years ago to live with his aunt and cousins. Since turning pro on the undercard of the first Resto-Warrick fight, he's 7 and 0 with 7 knockouts.

Codrington is friends with Curtis Stevens (6-0, 6 KOs). They train together at Brooklyn's Starrett City Boxing Club and are known in boxing circles as "The Chin Checkers" because of their all-knockout records.

"We've earned the label," Jaidon says. "We can punch, and we've got steel chins too. When we spar together, we push each other. Most of the time, it's just working on things. But when a fight is coming up and we're each in our own mental zone, we go at it a little harder. There's never been a knockdown either way between us, but we've rung each other's bell a few times."

"It gets competitive," Stevens acknowledges. "He's stunned me, and I've stunned him. Now, when we fight on the same card, we have a competition over knockouts. It used to be who got the fastest knockout. Now it's whose knockout is the prettiest. Anyone can have a quick knockout. So with us, it's whose knockout looks the best. That can mean knocking a guy cold; or maybe he goes down, gets up, and falls back down again. But we're good friends. For me and Jaidon to fight each other for real, we'd need a hundred million dollars."

"A hundred million apiece," Jaidon counters.

Codrington is a complete fighter. Everything he does works off his jab, but he has a full arsenal of weapons at his command. He can box, punch, and take a punch. He has never been stopped and has been knocked down only once, by U.S. Olympian Andre Dirrell. "He knocked me down; I knocked him down back; and he won the decision," Jaidon recalls.

Meanwhile, Lou DiBella (who co-promotes Codrington with Damon Dash) observes, "Jaidon is the kind of kid you love to promote. He's a skilled boxer with good punching power. He's articulate and thinks before he speaks. He gets along with everyone from television executives to guys on the street. He's determined, hard-working, and confident. And he's good looking. What more could you want?"

*Author's Note: On November 4, 2005, Jaidon Codrington journeyed to Oklahoma to fight Allan Green. Green was 18-0 with 12 knockouts. Codrington was also undefeated with nine knockouts in nine fights. Seconds into the bout, Green landed a left hook to Jaidon's temple. The blow landed in a freakish way that left Codrington senseless but still standing with his arms frozen upright. Green then landed several more blows and Jaidon pitched forward face-first into the ropes where he was entangled on the bottom two strands. Several spectators pushed him back into the ring. His body looked lifeless and his neck was twisted grotesquely so that his head was tucked beneath his torso.*

*"I thought he was dead," Showtime boxing analyst Steve Farhood, who*

*was at ringside, later acknowledged. Jaidon was unconscious for several minutes and was carried from the ring on a stretcher. Fortunately, neurological tests and CAT scans came back negative. He plans to fight again, but as this book goes to press, he has not yet returned to the ring.*◻

*John Duddy is already being talked about as the most crowd-pleasing young fighter since Arturo Gatti. Except his team hopes that he doesn't get hit as often as Gatti.*

# JOHN DUDDY

If a Hollywood studio needed a fighter to play the hero in an oldtime boxing movie, the search could begin and end with John Duddy.

Duddy was born and raised in County Derry, Ireland. He's 25 years old with a thick Irish brogue, charisma, and matinee-idol good looks. "My home will always be in Ireland," he says. "But New York is home to me now. I'm here for one thing and that's business. I'm here to box. People come to me all the time and say, 'I'll get you in movies.' They promise me this and they promise me that. And I tell them, 'After boxing.'"

Duddy is likeable, gracious, and charming. Two years ago, when he came to the United States to pursue his dream, he brought his girlfriend with him. "People ask me whether I'm married or single," he says. "I just tell them I'm in love with Grainne."

Asked to describe himself further, Duddy notes, "I try to keep things simple. I don't look too far into the future. I'm confident and straightforward. I don't like liars and phonies. I'm very focussed on my career. And I believe that a fighter needs passion, not cruelty, to be great."

And, oh yes. Duddy has nine knockouts in nine pro fights, seven of them in the first round. Most of those victories came against soft touches. But last Friday night [March 18, 2005], in a fight featured on ESPN2, Duddy knocked Lenord Pierre out in 83 seconds. Prior to that bout, Pierre had 16 wins and no losses with 11 knockouts.

Duddy's interest in boxing began with his father, a club fighter in the early 1980s, who posted a 3 and 4 record with 1 KO.

"He took me to the gym," Duddy recalls. "Watching him is how I got involved with boxing. I started training for the fun of it when I was five and had my first fight at seven. It was against a 12-year-old who quit after the first round. When I got in the ring, everybody was looking at me. And when they raised my hand, I liked that. I liked it a lot. From then on, I loved boxing."

"My father never put pressure on me to box," Duddy continues. "He allowed me to do it, but he also encouraged me to play other sports and do other things. And he always made it clear that I could stop if I wanted to. But sooner or later, the other things I did would fall by the wayside and boxing stayed with me. No other place in the world smells like a boxing gym. It's unique; I love it. The sweat, the leather; it's the smell of success." Duddy smiles, which he does a lot. "I remember my mother saying to me, 'If that's the smell of success, go outside and put a hose on it.'"

Duddy fought in 130 amateur bouts, winning 100 of them. He had some success in international competition, but eventually suffered from burnout, a common affliction among fighters who start young.

"It was the same thing again and again," he remembers. "The same bad hotels; the same planes; the same busses; the same bad food. It wasn't fun anymore, and I wasn't getting better as a fighter."

Then he met Eddie McLoughlin, an Irishman living in Queens, who's in the construction business.

"I was friendly with John's trainer," McLoughlin explains. "He told me he had a kid and might be interested in moving him to America in the future. Then, maybe a year later, he called and said, 'The kid needs to get out of here. He's at a state where you mention boxing and he just cringes his teeth.' So I said, 'Send him here and we'll see if he likes it.'"

Duddy came to America in March 2003. "That was my dream," he says. "I'd been to America a few times as an amateur and knew this was the place to be. The best trainers, the best sparring, the best of everything in boxing is here. Eddie opened that door for me and he's looked after me ever since."

Duddy turned pro with a first round knockout of Tarek Rached at Jimmy's Bronx Cafe on September 19, 2003. He fights at 160 pounds, which will be his weight for the foreseeable future. He has power in both hands, a jab that he doesn't use often enough, and a free-swinging style that leaves him open to counterpunches. That's a switch from the amateurs, where he was more of a boxer than a puncher.

He's also tough. His jaw was broken in an amateur fight, but he fought through the pain and won. "There were a few times in the amateurs when I was telling my legs to stand still and they were wobbling," he acknowledges. But he has failed to go the distance only twice: once in a fight stopped by the referee when he was ten years old, and once on the 15-point rule in the European championships (in international competition, if a fighter falls behind his opponent by more than 15 points, the bout is stopped).

The only stumbling block in Duddy's professional career so far was a seven-month period last year when he was exiled from the United

States. "I overstayed my visa," he says. "I was told it would be all right, and it wasn't. I really thought the dream was over. While I was back in Ireland, my father offered to work with me in the gym, but my heart and spirit weren't in it. Nothing could make me pursue my career in Ireland. Ireland will always be home to me. It's a wonderful country. But for boxing, the right people and the right knowledge just aren't there. So I worked as a bouncer, a postman, and a lifeguard until I was able to come back to New York."

Duddy's trainer, Harry Keitt, evaluates his charge with the thought, "John's not the most skilled fighter in the world. But he's focussed; he doesn't play games; and he's the most determined fighter I've ever worked with."

Duddy, for his part, says simply, "I'm learning and getting better every day. As the months go on, I realize that I'm doing well and holding my own. We'll see how far I get. If I'm not the best, I'll be close to it." Then he adds, "I'm happy; I'm living my dream. Boxing has taken me a long way. It's a tough job, but it's a good job. And I'm very lucky; I'm from Ireland. That means, wherever I go, I have Irish people offering to help and cheering for me."

*ADDENDUM*

On June 11th at Madison Square Garden, John Duddy faced his most difficult test as a pro—a well-conditioned fighter named Patrick Thompson.

Duddy arrived at the arena two hours before fight time and sat quietly in his dressing room. Neither he nor trainer Harry Keitt spoke as Keitt taped his fists.

"The entire day of a fight, I'm in a zone," Duddy said afterward. "I don't like talking. I'm focussing on what has to be done. It's like a dream, really. The world gets narrower and narrower until all I see is the ring and me and my opponent."

When the taping was done, Duddy examined his fists the way a gunfighter in the old west might have examined his guns. Then he went out and gave his best professional performance to date. He threw a good mix of punches, kept his power late, was the aggressor throughout, and won every minute of every round. All three judges scored the bout 80-72 in his favor.

"I don't mind losing the knockout streak," Duddy said when the fight was over. "You get more respect from people when you prove you can go the distance. I can go ten or twelve rounds in the gym, but I was glad to do it in a fight."

Duddy still has flaws. He doesn't move his head enough, which enabled Thompson to land lead righthands when he got off first. He also stands upright and is disinclined to bend at the knees, which leaves him susceptible to left hooks. That's part of what has led critics to contend that "Clan Duddy" is made up of amateurs. But Keitt, Irish Ropes promoter Eddie McLoughlin, and advisor Jim Borzell just keep doing their job. Meanwhile, powers-that-be like Top Rank, Don King Productions, and Main Events are calling.

"If I keep doing the business in the ring, the business outside the ring will take care of itself," Duddy said on Saturday night. "Everything is good. I'm on track. I've gone eight rounds now and I've won in Madison Square Garden."❑

*There were no titles on the line when Wladimir Klitschko and Samuel Peter met. But it was an intriguing match-up between two foreign-born heavyweights that captured the imagination of boxing fans in America.*

# WLADIMIR KLITSCHKO VERSUS SAMUEL PETER

Knockout power is an aphrodesiac in boxing.

Boxing is starving for a marketable heavyweight.

Because of those realities, a lot of dreams were riding on Samuel Peter's broad shoulders when he arrived at Boardwalk Hall in Atlantic City last Saturday night (September 24, 2005).

Peter is a likeable man with a ready smile and an almost childlike innocence about him. He was born into a middle-class family in Cross River, Nigeria. "I'm a happy person," he says. "I grew up with a good mother and a good father. They taught me to respect my elders and be humble. They loved me and taught me about God. To be a good person gets you to heaven."

Peter was a promising soccer player, fast and strong, until an adolescent knee injury ended his hopes for turf glory. Then he turned to boxing. "Boxing to me is a game," he says. "You hit me; I hit you. To knock somebody out feels better than scoring a goal. But boxing is a sport, not a war. In a war, I would run backwards. If you want to go to war, go to Iraq."

Peter came to the United States to pursue his ring career in 2001. He and his wife, Enobong, have two children; a 19-month-old girl and nine-month-old boy. "It's a great life here," he says. "Someday, I will be buried in Nigeria, but I am happy where I am now. To be a success in boxing, you must be in the United States. I want to make money. Money motivates me. To think about fighting for five or ten million dollars makes me run day and night. But to be the first African champion, to make history for my country and all of Africa, is also important to me."

So far, Peter has been spending his money on clothes and real estate; one hopes in inverse order. He gives the impression that his cell phone is surgically attached to his ear. One week ago, he had 24 wins in 24 fights with 21 knockouts. "In boxing, I have never been knocked down and I never will be," he said. "I am a special fighter. I don't think anybody can put me down. I don't compare myself with anybody because I'm special. One day, people will compare other fighters to me."

Peter's opposite number in Atlantic City was Wladimir Klitschko. The two men arrived at Boardwalk Hall on Saturday night within five minutes of one another. Samuel was wearing gray sweatpants and a white T-shirt with "www.samuel-peter.com" emblazoned in green letters across his chest. At 8:20, he entered his dressing room, lay down on the rubdown table, and closed his eyes.

Every fight is a journey into the unknown. The fact that the 25-year-old Peter was stepping up in class made this one particularly unpredictable. It was the first time in his professional career that he would be facing a fighter with tools comparable to his own. Samuel was aware of the risks and stakes involved. As he lay on the table, he looked smaller than his 243 pounds. At the weigh-in, his thighs had evoked images of giant oak trees. Now they looked more like human anatomy. Enobong came into the room and squeezed his hand. At 8:35, Samuel signaled for someone to turn on his music. Gentle sounds filtered through the air.

"Did I tell you that I love you. Did I tell you that I want you. Did I tell you that I need you. You make me feel like heaven is here on earth."

Samuel sat up on the rubdown table and began to sing. Assistant trainer Cornelius Boza-Edwards took a scissors and started cutting loose threads from the blue sequined trunks that his fighter would wear. Over the next two hours, myriad people came and went. The core group (manager Ivaylo Gotzev, trainer "Pops" Anderson, assistant trainer Kenny Croom, and Boza-Edwards) remained.

The standard rituals of boxing followed. A urine sample for the New Jersey State Board of Athletic Control. The referee's pre-fight instructions. From time to time, Samuel stood up and danced to the music, smiling at his own reflection in the mirror on the wall.

At 9:05 Vitali Klitschko and James Bashir came in with the intention of watching Boza-Edwards tape Peter's hands. Samuel continued to dance and sing.

"Anything that you can do, no one can do it better. Anything that you can say, no one can say it better."

Vitali was on edge. "It's easier for me to fight than to watch my brother fight," he'd acknowledged earlier in the day. "If I fight, I'm cool. If my brother fights, I'm nervous."

At 9:10, Peter sat down on a folding metal chair and the taping began. After the first roll of gauze had been applied, Samuel reached for his watch and handed it to Boza-Edwards, who stretched the heavy metal band around his fighter's fist in the manner of brass knuckles. Bashir's eyes widened. Samuel laughed. Cornelius removed the watch.

There was no change in Vitali's expression. He was measuring the man who, in less than two hours, would seek to destroy his brother; a man who he himself might someday face in the ring.

At 9:35, the taping was done. Time was moving slowly. Depending on the length of the co-featured bout between Miguel Cotto and Ricardo Torres, Samuel would be called to the ring sometime between 10:20 and 11:00. Once again, he began to dance and sing.

"It's the truth that I feel. My destiny is sealed. I know I can move any mountain . . . Lord, when I thought it was over for me, you gave me strength and lifted my burdens. Thank you, Lord, for giving me strength to carry on."

There was no television monitor in the room. Word came that Cotto-Torres was underway. Samuel began his stretching exercises. Then he gloved up and hit the pads with Croom.

Over the next half hour, there were reports on the progress of the co-feature . . . "Torres is down in round one . . . Cotto is down in the second round."

Samuel sat on a folding metal chair and stretched his legs out in front of him. Then he stood up and began dancing once more, watching his reflection in the mirror, keeping loose in a manner that seemed calculated to force his cares away.

"Cotto and Torres are in round five," he was told.

Samuel and Kenny Croom worked the pads again.

At 10:50, Cotto-Torres ended on a seventh-round knockout.

"You walk in five minutes," Team Peter was instructed.

Pops Anderson led the group in prayer.

At 10:55, Samuel Peter left his dressing room for the ring.

On paper, the fight was a fascinating match-up. Wladimir Klitschko was once considered the class of the heavyweight division. However, even when he looked good, there were danger signs. He totally dominated Jameel McCline and Ray Mercer, but appeared to bail out each time either man threw serious punches. Then he was knocked out in two rounds by Corrie Sanders, won comeback fights against Fabio Moli and Danell Nicholson, and was stopped in five rounds by Lamon Brewster.

The loss to Brewster was particularly troubling. Afterward, the Klitschko camp claimed that their fighter had been drugged. Brewster took a contrary view. "Wladimir Klitschko is a great athlete,"Lamon opined. "But Wladimir Klitschko is not a great fighter. There's a difference."

"We know the result of the fight," Klitschko said later. "Lamon Brewster won. But I have questions. My mind was crystal clear but my body and legs wouldn't respond. I couldn't breathe. I was fighting with myself just to move in the ring, not against my opponent. And the collapse came so fast. In the third round, it took effort to get up from my chair. It's important for me to know why. I want to find the answer to what was wrong with me. A man has to know the truth about himself. It's painful for me that people think, 'This guy, if he loses, he can't live with it; he will look to find any excuses.' But this is about myself and for myself, because I want to continue my career and I don't want the same thing to happen again."

Still, regardless of the reason for his failure against Brewster, in recent fights Wladimir had looked as though he were skating on thin ice each time he entered the ring. He'd shown an inability to take big punches, and there were those who thought that he no longer took little punches well either. "From nothing to everything is a very long road in boxing," he acknowledged. "But from everything to nothing is just one short step."

Klitschko voiced the opinion that his fight with Samuel Peter was "where I will regain my stature." However, the odds suggested otherwise. Samuel was a 7-to-5 favorite based on his punching power and Wladimir's suspect chin. But many of Peter's partisans were counting on Klitschko's weaknesses rather than Samuel's strengths as the key to victory. And others wondered how Peter would deal with adversity if it came his way. Real adversity. Not just being outpointed, but being tired and getting hit by a big man who could punch. Dishing it out is great, but could Samuel take it if his resolve were tested?

As expected, Emanuel Steward (who trained Klitschko) predicted that his man would win. "Boxing is so desperate for excitement in the heavyweight division that people are building Samuel Peter up beyond all reason," Steward declared. "Peter is nothing more than a ten-month sensation; and in my mind, he hasn't even been that sensational in those ten months. Samuel thinks he'll overpower Wladimir, but that won't happen. When you get to a certain level, you can't win fights on power alone. You think that all it takes is one of yours to make everything go your way. But being able to punch hard is only part of what world-class boxing is about. At the highest level of the sport, you don't just knock people out. Wladimir will control Samuel for the entire fight. Getting hit by a 250-pound man who knows how to fight will be a new experience for Samuel. After two rounds of eating the kind of punches that Wladimir is hitting him with, he won't want to fight anymore."

In the end, neither fighter was as flawed as the other side expected. And neither lived up to the high expectations of his backers. Peter was the aggressor for most of the night, but it was often ineffective aggression. As a person, Samuel is straightforward and honest with little artifice about him. Unfortunately, that's also true of his ring style. He rarely feinted and was often off-balance after missing with wild looping punches. That left him wide-open for counters. But since Wladimir bailed out when punches were fired and did his impression of a Ukrainian John Ruiz when Samuel got inside, the counters rarely came.

Klitschko did his most effective work with his jab. On occasion, he landed solid rights; most often, when Peter stopped punching. But when Wladimir landed, Samuel took the punches well. In round five, a clubbing left hook followed by a right hand to the back of the head put Klitschko down and "Dr. Steelhammer" became Dr. Wobbly Legs. A second knockdown that was more of a push followed. At that point, it looked as though the Klitschko strategy of "jab and grab" might become "hold and fold." But for the next four rounds, Wladimir stayed on his bike, jabbing, and holding when necessary, while Peter was unable to cut the ring off.

After round nine, Peter was visibly tired and his right eye was closing, so Steward suggested that Klitschko pick the pace up a bit and give Samuel a reason to fall. That seemed to violate one of boxing's cardinal rules; to wit, "There are times when a fighter has to punch with a puncher, but he should choose those times very carefully."

To put his opponent away, a fighter has to stay in the danger zone. So when Klitschko by his deeds said, "I'll punch with you," Samuel answered "WHACK" and Wladimir found himself on the canvas for the third time. At that point, discretion being the better part of valor, Dr. Steelhammer became elusive again.

All three judges scored the bout 114-111 for Klitschko, who connected on 129 jabs to 26 for Peter. The numbers were even on "power punches." Samuel showed heart and that he can take a good punch. When Wladimir landed, Peter took the blows well. But Samuel revealed himself to be a work in progress, not a finished fighter. Klitschko won because he was a technically more proficient boxer. And Wladimir did something that he had been unable to do before. He came back from adversity to win a fight. He proved his courage if not his chin.❏

*Tarver-Jones III was the thirteenth time that I saw Roy Jones fight in person.*

# ROY JONES JR. AND ANTONIO TARVER

Over the years, it has become increasingly difficult for me to watch fighters I care about in the ring. Maybe that's because I've seen two men beaten to death in front of me. Maybe it's because, as I've grown older, I've been imbued with a greater sense of mortality coupled with a fuller understanding of loss. When Lennox Lewis fought Mike Tyson in Memphis, I sat ringside and felt my heart pounding. During the early rounds of Jermain Taylor versus Bernard Hopkins, my hand was shaking so much that my notes were an almost-illegible scrawl.

In that vein, there came a time when I felt that Roy Jones Jr. should retire from boxing. "You're not Roy Jones in the ring anymore," I told him. "I'd like you to stop fighting while you're still Roy Jones out of it." Roy thanked me for my concern. Ultimately, he fought again.

On the night of October 1, 2005, I was in Roy's dressing room as he readied to fight Antonio Tarver for the third time. "Tom Hauser," Roy said, looking across the room at me. "I thought about what you said. I ain't got good sense, but don't worry about me. I'll be all right."

Roy Jones at his peak was one of the most gifted fighters of our time. He gave the impression of being able to ride bareback on a tornado without wrinkling his gleaming satin trunks. He could fight an opponent as good as James Toney and make boxing look like a game instead of the brutal competition that it is. He stood for the proposition, "When I go in the ring, that space is mine."

Given proper motivation, Jones went in tough. He did it against Bernard Hopkins when he wanted the middleweight crown. He did it against James Toney to establish his "pound-for-pound" credentials. Many of Jones's lesser opponents were greater risks than he has been given credit for. Eric Harding was good enough to beat Antonio Tarver. Julio Gonzalez beat Dariusz Michalczewski. Clinton Woods stopped Rico Hoye and fought Glencoffe Johnson to a draw.

And there was Jones's domination of John Ruiz in 2003 to capture the WBA heavyweight belt. Even Roy's most severe critics had to acknowledge his skills that night. Ruiz isn't pretty to watch but he beat Hasim

Rahman and Evander Holyfield. "I don't hit that hard," Jones said mockingly after the Ruiz bout. "Everyone knows that. So when you fight me, go ahead. Charge! Attack! It was a punch from the referee that broke John's nose."

"When the heavyweight thing happened," Jones said later, "that felt so good."

The biggest edge that many great fighters have is their ego. But ego is the greatest flaw that many fighters have too. Ego can lead a champion to undertrain for a fight. Ego allows a fighter to get careless in the ring against an opponent who's more dangerous than thought.

After Jones beat John Ruiz, he trained less arduously than he should have and won a narrow decision over Antonio Tarver. Six months later, in Jones-Tarver II, Roy learned that any fighter can be knocked out. He was stopped in two rounds. Next, he stepped into the ring with Glencoffe Johnson after hardly training at all. Against Johnson, Jones was Frank Sinatra fumbling the lyrics and Luciano Pavarotti unable to hit the high notes. In round nine, he was knocked unconscious. He lay on the canvas for eight minutes and sat on his stool for 24 minutes more before leaving the ring.

Those two knockouts shook Jones to his core and threatened to undermine his belief in himself. They became the dominant factor in his life. "Forced humility," writer Tim Graham called it. The question was, would Roy return to the ring?

"If I was looking at this from the outside," Jones acknowledged one week after the Johnson fight, "I'd say to myself, 'He was good; he did his thing; now it's time for him to move on to something else.' This is a killer game. When I was hungry and in the hunt, nothing could stop me. But I don't have that hunger anymore and reflex-wise I've lost something. People say, 'You can't go out like that.' And I say, 'Yes, I can if I want to.' I don't feel like I have to fight again. I don't have to do anything I don't want to do. So unless I do, I won't. I'll take some time off and decide what I want to do."

"I really thought Roy was going to retire after the Johnson fight," Alton Merkerson (Jones's longtime trainer) said recently. "That's what he told me, and I believed it. Then, in June, I went out to his farm. Roy wasn't there. I asked where he was, and his uncle said that he was out doing roadwork. A few weeks after that, Roy got the gym cleaned up. Then he started training; and the next thing I knew, there was a fight."

If Jones wanted public vindication, either Antonio Tarver or Glencoffe Johnson would have sufficed as his opponent. Roy opted for Tarver, the tougher of the two challenges. "If I can't beat the best, I don't want to be in there," he said. That was ironic in that, when Jones was at his peak, the knock against him in some quarters was that he fought too many soft touches. But the other side of the coin was, in some respects, beating Tarver would be an even bigger conquest for Roy than his victory over John Ruiz.

"I couldn't live with myself if I didn't do this," Jones said. "Do you want me to jump off a building or do you want to see me fight?"

To some observers, those options were similar.

Antonio Tarver presented a formidable challenge. He was born in Orlando to a single-parent mother who raised him and three daughters on her own. "She and my father never lived together," Antonio remembers. "He was a Vietnam vet. It's hard to say he was my father because he was never there. Biologically, he donated but that's about all. We never saw much of each other, just a phone call here and there, so I never had that male figure in my life. That was a void I had to live with."

Tarver learned to box at the local Boys Club when he was ten years old. "Kids would get into fights," he recalls, "and the way the director dealt with it was to put us in the ring with oversized gloves that were as big as we were. That happened to me a few times. After a while, the director saw I was good and I liked it, so he directed me to the Boys Club boxing team. In my first amateur fight, I knocked my opponent out in forty-five seconds. I was lefthanded but I fought in an orthodox stance back then and I had a hellacious left hook."

Tarver and Jones met in the ring for the first time as 13-year-olds at the 1982 Sunshine State Games. "I won the first round," Antonio asserts. "Roy won the second. The third round was close and he got the decision. Then, when I was fourteen, my mother moved us to a better section of Orlando that was thirty miles from the Boys Club. There was no way for me to get to the gym, so I gave up boxing and concentrated on other sports. I played quarterback and wide receiver in football and shooting guard on the high school basketball team. In my mind, I was good. But I wasn't as good as I thought."

That led to problems. Like many inner-city youths with athletic dreams, Tarver was ill-prepared to deal with the future. After high school, he was passed over in the hunt for a college athletic scholarship and began to drift. He fathered a son (who he spends time with and supports financially). He went from odd job to odd job. And he got into drugs.

"I abused drugs for about seven months," Antonio admits. "It started in the summer of 1987 when I was nineteen years old. I was out of school, running around with the wrong crowd. I was doing lace [a mixture of crack and marijuana]. And what happened was, in my mind, the drug became the only value that mattered. I was involved in something that I'd lost control over. My responsibilities become secondary to the drug. I began to change as a person. I was acting crazy. Finally, one night, I went into my mother's room when she was sleeping, woke her up, and told her, 'Mom, I'm in trouble. I have a problem.' She was like, 'What are you talking about?' And I said, 'Mom, I'm messed up. I'm using drugs.' We cried all night. She was very hurt, and I felt horrible because of the shame and hurt I was bringing her. Neither of us was educated on the matter, but we found out where I could go to get help. I went into a residential rehab program for six months. I had to do some rebuilding. They educated me about my problems and my purpose in life. I'm a better person now because of the experience. I learned from my mistake and put it behind me. I could have given up on myself. I know people who have battled drugs for years and never kicked the habit. But I beat it. It never resurfaced, and I'm very proud of that."

Then came a defining moment. In 1988, Tarver saw Roy Jones on television at the Seoul Olympics. "It touched me, " he says. "Because in my heart, I knew that I was just as good as Roy was when we'd fought. And I could see how he was advancing with his career while I was doing nothing."

Motivated again, Tarver resumed boxing. Eight years later, he made the United States Olympic team and won a bronze medal at the Atlanta Olympics. Then he turned pro, but it was a difficult passage.

"The talent and skill were always there, but I took shortcuts," Antonio acknowledges. "If I made weight, I thought I was in shape. I won my first sixteen fights on talent alone. Then I fought Eric Harding. That was a wake-up call. He broke my jaw. I knew I was hurt bad. There was pain from the bottom of my feet to the top of my head. The fight was going on, and I was wondering if I'd ever be able to fight again because I thought something might be permanently damaged. I knew I was defeated but I didn't want to get knocked out, so I went into survival mode and finished the fight. Then, after the loss, I asked myself, 'How bad do I want it? What am I willing to do to get it?' I started taking better care of my body and working harder. I worked my way back to being the number-one contender. I could have just sat back and waited for a title shot. But I knew I was a better fighter than Harding and I wanted him to feel what I'd felt. So I signed to fight a rematch against him and knocked him out."

On April 26, 2003, Tarver decisioned Montell Griffin to pick up the WBC and IBF 175-pound titles that had been vacated when Roy Jones went up to heavyweight to fight John Ruiz. At that point, Antonio had been watching Jones do his thing for fifteen years and telling himself, "I can beat him." On November 8, 2003, he got his chance but Jones prevailed on a split decision. Six months later, they met again. Moments before the bell for round one, Antonio earned a spot in boxing's sound-bite hall of fame.

"I gave you your instructions in the dressing room," referee Jay Nady told the fighters. "Do you have any questions?"

"I got a question," Tarver said. "Do you got any excuses tonight, Roy?"

"I thought about it the night before," Tarver explained later. "And decided I didn't want to do anything that would cost me points or get me disqualified. But then we got in the ring and the adrenaline was flowing and the stage was set and I felt it was my night." A bemused look crosses Antonio's face. "It's a good thing I won. Can you imagine if it was me that got knocked out that night?"

After defeating Jones, Tarver lobbied for a rubber match between them. "If I got knocked out and didn't try to even the score," he said, "there's no way I'd be able to sleep at night. I'd even things up or get knocked out again trying."

Jones wouldn't bite. So in December 2004, Tarver opted to fight Glencoffe Johnson, who by then had defeated Jones. Johnson is a one-dimensional fighter, but opponents don't beat him by just showing up. He makes them earn it. Against Antonio, Glencoffe fought aggressively, throwing punches in bunches and going to the body throughout the night. Meanwhile, Tarver seemed in less-than-top shape and fought like a man who knew how to win rounds but wasn't willing to pay the price. He spent much of the bout in retreat, jabbed less frequently than he should have, and didn't let his hands go often enough. Johnson outworked him and won a narrow split decision. Six months later, Tarver avenged the loss with a 116-112, 116-112, 115-113 triumph.

"Good things happen when you believe," Antonio said afterward. "A long time ago, I had a vision. I don't just want to be a champion. I want to be a superstar. I have the ability to be spectacular every time out. I did without for a long time. I struggled; I came up on the dirt road of boxing. I'm a hard worker; I'm goal-oriented. When I set a goal, I'm totally consumed by it. Failure isn't an option."

The kick-off press conference for Tarver-Jones III was scheduled for August 9th in New York. Everything went as planned except for one small detail. Jones didn't show up.

Roy can be gracious and generous with his time, particularly when schoolchildren are involved. But over the years, his penchant for arriving late (and sometimes not at all) has ruffled feathers. His failure to appear in New York aggravated HBO Sports president Ross

Greenburg, who took the microphone and declared, "I'd like to admonish Roy Jones for not being here. Hopefully, on October 1st, he'll get his little rear-end to Tampa."

That left the stage to Tarver, who is on the short list with James Toney and Bernard Hopkins as boxing's best sound-for-sound talkers. Among the thoughts Antonio offered were:

● "I've mastered my trade. I'm on top now. This is the pinnacle but the roles have been reversed. Once upon a time, Roy was that king lion on top. Now I'm the king lion, and it's up to him to knock me off my throne. They say it's lonely at the top, but I like it here and don't plan on coming down any time soon."

● "It was never personal for me as far as Roy was concerned; only business. I think Roy is a good person. He takes care of his kids and does a lot of good things. And I respect Roy for the champion he was. He set the bar high and gave me something to reach for. But I find it hard to respect Roy now because he's showing me no respect. It bothers me that he hasn't been able to say, 'Hey; I got beat by a better fighter that night.' I don't know why he won't give me my due. He didn't give me credit for the first fight either. Roy needs to recognize that there has been a changing of the guard."

● "If you don't believe, you can't achieve. I challenged Roy like no fighter ever challenged him before. Do you think Michael Jordan lay in bed at night telling himself he wanted to be almost as good as Dr. J, or did he tell himself he wanted to be better?"

Was Jones shot?

"That remains to be seen," Tarver answered. "Roy didn't give himself enough time off before he fought Glen Johnson. Now he's had time to rest, physically and mentally. He looks good; we know he's serious. A desperate fighter is a dangerous fighter, and Roy is desperate now. If he loses this fight, it's all over for him so he's going to prepare like he's never prepared before. I'm training for the best Roy Jones ever. If he's less than that, so be it. If he's a shot fighter, I'm the one who shot him."

But Tarver also expressed resentment and would continue to do so in the weeks ahead. The source of his anger was the belief that he was toiling in a perpetual shadow that existed as a consequence of the media in general, and HBO in particular, creating and then showcasing a select few superstars.

"I didn't proclaim Roy to be the greatest thing since Sugar Ray Robinson," Tarver declared. "You all did. The media and the politics made Roy out to be what he is. Roy Jones's greatness is a myth.

Sometimes I think the people at HBO have dementia. They're the ones who have made the great Roy Jones an icon, but I never looked at Roy Jones through the media's eyes."

Still, even Tarver was forced to concede, "This fight is more about what Roy Jones lost than what I took, and that's a bittersweet pill to me. I feel that I don't have the respect that I deserve when you look at all the things I've accomplished. I'm fighting to settle the issue of my own legacy."

As the fight approached, those who believed that Jones was never a great fighter were picking Tarver in a walk. Those who took a contrary view weren't so sure. Many in the latter group felt that Roy had lost to Johnson because he hadn't trained properly and that, against Tarver, he simply got caught.

"As strange as it sounds, Roy wasn't motivated for those two fights," Alton Merkerson said. "Roy is either self-motivated or he's not motivated at all. For those fights, he was bored. He was tired of pleasing other people. The second Tarver fight, he figured he'd beaten Tarver the first time when he was weak and had trouble making weight so now it would be easy. I didn't get what I should have gotten out of him in camp. And with Glen Johnson, it was the same thing. You can't make a fighter train if he doesn't want to. He might come to the gym but he won't work right while he's there."

"This camp, we had the Roy Jones I saw when I first started training him," Merkerson continued. "He's energetic; he's focussed. He put a lot of things to the side for this fight. If you take an exam without studying for it, you might get by or you might fail the test. When you really want to pass a test, you study harder. Training for a fight is the same thing. Roy's attitude has changed for this fight. This time, he's ready."

"We expect Roy to be ready," countered Tarver's trainer, Buddy McGirt. "But Roy just didn't get beat last time. He got knocked out. He didn't get TKO'd. He got KO'd. If Antonio fights Roy three more times, he'll beat Roy three more times."

Tarver was in accord. "I'm here to tell you; I don't think that at any point in Roy Jones's career, ever at any time, was he able to beat me," Antonio declared. "I'm not expecting to knock him out with one punch. Lightning only strikes once. But I will go in there, back him up, put pressure on him, and break him down. I know Roy will make adjustments from what he did in our last fights. But there's a limited number of mistakes he can make because, if he makes the wrong mistake, it's over."

Boxing fans are fond of saying that an aging great fighter who's on the decline often has one last great fight in him. But in truth, that's seldom the case. It's rare for a great fighter to come back after having been perceived as over-the-hill. Evander Holyfield did it at age 34, when he beat Mike Tyson after dismal performances against Michael Moorer and Bobby Czyz. And of course, George Foreman scored a one-punch knockout over Michael Moorer to become heavyweight champion at age 45. But boxing is a sport that eats its young, and the old have even less of a chance.

The conventional wisdom was that, at some point in fight, Tarver would crack Jones on the chin and the fight would be over. Clearly, Roy had trained harder for this encounter than for any fight in years. But there are no exercises a fighter can do for his chin.

Also, to some, Jones was acting strangely. There were reports that he had injured his left hand while training, which led to rumors that he might pull out of the fight. And after failing to appear at the kick-off press conference, he remained largely invisible. Not since Mike Tyson readied to fight Lennox Lewis had a boxer been so disrespectful toward the commercial imperatives of promoting a major fight.

Jones, by his conduct, said, "You're paying me to show up and box. Nothing else matters." That reduced Tarver-Jones III to its essence, and it certainly was "Roy being Roy." But for HBO, the fight was first and foremost a television production. Jones has a lucrative TV contract that can pay his bills far into the future. And some people thought it wasn't a good idea to shortchange the business end of things and piss off the man (Ross Greenburg) who hires and fires for HBO.

Then, for good measure, Jones blew off the final pre-fight press conference. Earlier, he had demanded and received the concession that he and Tarver would meet separately with the media. That led Buddy McGirt to observe, "If you could get Ali and Frazier in the same room, you should be able to get anybody in the same room."

Regardless, two days before the fight, Jones walked into what was supposed to be his final pre-fight press conference at the St. Pete Times Forum in Tampa. It was his only public appearance since the fight had been signed. He hadn't shaved in seven weeks. His beard was shaggy and unkempt. He strode to the microphone, looked out at his audience, and said, "How ya'll doing? I ain't really got much to say. My hand is fine. I ain't got no excuses. I got no reason to be here but one reason. That's to kick ass. That's what I came for. That's all I've got to goddamn say." After seventeen seconds on stage, he left.

"I think it's a slap in the face to all the people that have pumped him up and glorified him over the years," Tarver said at his own press conference an hour later. "The guy has given nothing to the game. The guy has no compassion for the sport that made him a wealthy man and an icon. Roy Jones disrespects the fans. He disrespects the media. He disrespects the sport. Shame on him." Then Tarver added, "I don't think Roy is as confident as people make him out to be. He seems to be very fragile right now."

The whole thing bothered a lot of observers.

"Do I fear for Roy's safety?" HBO commentator Jim Lampley told writer Eric Raskin. "Absolutely. How could you watch him lie still on the canvas for such a long time after getting knocked out by Glen Johnson, watch his feet quiver like that, and not be concerned? He couldn't be any worse than he was against Glen Johnson. I don't rule out that he could beat Antonio Tarver. I just don't think it's worth taking the risk. I would prefer not to see him get hit in the head again."

Others took a harsher view. Kevin Iole of the *Las Vegas Review-Journal* wrote of the fight, "You'll get an arrogant over-the-hill light-heavyweight who thinks so little of the fans that he shuns them consistently and who has been knocked out cold in his last two fights against a guy who is bigger, stronger, and, quite simply, better. Why HBO is allowing this fight to happen is a mystery. The Florida Athletic Commission should be ashamed of itself for sanctioning the fight. Jones doesn't deserve your money; there doesn't seem to be a way the fight can be competitive; and the specter of a disaster looms large. Save your money. If Roy Jones Jr. wants to kill himself, you don't have to pay fifty bucks to watch him do it."

And the most impassioned words came from Tim Smith of the *New York Daily News*, who declared, "Leavander Johnson will be buried on Saturday in Atlantic City, eight days after paying the ultimate price for participating in his sport. Later in the day, Roy Jones Jr. will take on Antonio Tarver in Tampa, ostensibly to regain his status in the same sport. The parallel of those two events disturbs me greatly. I remain saddened by Johnson being beaten to death in a sanctioned sporting event and Jones, who has been knocked out in his last two bouts, willingly putting himself in the same position. I don't understand why there was a need for Tarver-Jones III. I saw everything I needed in the second match when Tarver knocked out Jones in the second round. After Glen Johnson left Jones lying on the canvas with his arms folded across his chest like he was in a coffin, I never wanted to see Jones in the ring again. That image keeps flashing in my mind. Humanity is lacking in boxing. What do you expect in a sport in which the purpose is to render your opponent unconscious? But when did common sense take a holiday? Someone convinced the executives at HBO Pay-Per-View that a third match against Tarver was a good idea. It isn't. It never was. It is a shameful disgrace. I will cover Jones-Tarver III. It is what I do. I'm not proud of that, and I do so reluctantly. Jones may get into the ring against Tarver and be masterful again. But I'm not going to say I was wrong or that I'm sorry for not wanting Jones in the ring again. I'm ashamed that I cover a sport in which humanity is lacking and common sense is on permanent vacation. Forgive me, but I never want to see another man killed in a boxing ring."

State of mind is more important in boxing than in any other sport. To some, it seemed as though winning this fight had become a matter of personal survival to Jones. They thought that everything he believed about himself and had created in the first 36 years of his life was on the line. But the assumption in some circles was that Jones was on some sort of weird mental journey. And even in boxing, mind can't overcome matter. Thus, the question was asked, "Is Roy Jones living in a fantasy world? *The Matrix*? Mind over matter?"

"The frame of mind that Roy is in now," Alton Merkerson said in response, "is that he's tired of talking; he's tired of listening. He's not going to tell Tarver what he's going to do. He's going to show him. Roy wants to prove to everyone, and especially to himself, that he's not washed up; that he's still capable of being pound-for-pound the best fighter in the world. He's in the same state of mind now that he was in the early 1990s."

How would the two previous knockouts affect him?

"Soldiers have to deal with emotions like this before they go into battle," Merkerson answered. "You can be the best soldier in the world, but if you stay in combat long enough, you'll get hit. What you do then, if you survive, is you soldier on and hope it doesn't happen again. Sometimes it does, and sometimes it doesn't."

And there was one final element in the psychodrama. After years of estrangement, Jones was training again with his father.

Roy Jones Sr. ("Big Roy" as he's known in Pensacola) owned a farm when Roy Jr. was growing up and also did some long-haul trucking. There was a time when he put considerable time and effort into teaching youngsters, including his son, how to box in a makeshift gym without plumbing. When he took the kids to out-of-town tournaments, they ate peanut-butter-and-jelly sandwiches on the road and slept eight in a room.

Big Roy trained his son for thirteen years. Then they had a falling out. Alton Merkerson had trained Roy for twelve.

Meeting Roy Jones Sr. for the first time can be a disarming experience. When he chooses, he's friendly and charming. But Big Roy can also be a gruff forbidding presence. He lives by the code, "You do it my way or get the hell out of the way." He has a saying: "If you break a plate at my table, you're never coming back."

Big Roy trained Roy Jr. to box from the time he was six years old. He put a lot of pressure on him, sometimes taunting him and forcing him to fight back. There are oft-told stories of Big Roy whipping his son's legs while he did roadwork and shooting Roy's dog.

"I met Roy's father once," says Jim Lampley. "And I think that Roy's relationship with his father is still at the heart of what Roy does. But at the end of the day, he's trying to prove himself to a father he'll never really please."

"My father had his way of control," Roy says simply. "It wasn't nice; and when I was in his house, I had to take it. But I vowed that, once I got out from under my father's control, I'd never be controlled by anyone again."

In the weeks leading up to Tarver-Jones III, Roy ran in the mornings, had breakfast with Merkerson, and went to his father's gym to train. Then, late in the day, he'd go to the Square Ring Gym and train with Merkerson. Big Roy attended the latter workouts as well.

"I'm still with Coach Merk," Roy explained. "My father said he wanted to come in and help out. I'm not going to deny him that because he's my father. He's the one who got me into this and he understands me better than anybody. It has made a little bit of difference, him being there, because it's brought out some of the older things that I used to do that I pretty much don't do any more. Bringing Pops back to the corner has been good, but I'm still with Coach Merk."

"Roy needed me; he needed my help," Big Roy said. "I'm his father and I'm there for him and always will be. He told me that he signed to fight Tarver and that it would happen within eight weeks and that was that. He's my son. I don't see where Roy needs to do much different than what he used to do. What he needs to do is be better prepared. Roy only trained four or five good days for Glen Johnson. You just can't do that. If Roy is prepared, I don't think Tarver can beat him. If he trains hard and touches up his skills a little bit and goes in there with the right mindset, you'll see a different outcome."

That put Merkerson in a delicate situation, but he handled it with grace. "If Roy wants his father back, that's fine with me," Merkerson said. "It's working fine. Big Roy has his job, and I have my job. He does the things that he does, and I do the things that I do. We're both helping Roy."

Who would be the chief second during the fight and speak to Roy between rounds?

"That's up to Roy," Merkerson answered. "He hasn't told us that, and I don't know that it matters. I cannot fight for Roy, and Roy Senior cannot fight for Roy. Who's in charge doesn't matter. As long as it's a winning team, no one cares who's in charge."

On the night of October 1st, Roy Jones entered his dressing room moments after 9:30. He was wearing blue-jean shorts, a green-black-and-white horizontally-striped polo shirt, and white sandals. The mountainman beard was gone, replaced by a neatly-trimmed goatee and mustache.

The setting was familiar. A large room with industrial carpet, blue lockers set against white cinderblock walls, a dozen grey-metal folding chairs with blue cushions, and a mahogany-colored leather sofa. There were two small television monitors, both without audio.

Jones circled the room and touched fists with everyone. The first televised fight of the evening, Brian Minto versus Vinny Maddalone, was underway. The roar of the crowd was audible through the walls.

Roy took off his shirt. The day before, he'd looked remarkably fit, weighing in at 175 pounds. His biceps had biceps.

Larry Merchant came in for a brief HBO interview. Moments after he left, the television monitor showed a tape of Tarver entering the arena. Roy watched impassively. Then he put on a black undergarment, white socks, black-and-white Air Jordan shoes with matching tassels, and black trunks with white trim.

Andre Ward versus Glenn LaPlante (the second televised fight) began. LaPlante, a 37-year-old bellhop, had no business being in the ring with Ward, and everyone knew it. At the end of round one, Ward knocked him woozy. The fallen fighter lay flat on his back as medical personnel rushed to care for him. Jones turned away from the screen. Alton Merkerson stepped in front of the television monitor.

The cornermen for the night would be Merkerson, Roy Jones Sr., Lemuel Jones (Big Roy's best friend), and Dr. Richard Lucey. Each of them was wearing black warm-up pants, black shoes, and a black jacket with "RJ Jr." inscribed in white on the back. Merkerson was doing all the hands-on work—helping Roy get dressed, rubbing Vaseline on his body.

At 9:55, Roy Jones Sr. spoke up for the first time.

"It's quiet in here."

Rhythmic clapping began

"Whose house?" Merkerson demanded.

"Jones house!" the chorus replied.

"Whose house?"

"Jones house!"

"Whose house?"

"Jones house!"

"It's all over but the shouting," Merkerson cried.

Roy stood up, walked to the center of the room, and started circling as though he were in a boxing ring.

Applause and cheers sounded.

Roy looked happy. "There's been a lot of talk for a long time," he said. More cheers.

It was ten o'clock. Except for his hands, which had yet to be taped, Roy looked ready to fight. But the earliest he would be called to the ring was 10:55.

Nate Campbell versus Almazbek Raiymkulov, aka Kid Diamond, began. Jones looked at the television monitor. "Get that bullshit out of the ring," he demanded. "I got something I got to do tonight."

Again, there were cheers followed by chants and rhythmic clapping.

"Uh-huh!"

*Clap-clap.*

"Uh-huh!"

*Clap-clap.*

Roy began to shadow-box, his hands moving like lightning. "Too fast," he shouted.

"Uh-huh!"

"Too fast."

"Uh-huh!"

"Too fast."

"Uh-huh!"

"Whose house?" Merk demanded again.

"Jones house!"

"Whose house?"

"Jones house!"

"History is going to be made," Big Roy shouted in a voice that rose above the din.

At 10:10, referee Tommy Kimmons came in to give Jones his pre-fight instructions. Quiet fell. Roy sat on a chair. Kimmons waited for a signal from the HBO cameraman.

"Speed it up," Merkerson said. "We're in a flow."

Kimmons (who would do an excellent job of refereeing the fight) began, was interrupted by feedback from HBO's sound equipment, waited for another signal, started anew, and proceeded to recite what seemed to be every rule in the book. He left at 10:20, and the chanting resumed.

"Whose house?"

"Jones house!"

"What time?"

"Jones time!"

Merkerson began taping Roy's hands.

"Whose house?"

"Jones house!"

"What time?"

"Jones time!"

At 10:30, the taping was done. Roy stood up, raised his fist in the air, and bowed his head. "Come together, everyone," he said. A circle formed around him. Those who could not touch him touched those who could. There was a prayer with the "amen" at the end sounding like a battle cry.

Roy circled the room again, shadowboxing with greater intensity. "We got about thirty minutes before you see it all," he promised.

There were cheers followed by voices.

"That boy's so fast, he'll hit a ghost in the head."

"Tarver ain't been where you're gonna take him tonight."

"You done the work. The fun part is coming up now."

On the television monitor, Nate Campbell emerged victorious over Kid Diamond. Merkerson patted Roy's brow with a towel, sat him down, and gloved him up.

At 10:50, Roy circled the room one last time and embraced everyone. One wondered if he was harboring any self-doubt. The dressing room was safe. A boxing ring isn't.

Ten minutes later, Jones entered the main arena to a thunderous roar. Tarver followed to more boos than cheers. In Antonio's hometown, the sell-out crowd of 20,895 belonged to Jones. For the first time in his career, Roy was an underdog. The odds were 9-to-5 against him. When the bell rings, a fighter can't live on his past.

Round one was a feeling-out process with Tarver the aggressor. There was drama but little action. Antonio landed only three punches and Jones one less.

Then came a surprise.

"Going to the ring," Merkerson said later, "I was the guy who was supposed to be inside the ropes between rounds. And after the first round, Big Roy just pushed his way past me and got in. I didn't like it but it wasn't the time to make a fuss." For the rest of the fight, Big Roy was in the ring after every round. "We couldn't both be talking." Merkerson acknowledged. "That would be like having two men in one household. We all know that doesn't work. So I figured one of us had to be man enough to step back, and I was that guy."

In round two, Tarver remained the aggressor. Near the end of the stanza, he pinned Roy in the corner and seemed to hurt him. Jones looked to be headed toward another "KO by."

Round three saw Tarver continuing to stalk while Jones remained elusive. Round four was more of the same, but Roy got Antonio's attention with some good body shots near the end.

In round five, everything changed. For one shining interlude, Jones looked like the original Roy Jones Jr. again. He scored with vicious body blows and some good shots to the head interspersed with taunting moves like one of his fighting cocks. With a minute left, Tarver seemed confused by Roy's speed, a bit shaken, and was up against the ropes. Then, instead of pressing his advantage, Jones backed off. At the end of five rounds, Roy was up 48-47 on two of the judges' scorecards and trailed by a point on the third. It seemed as though he could win, would win, the fight.

In the old days, Roy Jones had eight or nine rounds per fight like round five. This time, he had one. Round six marked the final turning point in Tarver-Jones III. Antonio came out aggressively and took control again. In the previous round, he had been hit with Roy's best, and Roy hadn't been able to break him. Once again, there was a feeling in the air that Tarver could dramatically change the flow of the fight with one punch and Jones couldn't.

Rounds seven through ten were copies of one another. Tarver moved forward behind a stiff jab, while Roy seemed reduced to gimmicks and tricks. In the past, Jones's speed was his greatest offensive weapon. Opponents didn't have time to think against him. They were always under siege. He could strike at any time. But here, Roy used his speed largely for defensive purposes. He circled the ring, stayed out of harm's way, and avoided the ropes. He wiggled his hips, stuck out his tongue, feinted, and smiled a lot. What he didn't do often enough was punch.

Jones landed only one punch (a jab) in the entire seventh round. In rounds seven through nine, he connected a total of seven times. Meanwhile, Tarver fought a patient fight. On occasion, Roy scored with blows that made Antonio think twice about being overly aggressive. But for most of the night, Jones let Tarver engage when he wanted to engage and rest when he wanted to rest. As the fight went into the late rounds, it looked as though Roy was fighting to go the distance, not to win.

With two minutes left in round eleven, Tarver staggered Jones with a big right hook. Roy was badly hurt. For the next thirty seconds, Antonio battered him from post to post. But Roy took it and came back as Tarver appeared to tire. At round's end, Antonio appeared to be in a bit of trouble.

The logical time for a fighter who wants to win to gamble is when time is running out and he's hopelessly behind on points. That's when he should try to land his most powerful punch, even at the expense of defense, when the slightest opening presents itself. After round eleven, some listeners expected to hear Roy Jones Sr. tell his son, "You've got to suck it up and dominate this motherfucker. He's tired now. Knock him out."

Nothing of that nature was said. Roy won the twelfth round on two of the three judges' cards, but it wasn't enough. The scores were 116-112, 116-112, and 117-111 in favor of Tarver. This observer had it 117-112 (scoring the first round even and giving Roy rounds four, five, and twelve). Antonio threw 620 punches to Roy's 320 and outlanded him 158 to 85.

After the fight, Tarver was jubilant. "Roy is a great fighter and Roy beat some great fighters," he said. "I've benefitted from what Roy accomplished before he fought me. I hope that, when people look at our fights, they use them to build me up and not tear Roy down. After all, if Roy Jones is everything in the ring that his fans think he is, where do you put Antonio Tarver?"

But face-to-face competition isn't the best gauge of comparative greatness in boxing. Muhammad Ali and Joe Frazier were roughly even against one another. However, few observers place them on equal footing when ranking the greatest heavyweights of all time. Ali is usually mentioned with Joe Louis and, sometimes, Jack Johnson. Frazier, despite his accomplishments, resides on a lower level.

Meanwhile, after the bout, Jones was incongruously satisfied. "This is a new beginning for me." he said. "It's the first time I've felt good in the ring in a while. Tarver took advantage of a few things. My reflexes are slower. He wouldn't have beaten me in my prime, but he always would have given me trouble. There's a few more things I need to do. I was a little rusty but I felt like I was getting my old self back again. I liked what I saw. It became fun again. I think, if I continue to go on and get myself up, I can come back and be who I was. I hate to lose but I feel good."

Alton Merkerson left the dressing room quickly after the fight. He said nothing but the disappointment of the moment was etched on his face. "Roy was tentative," he said later. "We all know that things change as you get older, but he could have done more. He could have won the fight. Tarver was confused by Roy's speed; and to be honest with you, I think Tarver is a bit overrated. But if you've been knocked out in your last two fights and you're fighting one of the guys who did it, things go through your mind."

"I've been in combat [as a career military officer in Vietnam],"

Merkerson continued. "And believe me, once you've been hit, you do things different. If Roy had been busier and fought every round like he fought the fifth, he would have won. But I'm proud of him, and he still has a lot left. The next fight, if he fights again, you'll see more of the original Roy Jones Jr."

What about Big Roy taking over in the corner?

"Big Roy was trying to help his son," Merkerson answered. "He knows Roy as well as I do. There's things I might have said to Roy during the fight that were different from what Big Roy said, but that's the way life is sometimes."

Meanwhile, a bit of career evaluation is in order. Roy Jones was once a great fighter. His history can never be taken away from him. But Roy has now lost three fights in a row and hasn't won since November 2003.

Jones lost to Tarver for a number of reasons. First, Antonio is very good. Second, Roy hadn't been in action for over a year and there was a modicum of ring rust. Third, Jones is growing older. There were times when Tarver was open for counters and Roy didn't let his hands go. Whether it was physical ("I realize I lost a step," he conceded afterward) or mental, the counters weren't there. He couldn't, or wouldn't, pull the trigger for most of the night.

That, of course, leads to the supervening issue. In the past, Jones gave the impression of a fighter who would do what he had to do to win. In his first fight against Tarver, Antonio was physically superior. Roy was physically depleted but he was the mentally tougher of the two men. He walked through fire and won.

In Tarver-Jones III, the roles were reversed. Roy was in superb physical condition but Tarver's resolve was stronger. Indeed, there were times when it looked as though Jones wasn't fighting to win but rather to meet a certain standard of his own satisfaction. It was as though he wanted to prove to himself that he could still be Roy Jones in the ring; if not for a whole fight, at least for a few rounds. And above all, he didn't want to get knocked out. The two prior knockouts had changed him. He was unwilling to walk through fire again.

In sum, Jones was in his own parallel universe with his own private agenda from the beginning to the end of Tarver-Jones III. It's hard to recall another great fighter being as satisfied as he was after a loss. The fact that Roy treated his defeat as a moral victory speaks to how down he had been before the fight. But he did what he felt he had to do, and he's at peace with himself now.

That much was clear in the dressing room after the fight. Roy was sitting on a folding metal chair. Big Roy was talking at the far end of the room.

"Roy fought that fight for himself," Big Roy said. "I could have pushed him more in the corner but it was his fight. He knows his way around the ring. He's been fighting since he was a little boy. There wasn't anything I could tell him about the judges' scorecards that he didn't already know. The victory for him is in what he did. Tarver won the fight; but in his heart, Roy won."

Then Big Roy made his way through the well-wishers to his son's side. "That one was from his soul," he told the room at large. "Roy came back from two knockouts and a year off. Can you imagine what was going through his mind in the ring? Son, you're the best fighter I've ever known. Ain't nobody else I know could have come back from those things and performed like you did tonight."

Big Roy extended his hand, and Roy grasped it.

"I'm proud of you, son."

Roy's face lit up.

"Take a picture with me, son. I want something I can look at when I think of tonight."

Roy Jones Jr. stood up and Big Roy draped an arm around his shoulders. A camera flashed. Little Roy was smiling but there was mist in his eyes.❏

*When Jermain Taylor fought Bernard Hopkins in the last big fight of 2005, once again I was given full access to the Taylor camp.*

# JERMAIN TAYLOR DOES IT AGAIN

On July 16, 2005, Jermain Taylor stood in a boxing ring at the MGM Grand Garden Arena in Las Vegas and awaited his fate. He had just fought twelve hard rounds against Bernard Hopkins, the undisputed middleweight champion of the world. In round five, Taylor's head had been split open by a head butt. The gash extended down to his skull and caused significant tissue damage. As the bout progressed, cutman Ray Rodgers' bucket looked like it belonged in a hospital emergency room.

"I was just hoping I had enough blood in me to finish the fight," Taylor said afterward. Tired and bleeding badly, he fought the final rounds on heart.

"Ladies and gentlemen, we have a split decision," ring announcer Michael Buffer told the crowd. "Jerry Roth scores the bout 116 to 112 for Hopkins."

Taylor's trainer, Pat Burns, patted his fighter's cheek. "Don't worry, that's just one."

"I knew the next one would be for me because that's the way they read them," Jermain said later.

"Duane Ford, 115-113 for Taylor."

"Okay, here we go," Jermain told himself.

"Paul Smith, 115-113 to the winner by split decision and NEW . . ."

"All I heard after that was the cheering," Jermain remembers.

"He pulled it off! He pulled it off!" HBO commentator Jim Lampley shouted to a national television audience. "The long reign of Bernard Hopkins is over."

In that moment, Jermain Taylor's world turned golden.

The adulation that comes from winning a fist-fight speaks to the primal and enduring nature of the sport. The first few weeks after winning the championship were the equivalent of a little kid opening presents on Christmas morning for Taylor. On July 22nd, a parade in Little Rock honored his accomplishments. Thousand more attended a rally at the end of the route. "That was the best feeling I ever had,"

Jermain said afterward. "It was amazing that all those people came out just for me."

Next came a trip to New York for an August 2nd meeting with fellow Arkansan Bill Clinton. "That was amazing too," Taylor recalls. "We walked into his office. Bill Clinton was at his desk, reading a book. He looked up. And I'm asking myself, 'Is this real? Am I watching TV or dreaming or is this really Bill Clinton?' He stood up and said hello. We shook hands. And I'm thinking, 'Damn! What am I supposed to say. This man was president of the United States. "But he started the conversation. He was very nice. Amazing! That's all I can say. It was amazing."

But Taylor received more than attention. He received affection. The embraces at social gatherings and chance meetings in stores or on the street made it clear to him that people liked him. "It really makes me feel like I'm somebody," Jermain said. "I've loved every minute of this."

But a cloud named Bernard Hopkins loomed on the horizon.

Taylor had never been truly tested in his first twenty-three fights. He was against Hopkins. In the ring, Bernard lives by the credo, "By any means necessary." And in their July 16th match-up, he'd employed every tactic and weapon at his command. Defensively, Hopkins backpedaled for much of the night. "That's the way I work; I'm careful," he said later. He was successful in neutralizing Taylor's jab. As the fight progressed, he landed myriad punishing blows. And there was more.

Some fighters throw punches from all angles. Hopkins uses his head and elbows from all angles. "I'm in the hurt business," he says. "I'm not looking to come out of this squeaky clean every time I step into that ring."

The clash of heads that caused Taylor's scalp wound appeared to have been accidental. But regardless of intent, it changed the flow of the fight. In the early rounds, Jermain had been overanxious and expended unnecessary energy by fighting in an undisciplined manner. "I was in the best shape of my life," he said afterward. "But I got tired because I was chasing him around the ring and wasting punches." Then came the collision of heads and gash.

Ernest Hemingway once wrote, "Courage is grace under pressure." When Taylor was cut, he showed his courage. "Blood was pouring from my head," he said later. "I'd never gone through anything like that before. After the head butt, it was like, 'Boy, these rounds are long.' In the twelfth round, I was dog-tired. No way of getting around it. I said to myself, 'Man, this is it. Either you've got it inside or you don't.'"

To the judges, it looked as though Taylor was trying harder and did more to take the belts than Hopkins did to keep them. "The first fight was too close for comfort," Jermain acknowledges. "But I think I won."

Hopkins thought otherwise. Immediately after the fight, he took to calling himself the "people's champion" and began a non-stop campaign to discredit Taylor's victory. Indeed, Joe Santoliquito (managing editor of *The Ring*) says that Bernard went so far as to lobby with him to have the magazine withhold recognition of Jermain as middleweight champion. The magazine refused Hopkins's request. And according to Santoliquito, there were repercussions.

"Bernard had promised me he would sign a pair of boxing gloves to be auctioned off to raise funds for the American Cancer Society," Santoliquito revealed. "It had been preearranged, and I brought the gloves to the [August 4th show that Golden Boy East was promoting at] the Borgata. Bernard put me off and he put me off. Finally, he told me, 'Fuck the American Cancer Society. Get Jermain Taylor to sign them.'"

Thus, outside the ring, the battle raged on. "Bernard is like a guy who's going through a divorce," Pat Burns observed. "He had four wives: the WBC, the WBA, the WBO, and the IBF. And one night, they all left him for another man. At first, he couldn't believe it. Then he became angry and, like a lot of people would, lashed out at the other man rather than blame himself. But no matter how Bernard reacts, the bottom line is that Jermain walked off with his women. They're living with Jermain now in Little Rock, Arkansas."

And Charles Jay wrote, "Bernard Hopkins is the former middleweight champion of the world; not because the judges bungled it; not because the entire world is against him; not because he came up against an unbeatable fighting machine. No, Bernard Hopkins is the former middleweight champion today because he made some serious miscalculations. He miscalculated about where he stood in the fight. He miscalculated about his ability to knock out an opponent. He miscalculated about what he had left, which just wasn't enough. Veteran champions with twenty title defenses under their belt and all the experience and savvy that are expected to come with it aren't supposed to make those kinds of miscalculations. Unless, of course, the guy with all that experience was experiencing something entirely different; in this case, a real live legitimate middleweight on his way to the top of the ladder and completely unwilling to be intimidated before or after the opening bell. That was something Hopkins hadn't seen in over a decade."

Still, many in the media bought into Hopkins's complaints. And with a contractually-mandated rematch ahead, the prevailing view was that Taylor-Hopkins II would be double-or-nothing. If Bernard prevailed in their second encounter, it would invalidate Jermain's victory in the first.

Meanwhile, one got the impression that, wherever Hopkins was on the day of the parade in Jermain's honor, he was hoping for rain in Little Rock.

At the October 11th press conference in New York to formally announce Taylor-Hopkins II, Bernard continued to complain. "Jermain Taylor didn't beat me," he proclaimed. "Duane Ford [the ring judge who cast the deciding vote] beat me. The credible witnesses at ringside thought that Bernard Hopkins won that fight. The only thing I didn't do was finish Jermain Taylor off when I had him on queer street. Everything from round one through round twelve was perfectly executed by Bernard Hopkins. A draw would have been a robbery. Giving it to Jermain Taylor was a rape. Jermain Taylor is the corporate champion. I'm the people's champion. Jermain Taylor got the victory but Jermain Taylor didn't beat Bernard Hopkins."

Meanwhile, Taylor was getting tired of the complaining. Initially, he'd responded to Hopkins's rants with the thought, "That's just Bernard being Bernard. If he doesn't give me respect, that's his problem, not mine. It says more about him than it does about me."

But now, Jermain ratcheted things up a bit. "You lost, man," he said at the press conference. "Stop complaining and take it like a man. A true champion would have said, 'I lost; I'm gonna do better next time.' If you feel you got robbed, do better in the rematch. If you want your belts back, come and take them from me."

Taylor also had some choice words regarding Hopkins's ring tactics.

"When I watched the tape, I saw very clearly how dirty he was," Jermain said. "Hitting below the belt; hitting behind the head; holding and hitting. He uses his head like a third hand. Bernard is an all-around dirty fighter. If I cut you with a head butt, that's not boxing. He cheats to win, and I don't consider that winning a boxing match. I lost all respect for him. He tried every trick in the book, which shows me he's not a true champion. Fight like a champion fights and keep your mouth shut."

Later in the day, Jermain added another thought. "Bernard Hopkins is the type of person you want to beat up," he said.

The rematch was slated for December 3rd at Mandalay Bay Hotel and Casino. It was the last big fight of 2005, and also Hopkins's last chance to leave boxing on his own terms as an active fighter. The week of the fight, Las Vegas was buzzing. And despite Taylor being the champion, the media attention was focussed on Hopkins.

Bernard is a great fighter, who has approached the inevitable end of his career with as much skill in the ring as any aging fighter ever. One month shy of 41, he's old for the sweet science but he doesn't fight like it. "Other men's fists have pounded his features into a perfect face for a fighter," LeRoy Neiman says. And in the ring, he's close to perfection.

Readying for fights has been Hopkins's life. He has gotten as much out of his natural gifts as possible. He's a superb defensive tactician, who embodies Archie Moore's maxim, "It's not the length of a career that wears a man out; it's the punches he takes."

Hopkins is also very good at beating people up. A punch here, a lot of punches there. Lest one forget, as Gene Tunney observed, "The strongest and best natural defense is a good punch."

During the course of his career, Hopkins has engaged in five defining fights. The first was against Roy Jones, when Bernard didn't takes the risks he needed to take and was outboxed over twelve rounds. Then came a courageous effort when he climbed off the canvas to salvage a draw against Segundo Mercado in the 9,252-foot altitude of Quito, Ecuador. Bernard's signature wins (against Felix Trinidad and Oscar De La Hoya) were against legitimate Hall of Famers, but Hall of Famers who had moved up in weight from 140 and 130 pounds respectively. Then there was Hopkins-Taylor.

Comparing fighters from different eras is a tricky business. Stanley Ketchel, who reigned as middleweight champion in the early 1900s, is justifiably regarded as a great fighter. But if Ketchel emerged unchanged from a time capsule today, he'd find that technique and conditioning had passed him by. Thus, in measuring greatness, one must look to a fighter's core and judge him by the standards of his own era. In that regard, three markers are of particular importance: (1) a fighter's historical impact; (2) his longevity; and (3) his record against other great fighters.

Hopkins scores his highest marks for longevity. One can argue all day about his place among the alltime greats. The bottom line is, set up a middleweight tournament with Hopkins, Sugar Ray Robinson, Marvin Hagler, Carlos Monzon, and Roy Jones Jr. Go further back in time for Ketchel, Mickey Walker, and Harry Greb (who would have taught Bernard a thing or two about dirty). Add Tony Zale, Jake LaMotta, and Charlie Burley. These men would engage in great fights.

Meanwhile, Hopkins is particularly adept at the media game and getting his message out. He's verbally gifted and has a good sense of humor. No fighter but Bernard would think to say, "James Toney is talking about how I'm not on his level. If he's talking about who can eat the most donuts, he's right."

"If I could talk a fight," Hopkins declared in Las Vegas, "I'd have 100 wins and no losses with 100 knockouts." But as Jim Lampley notes, "Bernard is a better talker than listener. And there's a difference between the world as it is and the world as Bernard proclaims it to be."

Thus, while Hopkins calls himself the "People's Champion," his conduct can be at odds with that notion. At the Boxing Writers Association of America awards dinner earlier this year, a fan approached Bernard with a boxing glove and felt-tip pen.

"Mr. Hopkins, would you sign this glove for me?"

"For twenty dollars," Hopkins told him.

"Please."

"For twenty dollars. Both of us know you can put it on Ebay and make a profit."

The fan took out his wallet and handed a twenty-dollar bill to Hopkins. Bernard took it, signed the glove, and put the money in his pocket. "I'm a businessman," he said. "Other fighters can learn from me."

This is a people's champion?

Hopkins has a vision of the world with himself at the center. His self-adoration is evident. Four days before the Taylor rematch, at a sitdown with reporters, he likened himself as an athlete and trailblazer to Jim Brown, Bill Russell, and Muhammad Ali. Throughout the week, this theme was linked to a constant lobbying effort vis-a-vis the judges for his upcoming fight.

"The judging in the last fight showed I'm not paranoid," Hopkins declared. "Just because a guy is running and looking back over his shoulder doesn't mean no one is chasing him. On July 16th, I exposed the industry to the point where they couldn't hide the dirty laundry anymore. July 16th exposed what I've been saying for years. After July 16th, I felt like some historical people who made great speeches right before they were assassinated."

"I exposed what happens in the sport if you don't play the game," Hopkins continued. "I stood up and looked the system in the face. Very few people can do that. Once you become a person of knowledge and you happen to be an athlete, you become a problem. But if you follow my history, you know that I'm at my best when I have to beat the system. My whole life has been adversity, victorious, adversity, victorious. I've always been up against this type of adversity."

But there was more. With increasing frequency, Hopkins was speaking in an ugly way about Jermain Taylor. Before their first fight, he had demeaned Taylor's ring skills. This time, he was demeaning Jermain's intelligence and character.

In a November 22nd conference call, Hopkins called Taylor "an impersonator who he thinks he's a champion" and added, "Just because you got the belts doesn't mean that you actually earned the belts." Then, for good measure, Bernard labeled Jermain an "idiot" and said he was "not intelligent."

It brought to mind a moment that occurred on February 5, 2003, when Hopkins testified before the United States Senate Committee on Commerce, Science, and Transportation in support of a bill to establish a federal boxing commission. Like the other witnesses, Bernard was asked to read a prepared statement explaining his views after which he would answer questions. Hopkins began to read, and it became apparent that he was struggling. A high IQ (which he presumably has) and good reading skills are two very different matters. Bernard never finished reading his statement. Midway through it, he stopped in frustration and told the senators that he would be happy to answer any questions they might have.

Now, in Las Vegas, Hopkins branded Jermain Taylor as "ignorant." At his Tuesday sitdown with reporters, he went further, declaring, "The establishment can control him. They got their boy who they can control. He's a yes-sir no-sir type of guy. There's modernized slavery and there's out-and-out slavery. Things have been tweaked as time goes on, but some people's hearts and minds haven't changed. I'm the guy in the fields. He's the guy who would be in the house."

The following day, at the final pre-fight press conference, Hopkins stayed on message. After likening himself to Hannibal "coming through the ocean on his elephants to attack the Italian people," he declared. "What a perfect script for Bernard Hopkins. This is the last stage of greatness. In boxing, when it's young versus old, young prevails but I'm different. I'm the Robin Hood of boxing. Physically, I can't knock out the system, but I can knock out the system politically. Whatever Jermain Taylor brings to the table, Bernard Hopkins is going to make sure that it backfires on him. I know everything about Jermain Taylor. I got this guy down pat. Jermain Taylor is a four- or five-round fighter. He's a front-runner. I'll get him hurt and finish him. When I leave boxing as an active fighter, I'll be taking Jermain Taylor's future with me."

Later, when Taylor was out of earshot, Hopkins called him "an ignorant fool" and "punk" and added, "The lack of intelligence that Jermain Taylor has, this guy totally don't get it." He also proclaimed, "Jermain Taylor gets the impression that, because he's in the house, he's special. But come Saturday night, he'll be out in the fields again."

Taylor was apprised of, and shrugged off, the insults. But there was concern in the Taylor camp that Bernard's incessant complaining about the decision in their first fight would have an impact on the judges in the rematch. In truth, the first-fight controversy primarily involved one round: Duane Ford's scoring of the final stanza for Jermain. But the threat implicit in Hopkins's constant criticism of Ford was, "Score the rounds you think are close for me. Because if you don't and you happen to be way off on one, I'll expose you to ridicule."

Thus, when it was his turn to speak at the final pre-fight press conference, Pat Burns took the microphone and said, "Bernard is trying to fight this fight outside the ring. He knows he can't intimidate Jermain, so he's trying to intimidate the judges. I'm confident that won't happen."

Then Taylor had his say. "A true champion takes his loss, goes home, and says, 'I'm going to do better next time,'" Jermain said. "But Bernard can't do better. He's an accurate puncher, but he's not a big puncher. He doesn't have the power to knock me out. If I'd been hurt last time, I'd say I was hurt. He caught me with some good shots but he never hurt me. I was tired more than anything else, and I don't think he can do anything different this time. Bernard should have gotten out when he was on top. Now it's too late."

And there was one last exchange between the fighters that spoke volumes. In an obvious attempt at verbal intimidation, Hopkins suggested that Jermain hug his wife and daughter before going into the ring on Saturday night in case he didn't come out whole.

"He told me to hug my wife and kids," Taylor said in response. "What's he gonna do? Kill me? Come on, man. This is a sport. I'm a fighter. I ain't trying to kill nobody. I'm sick of this man crying."

Then Taylor took a tape recorder out of his pocket, announced, "This is what Bernard Hopkins sounds like," and pushed the "play" button. The wails of an infant and laughter from the media resounded throughout the room. Next, Jermain produced a doll dressed in pink with "Cry-Baby Hopkins" written on its pajama top. There was more laughter.

Hopkins maintained a stone-faced silence. He might enjoy making fun of other people but he doesn't like being the butt of other people's jokes.

"This idiot doesn't know that, when he steps in the ring, he might not come out the same as when he went in," Bernard fumed afterward. "He don't get it. This idiot can't even grasp what I'm saying. I'm letting him know, this is the boxing game, buddy. When you go to war, and that's what I call it, you might not come back. I'm pretty sure that Leavander Johnson believed when he came to Las Vegas that he was going home."

Leavander Johnson, of course, was another piece of the puzzle and part of a subplot that surfaced from time to time during the build-up to the fight. Taylor was promoted by Lou DiBella, who had once been Bernard's promoter and had also promoted Johnson. DiBella and Hopkins despise one another and at times seem as obsessed with each other as Captain Ahab was with the white whale.

"If you're a promoter in this business and you don't have a superstar, you have nothing," DiBella once said. Hopkins had been DiBella's superstar. Then he left him, made ugly allegations of financial wrongdoing, and wound up on the wrong end of a $610,000 jury verdict in a libel action that DiBella brought against him in federal court.

A lot of people think that Hopkins agreed to the first Taylor fight because of his desire to destroy DiBella. Bernard seemed to say as much prior to that bout when he declared, "Everybody in their lifetime has the experience where they want to get revenge" and added that beating DiBella's fighter would be "like a second erection." When asked about Hopkins's motivation for facing off against Jermain the first time, Bouie Fisher (Bernard's longtime trainer) laughed and said, "You can use your own imagination on that one. All I'll say is, when you put personal opinions in business, it doesn't work."

After Hopkins-Taylor I, DiBella declared, "As far as Bernard is concerned, I feel like that horrible chapter of my life is finally over."

But it wasn't; not really, not for either man. In response to Hopkins's constant complaining that he'd been robbed by the judges, DiBella proclaimed, "Bernard knows a lot about robberies since he committed dozens of them before going to prison for five years; but in this case, he's wrong."

When potential sites for Hopkins-Taylor II were discussed, Memphis was mentioned because of its proximity to Arkansas. Four thousand fans from Jermain's home state had travelled to Las Vegas for Hopkins-Taylor I, and it was assumed that they'd travel in even greater numbers to Memphis.

"Hopkins can't even sell a fight in [his home town of] Philadelphia," DiBella opined at the time. "They'd have to have it in Graterford prison for the crowd to be on his side."

Then, on September 17th, Leavander Johnson was killed in a fight against Jesus Chavez, who is promoted by Golden Boy. Hopkins has an equity interest in Golden Boy East and, like DiBella, was on site for the Johnson tragedy. It was a sobering moment for both men and they agreed to cool the rhetoric between them. But at the final pre-fight press conference for Taylor-Hopkins II, Bernard's complaining was too much for DiBella. Talking the microphone, he looked Hopkins in the eye and told him, "Since the last fight, you've been a whining crying sore-losing baby."

And there was one more issue of note swirling around Taylor-Hopkins II. Bouie Fisher wasn't there. The 77-year-old trainer is one of the most respected men in boxing. He began working with Bernard in

1989 and guided him to greatness. Three years ago, they had a falling-out and Fisher filed suit claiming that he'd been underpaid $255,000 for Hopkins's title fights against Keith Holmes, Felix Trinidad and Carl Daniels. Sloan Harrison trained Bernard for his 2003 title defense against Morrade Hakkar. Then the case was settled and Bouie returned to the fold.

Hopkins claimed that Fisher was no longer in his camp because of medical problems. "Bouie is sick," the fighter said. "It's a personal thing so I'd rather not go into detail, but he's been sick since like three fights ago. People always want to bring negativity into the situation but let's call this for what it is."

Then, in a November 21st interview with Bernard Fernandez of the *Philadelphia News*, Fisher put the lie to Hopkins's story. "Bernard is a very difficult person to deal with," Bouie said. "He wants all the glory. He wants all the credit. He wants all the money. It's all about him, him, him. He's made some bad decisions in the past, and this is another one. The devil is always busy; the devil finds a way. I would be with Bernard right now if he was paying me right."

In Fisher's absence, Naazim Richardson assumed the role of lead trainer. "Brother Naazim is a world-respected guy," Hopkins told reporters on a teleconference call eleven days before the fight. "He's been the energy in the gym for the last nine or ten years. He's a guy that's been sort of fifty to sixty percent of the strategy. He's been the youth of this thing. He holds the pads; he holds the bags; he comes up with the movements. Bouie is seventy-plus-years-old. He can't hold pads or I'll knock his arm off."

Regardless, Fisher's absence made it difficult for Bernard to style himself as a good guy, and questions about the trainer's absence seemed to make him uncomfortable.

"Why did you fire Bouie?" Kevin Iole of the *Las Vegas Review Journal* asked during the November 22nd conference call.

"Who said I fired Bouie?"

"Bouie."

"Can we talk about the Jermain Taylor fight?" Hopkins pleaded. "I'm fighting Jermain Taylor, and Jermain Taylor is fighting Bernard Hopkins. People are coming to see this fight. They're not coming to see Naazim Richardson, Bouie Fisher, Pat Burns, or Lou DiBella."

On fight day—Saturday, December 3rd—Jermain Taylor awoke at 6:30 a.m. He ate a light breakfast, watched television, and took a short nap. At 2:30, he went downstairs to Raffles Cafe for a final pre-fight meal with family and friends.

When Taylor-Hopkins II was announced, Bernard had been installed as an 11-to-10 favorite. Now the odds were 6-to-5 in Jermain's favor, reflecting the view that the match-up was too close to call. As Jermain's wife, Erica, passed around color photographs of their eleven-month-old daughter, Nia Jay, Pat Burns considered the night to come.

Burns had been on the receiving end of some sniping after Hopkins-Taylor I, with critics suggesting that Jermain faded late in the fight because he'd been overtrained. But Jermain had reported to camp for that bout at 187 pounds and been required to work hard simply to make weight. This time, he'd begun training at 171 pounds and tipped the scales at the official weigh-in at 159.

"There were some Monday-morning quarterbacks and a trainer or two with big names who wanted to get their hands on Jermain," Burns acknowledged. "They made comments that they could do a better job than I'd done and strategically zeroed in on someone they thought was a weak link in the chain. But Jermain stood by me. I'm still here."

Burns had watched Hopkins-Taylor I on tape more than a dozen times, stopping and rewinding within rounds each time. "The first time, I looked at it as a fan," he said. "Then I studied it for Bernard's strong points and weak points; Jermain's strong points and weak points; what Jay Nady allowed and didn't allow. I watched it three times with Jermain, and Jermain looked at it a lot on his own. Bernard was a better fighter than Jermain that night. Jermain did not fight a good fight, but he made up for it with tenacity, speed, and power. I agree with the judges. I thought Jermain won seven rounds to five."

As for the night ahead, Burns opined, "I think Bernard is a better fighter now than he ever was. His coordination, reflexes, and balance are amazing for a forty-year-old man; and when he was in his physical prime, he didn't have the ring savvy he has now. But Bernard doesn't do much when you're genuinely aggressive against him. He's very cautious about getting hit and only throws punches when it's safe. And Bernard's problem is that he can only fight in spurts because time has caught up with him. So he might do a few things differently tonight to make it appear as though he's fighting more aggressively than last time. But I expect him to fight pretty much the same way he did then."

As for what Taylor might do differently, Burns offered, "Jermain learned more in the last fight than anything I could have taught him. Nothing can match the experience he got that night. He has much more potential for improvement over last time than Bernard does. One key thing we've worked on is for Jermain to worry less about throwing big power shots and concentrate more on utilizing his hand-speed and foot-speed."

What about head butts and other borderline Hopkins ring tactics?

"We've worked on that," Burns answered. "Seeing something on tape when you're preparing for a fight is different from going through it. Jermain has learned from experience now how Hopkins fights. If Bernard uses his head tonight, he might get an elbow in the eye."

Meanwhile, Taylor was looking forward to battle. "I'm a lot more relaxed than I was before the last fight," he said over a large bowl of pasta. "I'm not as worried; I'm much more confident. I still feel like I have a lot to prove, but there was more pressure on me last time. Bernard has a sneaky righthand, but I know now that he has no power. And Bernard is scared of getting hit. That's why he ran those early rounds and why he doesn't fully commit on his punches. I took his best last time. He hit me with his best punch when I was tired, and I still beat him. That's all he has, and he hasn't seen my best yet."

As the meal progressed, it became clear that the Taylor camp considered it significant that Bernard's most vicious attacks on Jermain's intelligence and character had been launched behind Jermain's back (at solo sitdowns with the media on Tuesday and Wednesday and during Thursday's satellite interviews).

"Bernard is trying to build his confidence by tearing Jermain down," Burns said. "But he's afraid to do it face-to-face."

That led to an observation by Dennis Moore, a Little Rock police detective who has known Taylor since Jermain was in sixth grade. Moore handles security for the Taylor camp and is ideal for the job. He's low-key and doesn't throw his weight around but has a presence that exudes authority and demands respect.

"Bernard is talking about the last fight like he's trying to convince himself," Moore posited. "There are bad calls in every sport. You might complain at the time; but after a while, you let it go. You don't complain forever. When did you ever hear a true champion complaining like this? Can you imagine Muhammad Ali or Michael Jordan or any true champion complaining like Hopkins has done. It tells me that he's struggling with some serious doubts inside."

The lunch ended shortly before four o'clock. "Is there a party tonight?" someone asked as Team Taylor was leaving the table.

"Yeah," Burns answered. "In the ring right after the fight."

Two hours later, at 5:55 p.m., Jermain Taylor entered dressing room #4 at the Mandalay Bay Events Center. With him were Pat Burns, Dennis Moore, training assistant Edgardo Martinez, Ozell Nelson (who had trained Jermain as an amateur), Joey Burns (Pat's brother), and cutman Ray Rodgers.

Initially, the small talk concerned Rodgers and his wife of two days. Ray is part-owner of a Little Rock company that sells and installs drywall for commercial construction projects. He has known Taylor since Jermain was twelve and been in the fighter's corner for all of his professional fights.

Rodgers became a widower in 1987, when his wife of 28 years died of breast cancer. That same year, he started seeing "the beautiful Carole" whose husband had been killed in an automobile accident four years earlier. They'd been a couple ever since. Finally, after eighteen years, Ray asked Carole to marry him. The proposal came on their flight to Las Vegas and took the form of, "After the fight, let's go back to Oklahoma [where Ray was born] and get married."

"Why don't we get married here?" Carole countered.

"Okay."

"She thought I was kidding," Rodgers said in the dressing room. "But we got off the plane and went to the courthouse. At three o'clock on Thursday afternoon, we were married by the county clerk right here in Las Vegas. I feel like a new man now."

The dressing room was eighteen-feet-squared with industrial carpet, hardwood benches, and a half-dozen chairs. A large gray sofa had been brought in for the occasion. "Let's get that sofa out of here," Burns said. "We'll need the space to warm up."

Two members of Team Taylor carried the sofa to the corridor. Jermain took off his warm-up jacket, sat on a folding metal chair, and stretched his legs out on another chair in front of him. He said nothing. From time to time, he leaned back, closed his eyes, and visualized the battle ahead.

At 6:35, Marc Ratner (executive director of the Nevada State Athletic Commission) entered the room and announced, "The Governor of Arkansas will be coming in before the fight to see Jermain."

"If the Governor is coming, get his ass in here now," Burns said. "I want no distractions later on."

Five minutes later, Ratner returned with Arkansas Governor Mike Huckabee and the Governor's wife. Jermain rose to greet them. "We're so proud of you," Huckabee said. They posed for a photo.

"Now how do I say this as politely as I can?" Burns began.

"I know," Huckabee said with a smile. "Get the hell out of here."

At 6:55, Naazim Richardson came in to watch with a commission inspector as Burns taped Jermain's hands. After the right hand was taped, Richardson objected that a seam in the tape extended more than the permitted three-quarters of an inch past one of Jermain's knuckles.

"I'm not re-taping," Burns said.

Ratner was summoned.

"I asked when I was doing this if it was okay," Burns explained. "No one objected and I'm not rewrapping."

Ratner examined the tape. "There's no advantage or disadvantage," he ruled. "It's okay."

Ratner left. Burns turned to Ray Rodgers to break the tension.

"How long have you been married now, Ray?"

Rodgers looked at his watch. "Fifty-two hours and a couple of minutes."

At 7:13, the taping was done. At 7:15, referee Jay Nady entered the room. Nady had been the third man in the ring for Hopkins-Taylor I. The Taylor camp felt that he'd let Hopkins get away with too many fouls, but they were pleased that he'd been assigned to the rematch. Nady was a strong no-nonsense referee who, like Jermain, would have a better understanding of Bernard's ring tactics the second time around.

Nady gave the pro forma instructions. Then Burns took him aside.

"I think you're a great referee," Burns said. "But I also think that last time you let Bernard get away with more than he should have. I have full confidence in you. All I'm asking is that you enforce the rules the way they're written because, if you don't, it will give an unfair advantage to the guy who breaks them."

"Last time, I missed a few head butts," Nady acknowledged. "I've seen the tape. I'll watch for that."

At 7:25, the final undercard bout ended. Jermain put on his trunks. "How much longer?" he queried.

"You won't go until eight o'clock," an inspector told him. "Maybe a few minutes later."

Jermain began to pace back and forth, occasionally shadow-boxing to loosen up. At 7:50, he gloved up.

"Let's do a set of mitts," Burns ordered.

Edgardo Martinez moved to the center of the room with pads on either hand. Jermain began to punch. Burns looked on, offering instruction.

"You want to make that forty-year-old man use his feet. Make sure you keep him moving . . . Step it up [Jermain's punching grew more intense] . . . We're getting there . . . That's it . . . Very good . . . Good short righthand . . . I like it . . . Very good; one more time . . . Be short . . . You know he's going to drop away from the righthand, so come back with the left . . . When he leads with his head, forearm up or a short stiff jab . . . Hands and feet working together . . . Speed kills. You're too damn fast for him. You'll pick him apart with speed . . . . [Taylor fired a short sharp right] . . . Oooh, beautiful! Goodnight, Charlie . . ."

But one thought went unspoken. In boxing, a single punch can change everything. That's all it takes to crack a rib, open a cut, or break a hand and send months of fine-tuning down the drain. Hitting Bernard Hopkins would be more difficult than hitting the pads with Edgardo Martinez holding them. And unlike Martinez, Hopkins would be punching back.

Minutes later, the fighters were in the ring. Taylor was dressed in white with red trim. Hopkins was wearing black trunks, a black robe with a large red "X" on the back, and a black executioner's hood. Michael Buffer made the introductions. The last words he'd spoken with the same two men beside him had been the high-point of Jermain's life. Now, 140 days later, the middleweight championship of the world was again at risk. Within an hour, Buffer would announce either that Jermain Taylor had successfully defended his title or that he was a former champion.

The fight that followed was a tactical one. That's the way Hopkins wanted it and he had the skills to make it that way. For most of the night, he fought defensively, keeping Taylor at bay with the threat of nasty counterpunches. When he spotted a flaw or momentary lapse, he attacked. His most effective punch was a lead righthand that he landed whenever Jermain stood flat-footed in front of him. But overall, Hopkins fought the same way he'd fought in July: one punch at a time. After six rounds, he'd landed only 40 punches and trailed on the judges' scorecards 60-54, 59-55, and 59-55.

The difference this time was that there was no big Hopkins comeback. Jermain was more disciplined and fought a more measured fight than the first time around. He was largely successful in using his forearm to ward off head butts. Except for one lapse late in the fight, he tied Hopkins up on the inside, thereby preventing Bernard from landing sharp clean punches as the fighters came out of clinches. And this time, there was no scalp wound caused by a head butt.

After round ten, when it seemed as though Hopkins had taken at least three of the previous four stanzas, Pat Burns told his charge, "You got to throw some punches now. You're just sitting there waiting to counterpunch him and it's not going to work. Suck it up."

Properly counseled, Taylor went after Hopkins more aggressively in round eleven and landed his most damaging blows of the fight.

Then came the decision. "Ladies and gentlemen," Michael Buffer intoned, "we go to the scorecards. All three judges—Dave Moretti, Chuck Giampa, and Patricia Morse-Jarman—score the bout identically, 115 to 113, all for the winner by unanimous decision and . . . STILL undisputed middleweight champion of the world, Jermain 'Bad Intentions' Taylor."

After the fight, Taylor returned to his dressing room and sat heavily on a long wood bench. Hopkins's lead righthands had left their mark. His face was bruised and swollen around the left eye. "I'm proud of what I did tonight," Jermain said. "Bernard is a very good fighter, tough; it's hard to hit him." Then Taylor smiled. "Next time I'm against Bernard Hopkins, let's play water polo or something."

Off to the side, several team members were talking about the judges' scoring. Each judge had given rounds one, two, three, six, and eleven to Taylor, and rounds seven, nine, ten, and twelve to Hopkins. That made it five rounds to four in favor of Jermain with three rounds up for grabs. Each judge gave two of those three swing rounds to Taylor. If anything, when it came to his pre-fight complaining, Hopkins had overplayed his hand.

"Bernard does that sometimes."

The speaker was Bouie Fisher, on the phone from his home in New Jersey. It was three days after the fight, and Hopkins's former trainer was in a reflective mood.

"I didn't see the fight while it was happening," Bouie said. "I was home in New Jersey, looking at the news on TV. A few people called while it was going on. When it was over, my daughter called and told me the result. The next day, she brought a tape by and I watched it. Bernard did the same thing as in the last fight. He lay back too much and, in certain instances, he should have fought more. There were things that could have been done and should have been done. Bernard had a little more in his arsenal than what he put out. But then again, maybe Jermain didn't let him put it out."

"Jermain did a good job," Bouie continued. "He was more confident than last time. His defense was better. Pat Burns did some excellent work with him. I can see Jermain getting better all the time. He's a great young man surrounded by good people. He wants to learn. If he stays with the things that got him to where he is now, he'll get even better. He can carry the load."

"Boxing is a great sport," Fisher said, turning to his own experiences with the sweet science. "It will always be a great sport. It's not easy, that's for sure. There's nothing easy about boxing. There's plenty of heartache. A lot of tears have been shed in this business. But I'm proud to have been part of boxing history, and I'm proud to have been with Bernard. I think he's one of the best middleweights since Sugar Ray Robinson. Marvin Hagler might have been tougher; but skillwise, Bernard could have fought with Hagler. Bernard's problems came when he began to think he knew everything there was to know. I'm still in school with boxing. No one ever learns everything there is to know about boxing. But I had a nice run with Bernard. It could have been better here and there. But I believe that right is right and, if you do right, everything will be fine. Right now, I'm sitting in my home, looking out the window at the sun melting the snow. I'm happy; I'm content. My health is good. This afternoon, I'll be in the gym teaching some young kids how to slip a jab. Everyone should be as happy as I am now."

Every decent person in boxing wishes Bouie Fisher well. And a lot of people in the sport are developing a similar fondness for Jermain Taylor. He's one of the best "feel good stories" of 2005. The more people get to know him, the more they like him.

In July of this year, Taylor beat The Man. Now he's positioning himself to be The Man. He's not there yet. He's still a few big wins away from superstardom. That might, or might not, happen. "There's a lot of unfinished business," Pat Burns acknowledges. "Jermain has enormous talent, but he's not as good a fighter as he could be and will be in the future." Still, beating Bernard Hopkins twice in one year is a pretty good accomplishment.

Meanwhile, Taylor is looking to the future. "I daydream about sitting in a lazy-boy chair someday with enough money that I don't have to work anymore." he says. "Just living in a big house with my wife and kids on a lot of land; a lot of land."

That probably will happen. Taylor-Hopkins II engendered approximately 410,000 pay-per-view buys. That means the gross income to Team Taylor will be roughly $5,000,000. Pat Burns, Jermain's management team, and Lou DiBella are entitled to forty percent of the total. Jermain's share will be in the neighborhood of $3,000,000. After taxes, that's about $1,800,000. Conservatively invested, $1,800,000 will yield $90,000 a year forever.

In other words, if Jermain Taylor handles his money wisely and doesn't spend wildly, he'll have a financial cushion for life. Let's hope the feel good story continues.❑

# ROUND 2

# NON-COMBATANTS

*Over the years, Jay Larkin has one of the good guys in boxing.*

# JAY LARKIN: THAT'S ENTERTAINMENT

It has often been said that boxing is showbusiness with blood. Jay Larkin's career has had its share of both. For years, Larkin has been the driving force behind Showtime boxing. But theater was his first professional love. His education includes stints at the Boston Conservatory of Music; the UCLA School of Theater, Film and Television; and a degree in theater and directing from C.W. Post. He was also a successful actor on Broadway, television, and national tours.

Larkin began work at Showtime in 1984 as a junior publicist for a series called *Broadway on Showtime.* "I stayed a publicist for about an hour-and-a-half," he remembers. "Then they put me in programming."

It was a good fit. At the time, entertainment specials were an important Showtime offering. Frank Sinatra, Paul McCartney, Paul Simon, The Rolling Stones, Diana Ross, Bob Hope, George Burns, Drew Carey, Jim Carrey, Ellen DeGeneris, and Tim Allen would all be featured on the cable network. And Larkin knew all aspects of the business. He could balance a budget and, the next day, walk on stage and know right away whether the lighting was right.

In the early-1990s, Showtime eliminated entertainment specials from its programming. Now they're back, causing Larkin to reflect on his experiences with some of the major entertainment icons of our time. Here, in his own words, is what it was like to work with Jackie Gleason, Paul McCartney, and Frank Sinatra.

### JACKIE GLEASON

"Jackie Gleason was a hero of mine. There's a reason they called him 'The Great One.' It's unbelieveable how deep his talent ran as a comedian and a serious actor."

"In the mid-1980s, Showtime stumbled upon a project that became known as *The Honeymooners: The Lost Episodes.* The episodes were televised on Showtime, and we created the largest marketing/PR campaign in the history of the network. As part of that, we contacted the four original stars. Art Carney wanted nothing to do with the project. Audrey

**135**

Meadows and Joyce Randolph were delighted with the series and did everything we asked of them and more. But the key to it all was Gleason. We asked if he'd become involved, and he told us, 'You've got me for one day. In that one day, I'll do whatever you want as long as they come to me and I don't have to go to them. Then lose my number and forget you ever knew me.'"

"Gleason chose the site for the interviews. He wanted to do them at 21 [a midtown-Manhattan restaurant]. The outpouring of media interest was staggering. I'd never seen anything like it before, and I've never seen anything like it since. For the first time in years, Jackie Gleason was going to talk about *The Honeymooners*. We had the three national morning shows with their cameras in separate rooms at 21. There was an army of print reporters. Local television stations, long-lead magazines; you name them and they were there."

"Gleason was true to his word. He did every interview we put in front of him. And all day long, whatever he did, he drank Cutty Sark and water from a large tumbler. To this day, whenever I see a bottle of Cutty Sark, I think of Gleason. His wife was with him. She was a former June Taylor dancer and never left his side. As the day went on, he put away a significant amount of booze. Meanwhile, she kept making sure that the drinks were more and more watered down until, by the end of the day, he was drinking little more than colored water."

"Gleason was a real pro. He was on from eight in the morning until eight at night and met our every expectation. Finally, it was over. Several of us walked Gleason to the elevator. He was standing there, leaning with his back against the elevator door for support. The elevator came, the door opened. Gleason fell backward onto the elevator floor; the door closed behind him. And that was the last time I saw Jackie Gleason."

### PAUL McCARTNEY

"I was in London for a pay-per-view telecast of a benefit concert called *Music for Montserrat* [a Mediterranean Island that had been devastated by a volcano]. The talent was incredible. Paul McCartney, Elton John, Phil Collins, Eric Clapton, Sting."

"On the day of the show, I was sitting in the Albert Hall with [Showtime vice president] Marina Capurro. The place was empty. We were the only ones there. Paul McCartney came in and walked across the stage. He was completely alone, carrying a guitar. Then he sat down on the edge of the stage and, with nobody but us listening, sang *Yesterday*. It was like seeing the Grand Canyon for the first time. You know it exists, but when you finally see it, it exceeds your imagination.

"Later that day, I was in the lobby, talking with some of our staff, when I heard Jock McLean behind me. Jock had toured with the Beatles in the 1960s, setting up their equipment. In London, he was our executive in charge of the show. Anyway, I heard Jock say, 'Paulie, come here; I want you to meet the boss.' Then Jock tapped me on the shoulder. I turned around. And there, with his hand extended to shake hands with me, was Paul McCartney. He said, 'Hi, I'm Paul.' And I turned into Ralph Kramden. I couldn't speak. I opened my mouth, and all that came out was something like 'hummada-hummada-hummada-hummada.' Paul looked at me with a big smile and said, 'I've heard how witty you can be.'"

### FRANK SINATRA

"I've always been a Sinatra addict; the music, not the man. His music is as good as it gets."

"In the mid-1980s, I was the network executive in charge of a Frank Sinatra special with Liza Minnelli and Sammy Davis Jr. We were on-site in Detroit for about a week. Minelli and Davis were cooperative and nice, extemely gracious to our entire staff. And Frank was Frank. No one was even allowed to talk to Sinatra. That was the rule. If you wanted to communicate with Frank, you did it through his friend, Jilly Rizzo."

"On the day of the taping, Sinatra was standing onstage next to Jilly and we had to do a soundcheck. So I walked over to them and said, 'Excuse me, Jilly. Would you please ask Mr. Sinatra whether he'd like to do his sound-check now or if I should just go fuck myself.' Jilly then turned to his left and said, 'Frank, the kid wants to know; would you like to do your soundcheck now or should he just go fuck himself.' Sinatra didn't acknowledge my presence. He just looked at Jilly and said. 'Tell the kid to go fuck himself.' That was Sinatra."❏

*For many boxing fans who came of age in the 1980s, Al Bernstein is "the voice of boxing."*

# AL BERNSTEIN

"I-i-i-t's Showtime!"

So proclaims Jimmy Lennon just prior to the main event on each *Showtime Championship Boxing* telecast. Clearly, the fighters are the most important element in the equation. But no one should underestimate the value of the authoritative yet relaxed and pleasant voice heard on air as the ring action unfolds.

Al Bernstein was born in Chicago on September 15, 1950. His father had a series of jobs that ran the gamut from owning a delicatessen to working as a dispatcher at a truck depot and writing comedy on the side (he even sold some jokes to Henny Youngman).

"I have good memories of my father," Bernstein recalls. "He loved sports and was a gentle easy-going guy. He died of cancer when I was eleven, and I often think that he would have gotten a big charge out of seeing all the sports stuff I've done since then."

Bernstein's mother never remarried and raised two children on her own. Al went to public school in Chicago and then the Chicago branch of the University of Illinois, where he was sports editor for the school newspaper.

"I wrote a column about how the Jets were going to beat the Colts in the 1969 Super Bowl," he remembers. "Much to everyone's surprise, I was right, and the sports editor of a small newspaper called *Chicago Today* called to offer me a weekend job. Then, to my mother's absolute horror, I left college without graduating to take a fulltime job at the *Skokie (Illinois) News.*"

More newspaper jobs followed. Bernstein wanted to write about sports, but he kept getting pushed up the ladder, covering political campaigns and eventually being named a managing editor. The only sports-writing he managed to do was as a stringer for the *Washington Star* and authoring occasional articles for boxing magazines. Then he quit the newspaper business and went to work as a public information officer for the town of Skokie. In 1980, ESPN entered his life.

"I'd been a boxing fan from the time I was nine years old," Bernstein reminisces. "I remember lying in bed, listening to Patterson-Johansson and Patterson-Liston on a small transistor radio. And of course, I remember watching Don Dunphy on the *Gillette Friday Night Fights.* Don Dunphy was my idol," Bernstein continues. "The greatest moment of my life might have been years later when Don Dunphy told someone that I was his favorite boxing commentator. When I heard that, it was like I'd died and gone to heaven."

Bernstein had also done some amateur boxing in Chicago. Starting at age sixteen, he'd had twenty fights over the course of three years and won fifteen of them. "Then I started facing better fighters," he acknowledges, "and decided I should stop."

Meanwhile, ESPN in 1980 was in an embryonic stage. And one of its flagship programs was *Top Rank Boxing,* which was televised with different local personalities doing color commentary from week to week. Here, sportscaster Sam Rosen picks up the story.

"We were doing a show from the Aragon Ballroom in Chicago," Rosen remembers. "I was the blow-by-blow commentator and Tommy Hearns was scheduled to be our rotating analyst that night. Before the telecast, the producer said to me, 'Look, Tommy isn't the most talkative guy in the world. If we don't get good commentary from him, there's a local writer named Al Bernstein who we can bring in to help out.' Anyway, the first TV fight started, and Tommy was a bit intimidated by the microphone. He was pretty quiet. So after a few rounds, I signalled to the producer, he brought Al in, and the rest is history. Al is a natural; he was great."

Bernstein quickly became a regular on ESPN's fights in Chicago; next in Las Vegas; and eventually, for all of them. But ESPN then was very different from ESPN now.

"Cable television was still in its infancy," Bernstein remembers. "No one knew who or what ESPN was. And on top of that, the old *Gillette Friday Night Fights* had been one hour, but we were doing two-and-a-half hours each week—on a shoestring budget, I might add—so we had to reinvent the format."

"Those early years were fascinating," Bernstein continues. "We were going from town to town, making up the rules as we went along. I did mostly color commentary but there was some blow-by-blow. My first regular partner was Sal Marchiano, who at the time was a pretty big sportscaster in New York. I was a nobody, and Sal was great to me. He couldn't have been nicer. There was Sam Rosen, Tom Kelly, Dave Bontempo, Barry Tompkins. I could go on listing guys I've worked with, but we'd be here forever. Over the years, I worked with dozens of partners. And in those days, there was a great core group of fighters on

ESPN; guys like Freddie Roach, Tommy Cordova, Terrance Ali, Donald Curry, even the young Mike Tyson."

Bernstein was a fixture on *Top Rank Boxing* until the series folded in 1995. Thereafter, he worked big fights for *SportsCenter*. But when *Friday Night Fights* was reincarnated in 1998 on ESPN2, Bernstein was passed over as a commentator in favor of a "younger" look.

"You have no idea how idiotic that was," says Bob Arum, who remains firmly in Bernstein's corner. "People forget that *Top Rank Boxing* made ESPN. In the early years, it was ESPN's top-rated show; and one of the reasons for that was Al Bernstein. Al was a no-bullshit student of boxing who knew what he was talking about. He was a great great commentator and still is. It was utter stupidity when ESPN let Al go. For ESPN to take him off the air because he had some gray hair shows how totally inane those moronic television people are."

Over the years, Bernstein has worked fifty-or-so pay-per-view telecasts, most notably Hagler-Hearns, Hagler-Duran, and Holyfield-Douglas. He has been the color commentator for *Showtime Championship Boxing* since May 2003.

"I've worked hard at being informational and anecdotal," Bernstein says, explaining his style. "During a fight, I think it's important to go with the flow. When things change, I adapt. I'm never married to one storyline. Rather than tell people what they just saw, I try to tell them what they didn't see. And I don't pontificate. I made a conscious decision a long time ago that, if I was going to be on ESPN fifty-two weeks a year, I'd have to wear well. That fit with my personality, so it was easy to make it part of my television style. I believe that there are gray areas in life; not just black and white. I seek out tranquility; I'm not into confrontations. I think people should get past their differences, whether they're personal or professional. That describes me professionally and personally."

Meanwhile, Bernstein has earned the respect of his peers by virtue of the quality of his work.

Teddy Atlas, who replaced Bernstein at ESPN, observes, "Unfortunately, in our business, not everyone who commentates knows what they're talking about; but Al does. He learned the game; he respects the game. Al was gone before I came in at ESPN. It's not like I took his job away from him. I was asked to audition for the job with dozens of other people. But when I got the job, I thought about what it meant that I was replacing a guy who was a solid pro and had been there for a long time. I asked myself, 'What were Al's strong points?' He was dependable, reliable, consistent, always prepared. And I tried to honor those qualities along with whatever personal qualities of my own that I brought to the job."

Barry Tompkins, who was paired with Bernstein for years on *Top Rank Boxing*, says, "Working with Al is a joy. He's the best guy I've ever worked with in boxing, and I've worked with a lot of great guys. And there's something else worthy of mention," Tompkins notes. "Over the years, wherever we went, it seemed like everybody in boxing and every boxing fan knew Al. He's a celebrity, and he handles that status with incredible graciousness. Al has a nice word for every single person who approaches him. He's one of the most decent big-hearted people I've ever known."

Dave Bontempo, Bernstein's last partner at ESPN, adds to the praise. "When I entered the business," Bontempo recalls, "Al was like a big brother to me. If you're at home, watching the fights on television, he comes across as a nice guy; but that doesn't tell the half of it. One thing he's done that's very important is, Al ushered in the era of people appreciating preliminary fighters. He has a way of conveying their story and the excitement of a four- or six-round fighter being involved in the fight of his life that makes people anxious to watch the whole program and not just the main event."

"I've never called a fight with Al," adds Jim Lampley, boxing's reigning blow-by-blow commentator. "But I've been on panels with him for fight preview shows and on radio with him many times. And I'll tell you what everybody in the business will tell you. Al is a generous warm likeable man. He's polite and unfailingly considerate in his dealings with other people. He's enthusiastic and knowledgeable about boxing but not dogmatic. And he's legitimately curious about other people's point of view."

Bernstein's first marriage lasted for ten years and ended in 1980. In 1988, he moved to Las Vegas. "I loved Chicago," he says. "But the winters were killing me and it was time for a change." He remarried in 1995 and has a five-year-old son named Wes with his second wife. He loves horseback riding and, as he puts it, "communing with nature." And there's one more passion in his life.

When Bernstein was young, he took voice lessons. In his late-teens and twenties, he performed in several Chicago nightclubs, singing old standards. Then he set his music aside. But as time went on at ESPN, he began to get frustrated because he wanted to do more than boxing.

"Finally, in 1987," Bernstein recalls, "I got together with the people at Caesars before Hagler-Leonard and they let me do a show in one of their lounges for three nights. I sang old standards, and that morphed into something I did later called 'The Boxing Party,' where I mixed in five or six musical numbers with video clips and fight trivia at some of the major hotels and riverboat and Indian casinos. I haven't done it for a while now. But it was fun; it was a good creative outlet for me; and I don't think I embarrassed myself."

Thus, the question: "In your fantasies, which would you rather be: a dominant heavyweight champion or Frank Sinatra?

"That's easy," Bernstein answers. "Frank Sinatra."❏

*Lem Satterfield is becoming a fixture at big fights.*

# LEM SATTERFIELD

Sometimes the lives of boxing writers are as interesting as the lives of the people we write about.

Lem Satterfield was born in Washington, D.C. on September 2, 1962. His father and mother, Cicero and Freda Lee Terry Satterfield, were born and raised in Mississippi. Cicero was drafted into the United States Army in 1941 and served as an airplane mechanic at the Tuskeegee Army Airfield in Alabama during World War II. Then he moved north, went to college, and took a job as a claims examiner with the General Accounting Office.

Lem grew up as the second-youngest child in a home with twelve children. When he was three, his family moved to Takoma Park, Maryland.

"Basically, it was an all-white neighborhood," he remembers. "There was only one other black family, and their kids had some criminal issues. So there were times when my brothers would be walking home from school and, through no fault of their own, got arrested and my mother would have to go down to the police station to get them out."

"My father worked constantly," Lem continues. "One way he demonstrated his love for us was by providing, and none of us wanted for any material thing. We were never poor; we were middle class. I never experienced what it was like to not have a meal. When my youngest sister was five, my mother got a night job as a radiologist in a hospital. That way, she was on a schedule where she could wake up, prepare dinner, be at work while we slept, get home to give us all breakfast, and send us off to school in the morning."

Satterfield was the first black Eagle Scout in his troop. At Montgomery Blair High school, he wrestled and posted an 18-and-3 record at 138 pounds in his senior year. After a brief stint in junior college, he enrolled at the University of Maryland. There he found trouble.

"I was a solid student," he recalls. "I was family-oriented. My family wasn't dysfunctional. I always had positive parental attention. But there came a time when I didn't want to deal with reality. A lot of stuff

**143**

happens on college campuses that's just as criminal as what happens on any street corner, and the kids go home and have a family dinner and everyone says they're good kids. I made a choice. Maryland was a pretty wild campus at the time. I allowed myself to be seduced by privilege and attracted by what I misperceived as excitement and drama. I started drinking heavily and getting in trouble. I'd wake up in the morning, and I'd slept through classes and couldn't remember what I'd done the night before. I was arrested three times for stupid things like public intoxication, but there were no real consequences. So my behavior got worse and worse to the point where it became life-threatening and totally irresponsible. I went from drinking to cocaine. That was my drug of choice, although I dabbled with a few others. I got in a lot of fist-fights. I never chose people who were smaller than me; and of course, I always felt that my conduct was justified. But I was a fight waiting to happen. I started losing friends. People started looking at me funny. At one point, I had a thirteen-foot Burmese python that I let slither around my room. I made enemies. I owed people money. I wasn't a bigtime dealer, but I dealt coke in small amounts to support my own use. Getting and using became the focal point of my existence. I won't say I was having a good time, because I wasn't. And I can't say I was in the wrong place with the wrong people because I was the wrong people. It wasn't my parents' fault. It wasn't my teachers' fault. It wasn't my friends' fault. None of it was anybody's fault but mine. I didn't get taught wrong. I chose to go in the wrong direction. I didn't realize how bad it was until I was caught in it. I'd lost myself. I'd become somebody I didn't want to be. I didn't like myself. Thank God, I didn't meet a woman I really cared about or have kids or do anything else that irrevocably damaged someone else's life."

Two events led to a turn in Satterfield's life.

On June 19, 1986, one day after he'd been selected by the Boston Celtics with the second pick in the NBA draft, Maryland basketball star Len Bias died of a cocaine overdose. "That had a profound effect on me," Satterfield acknowledges. "To a lot of us, it was like Kennedy getting shot. It was a total shock."

Then came a more personal horror. In November 1986, Satterfield got in another fight. He and the man he was fighting with went through a plate-glass window. Lem's thumb was hanging to his hand by threads of flesh. He needed plastic surgery. To this day, his arm is scarred.

Lem's sister Felicia picked him up at the hospital afterward. It was a Sunday morning. She was dressed to go to church.

"In the car going home," he remembers, "she asked me why I was actively pursuing my own death. Then she began reciting scripture to me. There's a passage in the Bible, in the book of Proverbs, about King

Lemuel and advice his mother gives him that could have been written for my mother and me. When we got home, the whole family was there; my brothers and sisters, nieces and nephews. Every one of them who is old enough to remember that day will always remember it."

Later that month, Satterfield sought help through Narcotics Anonymous and entered its twelve-step program. That required a searching moral inventory and the acknowledgment that his life had become unmanageable as a consequence of alcohol and drugs.

Narcotics Anonymous has a strong religious component. "We were raised as Baptists," Satterfield says. "I believe in God; I believe that God has always been in my life; and I lean toward being a Christian. I don't accept the Bible literally. I'm more spiritual than religious, but I was comfortable with the program. I've worn an Narcotics Anonymous necklace and been sober now for eighteen years. When I drink, it's Coca Cola and virgin pina coladas. The truth is, I'm very fortunate to be alive. I'm not ashamed of my past, but I feel awful for some of the things I did."

Satterfield graduated from the University of Maryland in 1987 and took a job stocking shelves at a local Price Club. "My father was disappointed and really pissed," he acknowledges.

Then fortune smiled. Lem had always liked writing. He'd written his first newspaper story in high school—an article for the school paper that examined why no one came to the wrestling team's matches anymore. In college, he'd also written for the school paper.

In autumn 1987, one of Satterfield's college fraternity brothers (who'd become an editor at a semi-weekly newspaper) asked if he wanted to write about high school sports. Lem began at a salary of $13,000 a year. From there, he went to a newspaper in Howard County. In February 1989, he took as job as a high school reporter for the *Baltimore Sun*.

Satterfield was tutored at the *Sun* by veteran newspaperman Alan Goldstein. His first major boxing assignment came by luck. On April 29, 1995, there was a card at the USAir Arena in Landover, Maryland. Bernard Hopkins won the vacant IBF middleweight title by knocking out Segundo Mercado. Vincent Pettway stopped Simon Brown for the IBF 154-pound crown. John David Jackson, James Green, Freddie Pendelton, Darryl Tyson, William Joppy, Maurice Blocker, and Oba Carr were all on the card.

"One day earlier," Lem recalls, "my wife and I had moved into our new house. My wife was pregnant; she was expecting in three weeks. On the day of the fights, Al Goldstein found out that Panama Lewis had been barred from working in Simon Brown's corner because of his suspension in New York for tampering with a fighter's gloves. Al told me, 'Lem, I'm covering Brown-Pettway and Panama Lewis. You'll have to write the other fights.' That was my baptism by fire."

Satterfield still writes high school sports and boxing for the *Sun*. "I don't think I'm a great writer," he says. "But I'm fortunate to sit from time to time in the company of some guys who are. I work hard. I have a great editor. I love my job, and it's particularly satisfying when I feel I've covered all the bases and written a story well."

As for his philosophy of writing, Lem says, "I try to put myself in the position of the person I'm writing about and understand where they're coming from. You won't find me writing someone off as a bad person because of one or two incidents. If that were the case, I'd be a loser forever. I've learned through my own life that any life can be salvaged. And I also know that, when I write about someone, their livelihood and privacy are in my hands, so I try to treat them with the same fairness that I'd want for myself."

"I make an effort to be particularly sensitive when I'm writing about high school kids," Satterfield continues. "I'm paid for my expertise and objectivity. And let's be honest, sometimes a kid blows a play at a crucial point in a game. But high school is a time in a young person's life when image is incredibly important, so I try to strike a fair balance."

As for boxing, much of Satterfield's writing about the sweet science has focussed on local hero Hasim Rahman. The first Rahman fight he covered was Hasim versus Oleg Maskaev on November 6, 1999. It was an inauspicious start. Maskaev knocked Rahman out of the ring and onto the HBO announcers' table for an eighth-round stoppage.

Nine months later, Lem had his first in-depth conversation with Rahman at the Round One Gym in Capitol Heights, Maryland, after Hasim had beaten Corrie Sanders. Then, on April 22, 2001, Rahman knocked out Lennox Lewis in South Africa. That led to a problem.

"After Rock won the heavyweight championship," Lem remembers, "it was discovered that he'd done some things that we hadn't known about. There were drug charges. There were gun incidents. So here we are. Baltimore is celebrating; there's a parade in Rock's honor coming up. And I have to call him up to ask for details about all those things so I can write about them in a newspaper story. Rock wasn't happy. That was obvious. But I said to him, 'Look, you're the heavyweight champion of the world. I'm the reporter assigned to write about you. I want to do the best job possible. It will be more difficult for both of us if we do this piecemeal, so let's address all of the issues now and get everything out.'"

"And that's what we did," Satterfield continues. "Rock was great. I've gotten to know him pretty well since then. I have a lot of respect for him. We talk about our kids all the time, so I know how devoted he is to his children and how much effort he puts into seeing that they do well in school and have good values. When Rock was young, he opted for a street life, and he's determined that his kids won't. I remember his telling me once that he stopped living the way he'd been living because, if he kept it up, it was just a matter of time before he wound up in jail or in a graveyard and he didn't want someone else raising his children."

Meanwhile, Rahman has strong feelings about Satterfield. He too remembers the conversation they had after he'd won the heavyweight championship and his past transgressions were about to be revealed.

"Lem was straight with me," Rahman says. "He was honest from the start. The story he wrote was the truth, but he came at it with humanity. He could have written something ugly. But instead, he wrote it in a way that made a positive out of some bad experiences in my life."

"Ever since then," Rahman continues, "I've considered Lem a good guy. He's persistent. No matter what the story is, he checks and double-checks the facts. He's interested in both sides. He has my respect. I might not agree with every word he writes, but he's always fair."

Lem's mother died in 1999. Cicero Satterfield is now 86 years old with 76 grandchildren and great-grandchildren. Lem's sister Eleanor died of cancer three years ago. All of his other siblings, with one exception, have graduated from college and are married with children.

Lem has been married for thirteen years. "My wife is awesome," he proclaims. "She's my best friend." Together, they have two children: Ada, age eleven, and Adam, ten.

"I'm always working at being a good husband and a good father," Satterfield says in closing. "That's the most important thing in life to me. My kids know my life story. My wife and I are determined to see them grow up to be happy productive citizens. And the best way to do that is through constant communication. I'm still in awe of the good things that have happened to me. My marriage is a privilege. My children are a privilege. Sometimes I feel like I'm living on borrowed time because of the things I've been through, so every day is precious to me. I'm truly blessed."❏

*Bobby Goodman is a "lifer" and one of the people who keeps boxing going.*

# BOBBY GOODMAN

In the pre-dawn hours of October 30, 1974, Muhammad Ali solidified his place in boxing history by knocking out George Foreman in the eighth round of their heavyweight championship fight in Zaire. In his dressing room after the fight, the first person he hugged was Bobby Goodman.

Goodman was born in the Bronx on June 8, 1939, but his lineage traces to Russia, where Moses Golubitsky was born. Moses began the voyage to America at age eight with his parents. His father died at sea of pneumonia. His mother opened a restaurant in the living room of their home to support her family in the new world. Moses Golubitsky's name was changed to Murray Goodman.

As a teenager, Murray worked as an office boy. By the time he was 21, he was sports editor for the Hearst wire service. Then the service folded. He became a publicist for Al Schacht (The Clown Prince of Baseball) and did some PR work for a Rocky Graziano fight. Madison Square Garden hired him as a publicist. Soon, he was MSG's director of public relations.

Bobby Goodman is Murray's son. "Boxing is in my blood," Bobby says. "I was literally conceived in a training camp at Grossingers. In those days, when a fighter went to camp for a big fight, the newspaper guys went with him. My father would coordinate both camps, so I grew up in boxing."

"When I was a kid," Bobby continues, "I was in camp with Joe Louis. It was like a personal hurt for me when he lost to Ezzard Charles. I was in camps with Sugar Ray Robinson. Ray was amazing. He'd do things a boxer just can't do. The guys in that era worked hard. Their camps were all business, although I remember Rocky Marciano playing ball with me. I'd pitch; he'd catch. We had imaginary batters and he called balls and strikes. Except one day, Charlie Goldman [Marciano's trainer] saw us and shouted at me, 'Bobby Goodman, what the fuck are you doing? That ain't a little league catcher. He's the heavyweight champion of the world.'"

Goodman has equally fond memories of Marcel Cerdan. "Cerdan was the guy who hooked me on boxing," Bobby reminisces. "He was training at the Evans Hotel in Loch Sheldrake, New York. Edith Piaf was with him. She was a very pretty lady, and the papparazzi of the day were always circling around her. Cerdan was nice to me. He'd put his arm around me. Even though we didn't speak the same language, his smile was infectious. There were times when the press was with him, and he'd call me over to sit with him and his translator. I remember going to his fight against Jake LaMotta when I was ten years old. Cerdan tore a muscle in his shoulder and they had to stop it. I cried that night. LaMotta meant nothing to me; he was just a tough guy from the Bronx. Cerdan was my hero, and my hero had lost. Then he died in that plane crash in the Azores, and I was devastated. My hero had been coming back to fight a rematch against LaMotta. I was going to see him again; he was going to be champion again. But it wasn't to be. When he died, it was like a family member died. I still get teary talking about it."

Goodman boxed in Catholic Youth Organization and Police Athletic leagues between the ages of eight and twelve. "I was a street kid," he says. "But growing up on the streets then was very different from what it is now." In 1958, after two years at the University of Miami, he enrolled in the Coast Guard so he could choose his branch of the service instead of being drafted. Four years later, he was discharged and opened a bar in New Jersey. At the same time, he began writing for *Ring* magazine. "I had a regular column," he says. "And if I wrote too many pieces for the same issue, I'd write some of them under the name 'Robert Arthur' [short for Robert Arthur Goodman]."

Meanwhile, Murray Goodman had left Madison Square Garden and worked briefly for Yonkers Raceway. Then he became an assistant to Harry Wismer, who was president of the New York Titans (now the Jets). After that, he promoted fights in New Jersey in partnership with Lou Duva. Finally, he opened a public relations agency called Murray Goodman Associates.

"At first," Bobby recalls, "I helped my father with PR during the day and worked the bar at night. Then I left the bar to work fulltime with my father. We did a lot of PR for Bob Arum. Then Don [King] came along. By the late 1970s, Don was taking up so much of my time that I left the agency to be with him fulltime."

As an adult, Goodman was no longer a hero-worshipper of fighters. Rather, he was their friend. Muhammad Ali, Joe Frazier, Larry Holmes, and others benefited from his services and took him into their confidence. Meanwhile, more than one inebriated boxing writer awoke from a hangover to discover that Bobby had written his story and filed for him.

In 1985, Goodman left Don King Productions to become a senior vice president and head of boxing for Madison Square Garden. There, he played a crucial role in the development of future champions like Buddy McGirt, Kevin Kelley, Junior Jones, and Tracy Harris Patterson. In 1993, he said goodbye to the Garden to set up his own promotional company (Garden State Boxing) with Dan Duva as a silent partner. In 1996, he rejoined King.

Goodman is now vice president for boxing operations and public relations for Don King Productions. His primary responsibilities are to (1) oversee match-making; (2) lobby and otherwise interact with the world sanctioning organizations; and (3) coordinate what happens on site before, during, and after each fight. He's a team player. And on fight night, with chaos around him, he's calm and reliable in the eye of the hurricane.

But Goodman will be 66 on June 8th (2005), and that leads to thoughts of retirement. "This is my last stop," he says. "I've said for a while that, when Don's done, I'm done; but I don't think I'll stay that long. Don works at his public persona. As he gets older [King is 73], he doesn't jump out of bed in the morning as easily as he used to. But Don will keep going until he dies, and I plan on retiring before then. My heart will always be in boxing. But I've been married for 42 years; I have four daughters and five grandchildren. I want to spend more time with my family and watch my grandchildren grow up. I'll always be available for consulting work. I'll come back for big fights if Don needs me. But retirement could come sooner rather than later."

As the words sink in, Goodman gets a bit teary-eyed. "Misty" is how he puts it. "I believe in boxing," he says. "I like to think that I've been good for the sport, that I've never hurt anyone or done anything to hurt boxing. A lot of the criticism of boxing today is based on ignorance, and I get angry when people who don't know what they're talking about badmouth the sport. Today's fighters are better than people say. Sure, the heavyweight division needs help. But if you took all of today's champions and weight divisions and compressed them into the way boxing was structured fifty years ago, this would be a golden era."

As for his own standing within the boxing community, Goodman notes, "I owe what I am to my father and to Don. They both gave me wonderful opportunities, and I got a great education from both of them. My father, and also my mother, were special people. My father was a great father and also my best friend. And Don is remarkable; he's a genius. I'm happy he's the man he is. Every day, I see a new side of him.

Just listening to him day after day is fascinating. Don is always a step ahead of the other guys. He never ceases to amaze me. He has more guts and character than anybody I know. He puts more of himself into the fights he promotes than anyone else in boxing. Don has been very good to me and my family. Don has never broken his word to me. And Don lets me be who I am."

In sum, Bobby Goodman's life has been framed by Moses Golubitsky from Tsarist Russia and Don King from the streets of Cleveland. He has been part of the sweet science from the 1940s into the new millennium. He's a sentimentalist at heart and a quintessential "boxing guy."

"Boxing has been my life, not just not my job," he says. "There's nothing I've ever wanted to do but be in boxing. I still get goosebumps when the lights go down and the ring announcer says, 'Ladies and gentlemen, for the heavyweight championship of the world.' I'm a very lucky guy. If I had to live my life all over again, I'd live it the same damn way."❑

*The general public has never heard of Mark Taffet, but he's one of the most powerful people in boxing.*

# MARK TAFFET

One day in 1993, Mark Taffet found himself sitting on a train beside George Foreman. The occasion was a press tour to publicize Foreman's upcoming fight against Tommy Morrison.

"This pay-per-view business is going to be enormous," Foreman told Taffet. "I wish I was ten years younger. And do you know who the beneficiary is going to be? That kid sitting two rows in front of us."

"That kid" was a 20-year-old junior-lightweight with seven pro fights under his belt who was fighting on the undercard of Foreman-Morrison. Oscar De La Hoya. Since then, De La Hoya has generated hundreds of millions of dollars in pay-per-view buys. So have Mike Tyson (the biggest must-see attraction of the 1990s) and Evander Holyfield (who stamped his heart and soul on the sport of boxing). But Taffet has made his own unique contribution to pay-per-view as HBO's resident expert on the subject. That much is clear from the thoughts of those who know his side of the business best:

● Seth Abraham: "Many boxing people turn themselves into business men. Mark is a businessman who turned himself into a boxing person. He's a fan, but he brings a sharp business perspective to everything he does. His skills in evaluating a fight as a business proposition are unique."
● Ross Greenburg: "Superstars today want pay-per-view fights because that's where the mega-paydays are. Mark has an exhaustive knowledge of how to work the pay-per-view-MSO [multi-system cable operator] world. He understands the intricacies of how to market and sell each event, and that has allowed us to fortify our entire boxing program."
● Lou DiBella: "I have a lot of respect for Mark. He's a good negotiator; he was there at the beginning; and he knows as much about pay-per-view as anybody in boxing."
● Jay Larkin: "Mark knows his business. It's as simple as that. People look at boxing from the outside and think how much fun

it is and how easy it must be to make big fights and sell pay-per-view. They have no idea how complicated and byzantine it really is. There's no one, and I mean no one, who's more fluent in the ins and outs of pay-per-view than Mark Taffet."

Taffet was born in New Jersey in 1957 and grew up in a lower-middle-class neighborhood financed by the G.I. mortgage bill. There were 450 houses, each one identical on the outside except for the color of the shutters. His father owned a succession of diners in Newark but never more than one at a time.

"They were family-run restaurants," Taffet reminisces. "My mother worked the cash register. I was taught to cook Jewish food in the kitchen by a Puerto Rican chef named Luis. Matzoh balls, kugel, brisket; you name it, and Luis taught me. My father used to say that, in the restaurant business, you do all of your business in three one-and-a-half hour spurts. That's when you make or break your business. The rest is planning. Sort of like pay-per-view."

The first pro fight that Taffet saw in person was Jerry Quarry against Ken Norton at Madison Square Garden in 1975. "I wasn't a big fight fan," he says. "But I was a fan of big fights. The Garden was showing Muhammad Ali against Chuck Wepner on closed-circuit television and put a live card on before it. I took the train in from New Jersey and had some slices of pizza at Little Nick's. I was sitting way up in the cheap seats, but the first impression I had was of serious drama. I'd never seen such singular focus before. The arena was dark. All I saw were the lights shining down on the ring canvas. I also remember that Quarry's wife, who was a strikingly attractive blonde woman, was sitting in the first row by his corner. She was wearing a long white satin or silk dress. And by the end of the fight, which Quarry lost, her dress was splattered with blood."

Taffet graduated from Rutgers in 1979 and, two years later, earned an MBA from Wharton. Then he went to work for General Foods. "I was the finance person for the Birds Eye frozen foods division," he remembers. "Our job was to develop and introduce new products. I spent a lot of time in supermarket aisles watching what women did and asking them why. But there came a time when I realized that I didn't have a passion for the product. I didn't love frozen foods."

In 1983, Taffet received a telephone call from a friend who had left Birds Eye to work for a company called Home Box Office. Was he interested in changing jobs? It seemed like a good fit, so he moved to HBO as a finance manager. "In finance," he recalls, "you supported one area of the company. Mine was sales and marketing. I developed financial models regarding what the cost for each new subscriber would be. Then I started getting calls to work on financial models in other areas of the company."

Taffet's introduction to sports came when HBO Sports president Seth Abraham needed someone with financial expertise to explore the possibility of making an offer for National Football League rights. Taffet was the guy, and Abraham was impressed with his work. At the same time, HBO's multi-fight contract with Mike Tyson was expiring and Abraham asked Taffet for help on that too.

Meanwhile, there was a fledgling business in a handful of cities called "pay-per-view." And the revenue it was generating was substantial in light of the small number of addressable homes. Taffet's next assignment was to prepare a business model for the entity that would ultimately become TVKO (the forerunner of HBO Pay Per-View). Once TVKO was formed, its first two employees were Taffet and Lou DiBella (who Abraham brought in from HBO's legal department). TVKO would revolutionize the way that boxing is televised.

Taffet is now HBO's senior vice president for sports operations and pay-per-view. Part of his job involves being the advocate within the company for HBO Sports vis-a-vis other areas of programming and marketing. The rest of his duties center on pay-per-view.

Boxing is the only major sport whose showcase events are unavailable to the viewing public unless they're willing to pay $44.95 to watch them. That's one of the reasons it's no longer really a major sport. But pay-per-view is an improvement over what came before. For years, fight fans who wanted to see big fights had to leave home, travel to a theater, and watch the fight on a smaller-than-normal screen without being able to hear what the announcers were saying. Compared to that, pay-per-view is a bargain.

HBO enters into two types of pay-per-view transactions with promoters. In some instances, there are "distribution" deals, where the network produces and distributes a show in exchange for a negotiated percentage of receipts. The other type is a "guarantee" deal, where the network puts up a fixed sum (in most instances, to cover the fighters' purses) and hopes to recoup that amount plus a profit out of its share of receipts.

Taffet has a low-key approach to his job and generally keeps a low profile. "All of the major promoters talk with us on an almost-daily basis," he says. "The most difficult thing for us is navigating the schedule. HBO can do six to twelve pay-per-view shows a year. In 2004, we did nine. Probably, we'll do ten this year. Obviously, the big block-buster fights are on pay-per-view. And there are times when we do a small niche-oriented fight to accommodate a promoter because he has a contractual commitment to a fighter and we simply don't have an available date on *HBO Championship Boxing* or *Boxing After Dark*."

As for what HBO buys and how much it pays, the network has the experience and history of more than a hundred pay-per-view fights to create financial models. There are times when it makes mistakes. Its worst blunder was Holyfield-Holmes in 1992, and it lost money on Vitali Klitschko against Danny Williams last year. "The lesson in that," says Taffet, "is no matter how sophisticated we get, what we do is still part science and part art. But we've had a ninety-eight percent success rate over the past thirteen years and hope we can be as good over the next thirteen."

One of Taffet's greatest strengths is his ability to reduce the storyline for a fight to a one-sentence message and get the media to repeat it. The core of his philosophy regarding pay-per-view is, "We're sellers, not buyers."

"If you buy a product from a promoter," Taffet elaborates, "you're separating your interests from his and losing the benefit of the promoter's entrepreneurial skills. The moment we sign a deal with a promoter, it's no longer an adversarial negotiation. From that point on, we're partners on the fight. We spend months working together to build the fight. There's naming the fight. There's choosing a visual image for marketing. Do we show one fighter as taller or more menacing than the other? Should they be standing side-by-side on the poster or should one of them be in the background? It's all part of the story that we're transmitting to the consumer. I love the storytelling involved in a pay-per-view fight; things that reach out and grab people's hearts. The history, the legacy, the traditions, the characters involved. And I've learned so much from working with promoters. Dan Duva taught me a lot of what I know today. Bob Arum understands the mechanics and nuances of the business better than anyone. Don King is the most difficult person in the world to make a deal with, but he's great to have on your side once the deal is done. Don is the most creative energetic person I've ever known."

A whimsical look crosses Taffet's face. "There's one moment with Don that I remember with particular fondness," he says. "We were at the Hyatt-Regency Hotel in Chicago as part of a ten-city press tour for Holyfield-Lewis II. The press conference was scheduled for eleven o'clock. No Don. Eleven-thirty. No Don. So I went up to his suite and knocked on the door. Don's personal assistant, who was a physically-imposing man named Isadore Bolton, let me in. Isadore told me to wait, so I waited in the living room for another thirty minutes while Don was in the bedroom putting on his tuxedo and jewelry. Then, from down the corridor, I heard a voice call out, 'Isadore, the comb.'"

"I think I believe what I saw next, but I'm not sure," Taffet acknowledges. "Isadore opened a leather attache case and took out a dark suede pillow with a silver comb on top of it. Then, with great ceremony, he carried the pillow and comb down the corridor to Don's bedroom. My only regret is that I didn't go with him. If I had, I would have seen what has to be one of boxing's greatest rituals."❏

*Ron Scott Stevens has been a key figure is transforming the New York State Athletic Commission from a microcosm of incompetence and corruption into a respected institution.*

# RON SCOTT STEVENS

It's fight night at Madison Square Garden, the most famous arena in the world. From a regulatory point of view, things don't just come together by chance on occasions like this. Someone has to make them happen. It's like getting everything and everyone in order for a circus parade.

An hour before the bell for the start of the first fight, Ron Scott Stevens, the chairman of the New York State Athletic Commission, gathers his troops together.

"This is a live event," he tells the NYSAC personnel in attendance. "It's not a play. It happens once and won't come back again tomorrow night, so everything has to be done right the first time."

For the next ten minutes, Stevens addresses his staff with regard to their responsibilities:

To the inspectors: "You're the eyes and ears of the commission at ringside and in the dressing rooms. Make sure the cornermen know they have to wear gloves. Look into the buckets; make sure the stuff they're using is kosher."

To the judges: "Forget about reputations. Forget about the crowd. Concentrate; make sure you're paying attention for every second of every round, and call it the way you see it."

To the referees (after making reference to several undercard fighters): "These guys are coming in as opponents. Give them a fair chance to win. But if they're getting hurt, do what you have to do sooner rather than later. The fans are entitled to see good honest boxing and that includes guys getting hit. But I don't want anyone taking unnecessary punishment."

"Be diligent," he tells the group as a whole. "Be professional. We're a team, and we operate as a team tonight."

Ron Scott Stevens was born in Manhattan on November 24, 1946. There's a school of thought that, in his present job, he has done as much for boxing in New York as anyone in the past thirty years.

Stevens's father was a small businessman who drifted from venture to venture. By the time Ron graduated from high school, his family had lived in Manhattan, Brooklyn, Queens, and Florida. In 1969, Stevens received a BA degree from Hofstra College. Thereafter, lacking career direction, he drove a taxi and worked as a waiter. Then he enrolled at John Marshall Law School but dropped out in 1972. After that, he worked as a carpenter's assistant, a bartender, and drove a cab again. "At one point," he recalls, "I even worked for an employment agency called Forbes Personnel. I couldn't get a decent job for myself, but I was helping other people get jobs."

In 1975, Stevens moved to Woodstock and took a job as a salesman at a clothing store. One year later, he began working for a local cable-TV station called Hudson Valley Television. He produced sports shows, sold advertising for the shows, and also did on-camera work for them. Among the shows he produced were telecasts of fight cards promoted by Lou Falcigno at the Westchester County Center. Stevens handled the blow-by-blow chores. His color commentator was an unknown phar-macist named Harold Lederman.

Then a radio station called WDST-FM opened in Woodstock. Five times a week at 5:55 p.m., Stevens read five minutes of sports news. He began writing a weekly sports column for the *Woodstock Times*. "And I was waiting on tables in restaurants," he adds, "to supplement my income so I could pay my bills."

That went on for four years. It was during this time that Stevens changed his name.

"My name then was Ron Rabinowitz," he explains. "There was a commentator for another cable network named Ron Rosenberg, and I figured the world didn't need Ron Rabinowitz to follow Ron Rosenberg. I had two brothers. Steven was older than me; Scott was younger. I told myself, 'I'll change my name to Ron Scott Stevens and make it for all three of us.'"

In 1980, Stevens decided to leave Woodstock and make a play for the big-time. He sent tapes of his work to television and radio stations around the country, pursued jobs in Miami and Denver, and wound up in Brooklyn again, waiting on tables.

"I was very down," he acknowledges. "I was 33 years old. I had no career. I remember very clearly asking myself one day, 'Ronnie, what are you going to do with your life?' And right then, a light flashed on in my head. It was a true epiphany. I said to myself, 'Boxing has always been the sport of the underdog; and I'm an underdog.' The next day, I was at Gleason's Gym, offering myself as a ring announcer, commentator, writer, anything. Every day after that, I was at Gleason's from ten in the morning till three in the afternoon, hustling for work. And at night, I waited on tables."

Slowly, the work dribbled in. Sciacca Promotions hired Stevens as a ring announcer. He began freelancing articles for boxing magazines and eventually became the editor of *Boxing Today* and *Boxing Beat*. Meanwhile, in 1982, a promoter named Elizabeth Barnett hired him as matchmaker for a small fight card on Long Island.

"I was born to make fights," Stevens says today. "Nobody taught me; I just knew how. I took to matchmaking like a duck takes to water."

Soon, he was matchmaking for other small promoters. Then Top Rank hired him for some shows in Atlantic City and he put together several cards for Main Events. He also became a substitute English teacher for the New York City school system, which enabled him to stop working as a waiter. And he began writing plays, two of which were performed in Actors Equity showcases.

Stevens's next step in the fight game came in 1987, when Gleason's moved from Manhattan to Brooklyn. Its owners, Ira Becker and Bruce Silvergalde, set up an arena a block from the gym. "And again, a light went off in my head," says Stevens. "I'd been networking in boxing for seven years. I'd seen how badly most club-fight cards were put together. So I decided to form my own promotional company and promote fights at Gleason's Arena."

Thus it was that Powerhouse Enterprises was born. Stevens's first show featured Felix Santiago against Bryan Nitz on May 20, 1988, with Alex Stewart on the undercard. Over the next eighteen months, Powerhouse promoted five fight cards at Gleason's. "But I couldn't make money," Stevens acknowledges. "I started with $25,000 from investors, and we made another $10,000 from a closed-circuit telecast of Mike Tyson against Michael Spinks. That gave us $35,000 to work with, out of which I paid myself a salary of about a thousand dollars a month. But at the end of eighteen months, Powerhouse was broke, so I dissolved the company."

In 1991, Stevens tried his hand at promoting again, this time with Cary Alex as his partner. "SportsChannel wanted to do boxing and offered me $7,500 a show for four shows," he remembers. "So I formed a new company called Stillman's Gym Inc. Over the next five years, we did twenty-five shows in the grand ballroom at the Pennsylvania Hotel, which seated a thousand people. We had some great fights with guys like Louis Del Valle, Kevin Kelley, and Julio Cesar Green. And we had great crowds. The problem was, half the people in the crowd were always there for free. Again, we couldn't make money, so I renewed my hack license and started driving a cab to make ends meet. Finally, in

1996, we dissolved the company."

Two more promotional efforts (Star Bouts and The Dukes of Boxing) followed with similar results. Meanwhile, Stevens started waiting on tables again and kept matchmaking when he could. In 1998, he telephoned Cedric Kushner to see if CKP would put cruiserweight Robert Daniels on one of its cards. Kushner said yes; but more importantly, his company needed another matchmaker and he wanted to know if Stevens was available.

In December 1998, Stevens began working for Cedric Kushner Promotions as a matchmaker, site coordinator, and jack-of-all-trades. It was the first secure job on salary in boxing that he had ever had. "At first, Cedric was doing well," Stevens remembers. "He had Hasim Rahman, Shane Mosley, Chris Byrd, Jameel McCline, Oleg Maskaev, Kirk Johnson. I started at $40,000 a year and, by 2002, was making $72,500. But then things got shaky for Cedric and I was approached about a job at the New York State Athletic Commission."

For eight years, beginning in January 1995, the New York State Athletic Commission had been widely viewed as a dumping ground for political patronage employees. Other than a nine-month period when Ray Kelly was chairman, the NYSAC, to put it bluntly, was an embarrassment. Kelly left his post in June 2002 and was succeeded by Bernard Kerik, whose lack of interest in boxing was becoming a national joke. Meanwhile, someone had to do the work. In December 2002, Stevens was brought in as the commission's community coordinator and director of boxing.

But more change was in the air. In March 2000, the Rackets Bureau of the New York County District Attorney's Office had referred allegations of improprieties at the athletic commission to the Office of the Inspector General of the State of New York. The inspector general conducted an extensive investigation and, in early 2003, issued a report highlighting no-show jobs, bloated expenses, and other forms of corruption. On April 11th, Kerik resigned. On June 10, 2003, Stevens was sworn in as his successor.

Stevens came into his position as chairman with a reputation for being fair-minded, honest, and having common sense. Also, unlike his predecessor, he understood the sport and business of boxing.

"Having been a promoter and matchmaker," Stevens says, "I was aware of the climate at the commission. I also knew that the climate could change but it needed someone to direct that change. My familiarity with boxing was my biggest asset. I wasn't afraid of boxing as a sport or a business. I knew what the commission did and what its parameters were. I also knew that most promoters in boxing struggle and aren't the Big Bad Wolf; that most of the rank-and-file people in boxing are decent people; and that we're all in this struggle together. So the heart of my philosophy was, instead of chasing people away, let's embrace them. I wanted the commission to enforce the law and not compromise its law-enforcement mission, but also to assist."

The New York State Athletic Commission has three commissioners, two of whom are paid on a per diem basis. The chairmanship is a full-time job, and there are seven other fulltime employees. Beyond that, Stevens can draw as needed from a pool of five deputy commissioners, thirty inspectors, thirty referees, thirty-five judges, eight timekeepers, nine medical advisory board members, and thirty ringside physicians.

"It's a good group," says Stevens. "Despite criticisms that might have been leveled in the past, I found some very talented people when I came to the commission. It was a question of getting them to buy into my team concept, which they readily did. And as time goes by, more and more good people are coming in."

As for the future, Stevens states, "I want to help resurrect boxing in New York. This isn't Little League Baseball. It's a tough hard dangerous sport, and you can't break the rules. That's a recipe for disaster. If a rule needs to be broken, then it should be stricken from the books. So we're going to enforce the law, but we're not bent on punishment. We want to fairly regulate the sport and create an environment in which the boxing community feels welcome and the sport can thrive. And I have to say, the governor's office has been wonderful in allowing me to shape the commission into what it's becoming. There has been no interference. To the contrary, I've gotten full support."

The results bear Stevens out. In 2002, there were no fight cards in the big arena at Madison Square Garden for the first time since the 1994 building renovation. In fact, MSG went 26 months (from October 2001 to December 2003) without a fight in the main arena. In 2003, there were only seventeen fight cards in New York State.

But 2004 (Stevens's first full year in office) witnessed a boxing renaissance. There were three major cards at Madison Square Garden and twenty-four shows throughout the state. 2005 is witnessing more of the same. In the first six months of this year, there have been two fight cards in the big Garden arena and thirteen shows statewide.

"Also," Stevens notes, "When I came in, there were three or four promoters licensed to do business in New York. Now we have fifteen licensed promoters and most of them are running shows here."

It's not all fun and games for Stevens. The nuts-and-bolts work of running a state athletic commission, when done properly, is extremely demanding. And there are times when circumstances require that hard choices be made. Twice, Stevens has felt compelled to place fighters he liked and respected (Evander Holyfield and Al Cole) on medical suspension. And he was responsible for overseeing the process by which James Toney was suspended after testing positive for illegal steroid use subsequent to his victory over John Ruiz. "Those were low points for me," Stevens acknowledges. "But high medical standards go to the heart of boxing."

Medical standards also play a role in Stevens's attitude toward the proposed federal boxing commission. "If all the states were as responsible as the better jurisdictions, a federal commission wouldn't be necessary," he says. "But many states are underfunded and understaffed and it's next to impossible for them to provide a true safety net for fighters. New York is the most generous jurisdiction in the world in terms of subsidizing medical costs for fighters. The promoter pays for the bloodwork and general physical examination and that's about all. New York pays for the MRIs and eye exam. We have an EKG machine and technician in the commission office."

"The variation from state to state on medical issues is unfortunate," Stevens continues. "Medical testing has to be standardized nationwide. Rules and regulations should be uniform and properly enforced throughout the country. If a state can't ensure proper pre-fight testing and have an ambulance and qualified ringside physicians at a show, then that state shouldn't have professional boxing."

"Also," adds Stevens, "another area of reform that has to be addressed is the enforcement of rights as they relate to the business of boxing. Other sports have mechanisms for participants to enforce their rights without spending hundreds of thousands of dollars in court. Boxing needs mechanisms that will enable licensees to enforce their rights in a fair economically-viable manner. A federal commission can succeed in these areas if it's financed properly and headed by the right people."

Meanwhile, the job that Ron Scott Stevens is doing as chairman of the New York State Athletic Commission shows what a huge difference one person can make.❏

*Over the years, Budd Schulberg has received numerous accolades for his boxing writing. He deserves them.*

# BUDD SCHULBERG

The press section at ringside these days bears little resemblance to the way it looked fifty years ago. The men no longer wear hats, suits, and ties. There are a significant number of women and a smaller contingent of newspaper writers. Computers have replaced typewriters.

But at big fights, there's one constant. Budd Schulberg is there, practicing his art.

Schulberg turned ninety on March 27, 2004. If he'd never written another line, he'd still be immortalized in boxing circles for the words spoken by Marlon Brando in *On The Waterfront*: "You don't understand. I could've had class. I could've been a contender. I could've been somebody, instead of a bum, which is what I am."

Schulberg, who authored those lines in his Academy-Award-winning screenplay, was born in New York and raised in Hollywood. After graduating from Dartmouth in 1936, he became a screenwriter at Paramount, where his father was head of production. In 1939, he returned to the east coast and wrote his first novel, *What Makes Sammy Run?*, which was the National Critics' Choice in 1941 as "Best First Novel of the Year."

Six years later, the most controversial period of Schulberg's life erupted. From 1937 through 1940, he had been a member of the Communist Party. In 1947, the Un-American Activities Committee of the United States House of Representatives began an investigation into Communist influence within the motion picture industry. During the investigation, ten men—Herbert Biberman, Lester Cole, Albert Maltz, Adrian Scott, Samuel Ornitz, Dalton Trumbo, Edward Dmytryk, Ring Lardner Jr., John Howard Lawson, and Alvah Bessie—were subpoenaed and refused to testify. Each was found guilty of contempt and imprisoned. Thereafter, screenwriter Richard Collins testified before the committee and named Schulberg as a former member of the Communist Party. Schulberg then sent a telegram to the committee offering to provide evidence as a cooperating witness. When that time came, he named fifteen former party members and testified that several of them had sought to influence the content of his work along political lines.

Schulberg's cooperation with the House Un-American Activities Committee allowed him to continue his screenwriting career, although he remained based on the east coast. His best-known work, *On the Waterfront*, followed. Directed by Elia Kazan (another former Communist Party member who "named names"), it was a scalding exposé of trade union corruption that won Academy Awards for Best Picture, Best Actor (Marlon Brando), Best Supporting Actress (Eva Marie Saint), Best Director (Kazan), and Best Cinematography in addition to Schulberg's Best Screenplay honor.

Topping the list of his other screenplays are *A Face in the Crowd* (which starred Andy Griffith, Walter Matthau, and Patricia Neal) and *The Harder They Fall* (based on Schulberg's novel about racketeering in boxing), featuring Humphrey Bogart in his final role.

Schulberg's work leads to the question: What are the origins of his interest in the sweet science?

"My love of boxing began with my father," he explains. "My father was a big fight fan. He went to the fights every week and started taking me when I was ten. And my father was a big shot at Paramount, so he brought all the important fighters to the studio and I got to know them pretty well. In fact, my mother introduced Jack Dempsey to Estelle Taylor [Dempsey's second wife]."

"It almost a cliché now," Schulberg continues, "but the best fighter I ever saw was Sugar Ray Robinson. Henry Armstrong came close, and I'd put the young Muhammad Ali near the top. The best fight I ever saw was the first fight between Joe Louis and Billy Conn. Over the years, I've met most of the legendary heavyweight champions: Jack Dempsey,, Joe Louis, Rocky Marciano, Muhammad Ali. And one thing that strikes me about all of them is, they've all been remarkably gentle and kind outside the ring."

As for Marlon Brando's immortal words—"I could've been a contender"—Schulberg recalls, "I remember writing that scene [with Brando and Rod Steiger]. The whole scene in the taxi was in the first draft of the screenplay, and that line remained unchanged. It came out of the fight game. I'd known boxers all my life, and seen that feeling in so many of them. The line itself, I made up; but the feeling was almost always there. 'It could have been different for me if just that one night had been different . . . That one wrong move; if it hadn't happened, my whole life would have changed . . . If I hadn't been overmatched . . . If I'd been advised differently . . . If he hadn't hit me with that lucky punch.' I had a friend named Roger Donoghue, a middleweight who I brought in to show Marlon Brando how to walk like a fighter, how to gesture like a fighter, how a fighter moves. Roger had been involved in a tragedy in the ring. He'd fought an opponent who died, and it had stopped his own progress as a fighter, so Roger had that feeling too. If. . . If. . . If. . ."

Schulberg remains active as a writer, authoring articles about boxing and other subjects close to his heart. He's also working with Spike Lee to develop a feature film about Joe Louis. But the best way to acknowledge his contribution to the sweet science is to repeat some of what he has written in the past. So herewith, a sampler of quotes from Budd Schulberg on boxing:

● "I know a good thing when I see it. Fistfighting is a good thing. Every great fight is a rare nugget. If our civilization is indeed declining and if it finally falls, it will not be because Joe Louis clobbered Max Schmeling or took the measure of Billy Conn."

● "Boxing is a mental sport. Think of a prizefight as a chess game of mind and body, and you are a little closer to it than if you compare it to a bloody brawl in an alley."

● [Recalling Archie Moore slumped on the canvas at the close of his 1955 title fight against Rocky Marciano]: "There was tragedy in the way he sprawled there with the fight and the will beaten out of him; a very old man of forty-two who, some thirty minutes earlier, had been such an astonishingly young man of forty-two."

● "Fights can be dumped in a dozen ways. Sometimes everybody but the fighter knows. Sometimes only the fighter knows."

● "Boxing doesn't need politicians to abolish it. It will abolish itself if it persists in its program of anarchy, chaos, and criminal neglect of the thousands who turn to it from the dark corner of discrimination and want. I hope for selfish reasons that boxing is not abolished. I'd miss it. But I would rather see it abolished than have it continue down the path to Beau Jack's shoeshine stand or the asylum where Billy Fox sleeps his troubled empty dreams."

● "Very few fighters get the consideration of racehorses, which are put out to pasture to grow old with dignity and comfort when they haven't got it anymore."

● "As much as I love boxing, I hate it. And as much as I hate it, I love it."

● "I've never lost that feeling about going to the big fights. There aren't as many magic matches now as there used to be. But every once in a while, there is a feeling just before a fight starts that it will change the fighters' lives and define them for the rest of their lives; that it has the potential to destroy either man or make him a legend."❑

*Several years ago, Jimmy Glenn was honored by the Boxing Writers Association of America for "long and meritorious service to boxing."*

# JIMMY GLENN

Jimmy's Corner is a blue-collar bar on 44th Street between 6th and 7th Avenues in Manhattan. It's open seven days a week from an hour before noon until to 4:00 a.m. The main room is dark and barely wide enough for people to pass behind patrons nursing their drinks at the bar. There's a smaller room with tables in back, but no food other than chips. Both rooms are ordinary except for the walls. Every square foot is covered with photographs of fighters and posters heralding long-ago ring confrontations.

"It's just a bar," says Jimmy Glenn, the soft-spoken man who owns Jimmy's Place and turns 75 today (August 18, 2005). "Just a bar is easier. You don't have to worry about food and cooks. I'd rather run a gym than a bar, but you can't make a living running a gym. The rent's too high."

Jimmy Glenn is a link to boxing's past. Over the years, he has owned bars, restaurants, and gyms. Despite never having made it to the top, he's one of the few people who's universally respected in boxing. I've written about the sweet science for two decades, and there are three people who I've never heard anyone say anything bad about: Eddie Futch, Al Gavin, and Jimmy Glenn.

Glenn was born in rural South Carolina on August 18, 1930. His grandfather was a sharecropper. His mother worked on the same farm. "My mother only had one child," he says. "But when I was ten, she married my stepfather and, after that, I had a lot of brothers and sisters on my stepfather's side."

Glenn's mother moved to Washington, D.C. in 1937 and left Jimmy behind. After she married, she sent for him and they relocated with her husband in Harlem. In December 1941, Pearl Harbor was attacked. The following year, Jimmy's uncles were drafted. So at age twelve, he went back to South Carolina to work with his grandfather on the farm.

Glenn stayed in South Carolina until the war ended in 1945. Then he returned to New York and got a job as a delivery boy in the garment district. He also began boxing in the Police Athletic League.

In the 1940s, boxing was a mainstream sport and deeply ingrained in the fabric of Harlem. Joe Louis ruled the world, but the local icon was Sugar Ray Robinson.

Glenn's face lights up when he discusses Robinson. "I used to watch Ray work out at a gym on 116th Street," he recalls. "Ray had magnetism. He was something special. He was a partying guy; and to tell the truth, I'm more of a homebody. But Ray made the whole community proud. Everybody in Harlem was happy just to look at him. The first big fight I saw was Sugar Ray Robinson against Tommy Bell [on December 20, 1946] at Madison Square Garden. Ray won his first championship that night, but it wasn't easy. Tommy made him work for it. Ray had to call on everything he had to beat him."

Boxing as an amateur, Glenn compiled a 14-2 record with two knockouts. "I was a fair fighter, not a good one," he admits. "I started at welterweight and ended up at middleweight. I could box but I wasn't much of a puncher." In his most memorable amateur match, he fought a middleweight named Floyd Patterson. "He beat me," Glenn acknowledges. "Knocked me down a few times, broke my tooth. But I went the distance."

Ultimately, Glenn quit boxing. "I wasn't good enough for it to make sense for me to keep fighting," he says. But the sport was in his blood. And when the Third Moravian Church opened a community center on 127th Street in Harlem, he volunteered to teach youngsters how to box.

"The church gave me the space, but it couldn't afford any equipment," Glenn remembers. "We had some dances and parties to raise money, but it wasn't much. We didn't even have a ring. I had to teach boxing on the regular floor, and we still had twenty to thirty kids a night, six nights a week. Then a lady from a foundation came up to see the place and liked what we were doing and gave us money to do things right. After a while, we started entering kids in the Golden Gloves. We won a team trophy and some individual trophies. And we kept doing it until the church got torn down in the 1970s."

Several years later, Glenn opened the Times Square Gym on 42nd Street in Manhattan. In the mid-1980s, that building too was demolished. Through it all, he has earned a living by owning restaurants and bars. Les Nanette's on West 43rd Street in Manhattan was the first. Two more establishments came and went. Jimmy's Corner has survived for three decades.

On the home front, Glenn has been married twice. His current marriage has lasted for 32 years. And while he himself dropped out of school in eighth grade, it's a point of pride for him that six of his seven children have graduated from college.

Meanwhile, Glenn remains committed to boxing. "The best thing about boxing is that it teaches respect," he says. "You take a kid off the streets. He's angry and scared and beefing about the system. But after a few weeks in the gym, it's 'yes, sir' and 'no, sir' and the lessons of discipline and hard work set in. Before long, the kid starts to make something out of himself and believe in himself. Kids in the gym want to learn. That's why they're there. People hear about the fighters who become champions. But a lot of young men who never go beyond the amateurs get good jobs and become good citizens because of boxing."

Over the years, Glenn has managed several fighters and trained many more (most notably, John Meekins and Jameel McCline). "There are times when it's frustrating," he acknowledges. "When you get a young fighter, everything you tell them the first few years, they listen. Then, with some of them, they become stars in their own mind. Everybody gets their ear, and they forget where they came from and what brought them from where they were to where they're at. They start wanting to change the way they train. You got to beg them to do things, and they still don't do it; or they do what you say, but they don't do it like they did when they were starting out."

There's also the business side of things. Two decades ago, Glenn spoke openly and eloquently about that aspect of boxing.

"Managers and trainers dream too," he said. "You teach a kid. You give him thousands of hours. The kid quits; you bring him back. He gets in trouble with the law or with a girl, and you help him out. You put a foundation under him. You give him your heart. Then the kid starts to look good. He turns out to be that one in a thousand who's really good. And all of a sudden, some guy walks in, offers the kid a salary, a bonus, and he's gone. That's always the way it is with amateurs on account of you can't sign an amateur to a contract. And with a pro, even if you have a contract, where are you gonna get the thousands of dollars in legal fees to enforce it? So you sell the contract or it isn't renewed when it expires. Guys like me dream of a champion. But when a fighter hits ten rounds, the big money pushes the little guys out."

"That's what boxing is," Glenn says when those words are read back to him. "That's the way it was then, and it's worse now. I'm not a pushy guy, and maybe I should be. In boxing, it helps to be that way."❏

*Craig Hamilton has worn many hats in the sweet science, from memorabilia expert to "management advisor" to fan.*

# CRAIG HAMILTON

Craig Hamilton is a Jesse Ventura look-alike. Strong, barrel-chested, fifty-three years old, with a clean-shaven head and deep booming voice. He's also one of the most knowledgeable and honest men in a business not known for candor. He's a boxing memorabilia dealer.

Hamilton was born and raised on Long Island. His parents worked for Grumman Aircraft. His sister was the second policewoman in the history of Suffolk County. Hamilton has taught high school history; worked as a laborer for the Long Island Lighting Company; was an investigator for the Suffolk County Department of Social Services; loaded and unloaded trucks; put in time as a claims adjuster for an insurance company; and been a partner in a real estate venture that purchased land for subdivision and the construction of new homes. He's now one of the world's foremost experts on boxing memorabilia.

Hamilton's interest in boxing began when he was young. His uncle, Frankie Ryan, was a welterweight who peaked in the 1920s and beat some highly-regarded fighters, including Jimmy Duffy and Phil "KO" Kaplan. Ryan was also a heavy drinker who lived the fast life. After retiring from boxing, he was working for the *New York Herald* when a ream of paper fell on him and crushed his chest. A subsequent stroke left him bedridden for life.

"I visited my uncle as often as I could," Hamilton remembers. "He told me of the great days of boxing and how he rode the rails from town to town. He claimed to have met Jack Dempsey when Dempsey was doing the same thing. My uncle was the person responsible for my taking up collecting. It started with his stuff; a few photos and a press release. Then I got into saving newspaper write-ups of fights, photos of different fighters, and boxing cards. Things mushroomed from there."

Hamilton now has what he considers to be one of the world's two best collections of boxing memorabilia. Stanley Weston, who owned *Ring Magazine* and died in 2002, amassed the other. "Weston had a fabulous collection of fight-worn gloves," Hamilton acknowledges. "Auctioned off side-by-side, I'd say that our collections would bring in comparable dollars. Put them together and you'd have Nirvana."

The strength of Hamilton's collection is in its diversity. He owns championship belts and trophies that belonged to James Jeffries, Jack Dempsey, Benny Leonard, Willie Pep, Joe Louis, Archie Moore, Sugar Ray Robinson, Sandy Saddler, Rocky Marciano, and Muhammad Ali. He also has robes, trunks, and gloves worn by Ali, Emile Griffith, Salvador Sanchez, Alexis Arguello, Sugar Ray Leonard, and Roberto Duran. The "paper" items in his collection include on-site posters for Clay-Liston I, Ali-Foreman, and Ali-Frazier I, II and III.

Hamilton has also assembled a library of two thousand books on boxing with titles that date to the sixteenth century.

"I've been collecting boxing books since I was a kid," he acknowledges. "Some of the favorites from my collection are *Pancratia* by William Oxberry and *Boxiana* by Pierce Egan, which is a boxed set in the original boards. I wouldn't claim that I have the best boxing library in the world, since I don't know what other collectors have. But it's a serious collection with a lot of rare titles, many of them in very fine condition. Boxing, in my opinion, has the finest written history of any sport, and I value my books above all of my other possessions."

In 1993, Hamilton founded JO Sports. Initially, the company was a vehicle for his own collecting. He bought as he chose, kept what he wanted, and sold off the rest. Now JO Sports is his primary business and occupies roughly seventy percent of his working time. He is also frequently retained by Sotheby's, Christie's, and other auction houses to document and authenticate boxing memorabilia prior to auction.

The past two decades have seen an explosion in the sports memorabilia market. In the late 1970s, a buyer who chose wisely might have been able to purchase a letter written by Jake Killrain for five or ten dollars. Now, that same letter sells for $3,000. The most valuable fighter's signature today is that of Marvin Hart, who reigned briefly as heavyweight champion in 1905. Once, Hart's signature was of minimal value. Now, because of its scarcity, a well-documented Hart signature in good condition can be sold for up to $10,000.

Hamilton himself purchased the belt that Sugar Ray Robinson was awarded by *Ring Magazine* when he beat Tommy Bell for his first world title. "It's probably the most significant piece I have," he says. "I bought it from Ray's widow, Millie, for $35,000. My guess is that it's now worth about $100,000, although Joe Louis's *Ring Magazine* belt is more valuable."

"James Corbett's gloves from his fight against John L. Sullivan sold for $60,000," Hamilton continues. "Ali's gloves from his first fight against Henry Cooper sold at auction for a bit more when the commission was added. That's the highest price for a pair of gloves that I'm aware of, although the right Ali gloves would go higher. Ali's trunks from the first Frazier fight brought a record $100,000, and his robe from Zaire was auctioned off for $160,000."

As for "paper" products, the most valuable fight poster that Hamilton is aware of is the on-site poster for Louis-Schmeling II. Depending on condition, it sells for $15,000 to $25,000. An uncut ticket for John L. Sullivan versus Jake Killrain goes for about $10,000. "Uncut tickets for Clay-Liston I are up there with Sullivan-Killrain," Hamilton explains. "But the problem with paper is, you never know what might show up. With a robe or a trophy, there's only one. But someone could be rummaging through a file cabinet and stumble across a whole stack of Clay-Liston tickets tomorrow."

And to prove his point, Hamilton recounts acquiring four on-site programs for John L. Sullivan versus James Corbett. "Guys who had collected fight programs for years didn't even know that a Sullivan-Corbett program existed until I found them," he says. Then he adds, "No Sullivan-Corbett poster is known to exist, but I have to think that there were some."

Meanwhile, Hamilton observes, "There's a whole new group of collectors today who have very little knowledge of boxing history and very little interest in it. They care about Muhammad Ali and no one else. When a good Jack Dempsey or Joe Louis item is available, two or three people might bid on it. With Ali, it's ten or twenty. Mike Tyson has a good fan base. No other active fighter sells at numbers close to Tyson, but his base isn't nearly as deep as Ali's."

Hamilton considers the championship belt presented to Cassius Clay by *Ring Magazine* for defeating Sonny Liston in 1964 to be the Holy Grail for boxing collectors. He has seen photographs of it, but doesn't know of anyone who claims knowledge of its whereabouts. "Many people think that Bundini [a member of Ali's entourage] sold it," he elaborates. "But no one really knows. I'd value the belt at a minimum of $250,000 and wouldn't be surprised if it brought a million dollars or more at auction. It would be an incredible find."

Hamilton's enthusiasm for collecting remains strong; although in recent years, it has diminished slightly as the result of a problem that plagues the entire sports collectibles industry.

"There's a ton of phony merchandise out there," he acknowledges. "Most of it is bad autographs. Ebay is the area of prime offense. It's the cesspool of sports collectibles. The listings on Ebay simply aren't screened sufficiently, so it's a true place for the buyer to beware. The bad material on Ebay flows like a rancid tide, and I've never seen it worse than it is today. A real Rocky Marciano autographed photo is worth eight hundred to a thousand dollars, but you see them on Ebay all the time for a hundred dollars. Marciano died in 1969. Buy one on Ebay, take it out of the frame, and it might be printed on paper that was manufactured in the 1990s."

"But it's not just Ebay," Hamilton continues. "A major auction house had an auction in 2003 that included a pair of boxing gloves that Joe Frazier supposedly wore for sparring while he was training for the first Ali fight. The first Ali-Frazier fight was in 1971. I know for a fact that the gloves were made after 1981 because of the design of the Everlast label on them. There was another glove in the same auction that Frazier supposedly wore in his fight against Jimmy Ellis. But if you look at photos of that fight, the glove is the wrong color. I hate stuff like that"

In retrospect, it was inevitable that Hamilton's love of boxing would lead him to become more directly involved with the sweet science. Thus, in addition to collecting, he has served in the past as a management advisor for heavyweights Michael Grant and Gerald Nobles.

"Michael was my first fighter," Hamilton recounts. "I came to know him in 1994 through Don Turner, who was his trainer at the time. Don wanted me to get involved but I didn't know enough about managing, so I took Michael to Bill Cayton. Bill, Steve Lott, and I formed a partnership. And although there came a time when we went separate ways, almost everything I know about managing I learned during the three years that Michael was with Bill, Steve, and myself. Say what you will about Bill Cayton; he knew how to manage a fighter. Everything he did was in the best interest of the fighter, and that's true of Steve too. Every time we had an issue, their approach was to ask the question, 'What's in the best interest of the fighter?' There might be disagreements as to the answer. But if you answer that question as honestly as you can, you'll make the right decision far more often than not."

Hamilton guided Grant to a multi-fight HBO contract and a multi-million-dollar payday against Lennox Lewis. He stayed with him through the transition from Don Turner to Teddy Atlas as the fighter's trainer and losses against Lewis, Jameel McCline, and Dominick Guinn. They parted ways in February 2004 because of what Hamilton felt was Michael's lack of gratitude and, more significantly, the lack of a serious commitment to boxing. Grant hasn't fought since, but the people who saw Hamilton do his job up close express their admiration for him.

"Craig is the absolute best," says Turner. "He's a stand-up guy who knows boxing and always, always, does what he thinks is best for the fighter. He's one of the finest people I've ever met in or out of boxing."

Atlas, who replaced Turner in late 2000, is equally complimentary. "I have a resistance to getting close to people," Atlas acknowledges, "and particularly to people in boxing. You give and you get involved and you trust, and then usually you're disappointed. But after Michael lost to Jameel McCline, I saw what Craig was about. I got to know him under the worst kind of disappointment and pressure. And under those difficult circumstances, Craig was a quality guy. He didn't panic. He didn't go looking for someone else to blame. He didn't just protect himself, run for cover, and leave his fighter out there alone. He kept his optimism but, at the same time, he was realistic and understanding. So I have a lot of respect for Craig. I like to see how people react when they're under fire and things are tough; not when they're on top of the world. And when things were tough, Craig faced up to what had happened and did what had to be done."

Meanwhile, Jim Thomas, who is still Grant's attorney, says simply, "Craig is one of those guys who restores your faith in the belief that there are some good people in the business of boxing."❏

*This piece was a precursor to Hopkins-Taylor I and also a look at one of the most intriguing people in boxing.*

# THE RESURRECTION OF SAINT LOUIS (DIBELLA)

Lou DiBella was once one of the most powerful people in boxing. As the number-two man at HBO Sports, he had considerable input into how the network's substantial financial resources were spent. He was also the driving force behind HBO's *Boxing After Dark* and an integral member of the team that elevated *World Championship Boxing* to an industry-wide standard.

In mid-2000, DiBella left the corporate world and went out on his own. He wanted to reform boxing and establish himself as a fighter representative. The watchword of his faith was, "A fighter should never make less money than the promoter or anyone else involved with a fight."

"I'll work for the fighter," DiBella said at the time, explaining his intended modus operandi. "I'll hire the promoter, who will be responsible for promoting each fight in accordance with the laws of the state in which the fight is held. The promoter will control the legal administration of the show, but I'll negotiate the site fee and close the television deal. In other words, the promoter will work for the fighter. I'm trying to make a point. I'm trying to rattle the cage and do things differently. I can't turn boxing upside down overnight. But it's as important to me now to shake this business up as it is to make money."

DiBella's detractors say that, when he went out on his own, he had trouble operating without the protective umbrella of HBO and ran a small business as though it were a large one. They also say that he gave new meaning to the word "lou-dicrous" and could start a fist-fight in an empty room. DiBella countered with thoughts like "being honorable is a death sentence in boxing" and "boxing is a dying business that's responsible for its own death."

Either way, DiBella had a rocky start. He put a great deal of time, money, and effort into developing Bernard Hopkins as a marquee fighter, only to be left at the altar after Hopkins beat Felix Trinidad to claim the undisputed middleweight championship. He also paid a $1,400,000 signing bonus to Olympic silver-medalist Ricardo Williams, who decided that it was too much work to train, lost two fights, and was recently sentenced to three years in prison for drug-trafficking.

But DiBella persevered and now finds himself in the second tier of promoters behind Top Rank and Don King Productions. That in itself is a switch from his original role as a "business representative." But DiBella proclaims, "The fundamental principles that I started my company on are unchanged. I still believe in fair contracts and open books and working on behalf of my fighters."

And DiBella is the same person he was five years ago. That means (1) he's still a good guy; (2) having a conversation with him on a bad day exposes a person to more profanity than gangsta rap; and (3) he's constantly on his cell phone. Recently, DiBella lost forty pounds. "I call it the misery diet," he says. "I like feeling like a fucking victim."

DiBella now has two dozen fighters under contract. The best-known are Jermain Taylor, Ike Quartey, Leavander Johnson, Jose Navarro, and Mark Johnson. In addition, he's working with a cadre of young boxers. Excluding journeyman Emanuel Augustus (who recently came onboard), DiBella's twenty-four fighters have a composite record of 505 wins, 38 losses and 5 draws with 312 knockouts. That's a pretty good base to build on.

DiBella has also entered into a joint venture with Damon Dash, who co-founded Rock-A-Wear clothing and the Rock-A-Fella record label. The two men are co-promoting three fighters. "For a long time, I've thought that something had to be done with marketing to revitalize the sport," DiBella explains. "The idea is to create a synergy between boxing, rap music, and urban style; particularly with African-American fighters. There have been attempts to sexy-up the sport for the young urban market before. But for the most part, they've been undertaken by white television executives, who are the wrong people for the job."

"I'm a much better promoter now than I was four years ago," DiBella notes. "I've learned the promotional end of the business in ways that I didn't understand when I was at HBO. I love working with fighters. But after my experiences with Bernard Hopkins and Ricky Williams, I approach fighters with more skepticism than before. I've learned that friendship only goes so far in boxing, so I don't take things that people do to me as personally as I once did. And I've started to make decisions based on realism rather than emotion."

"There's a certain pain that goes along with learning," DiBella continues. "I've been tempered by reality. I still think boxing is a miserable business. Everything is a deal. People lie all the time and don't even consider it lying. Sooner or later, virtually everyone in the business adopts a go-along mentality or they get crushed. I've come to the conclusion that I can't change the way other people do business. So I operate my own company consistent with my conscience and no longer get a stomach ache every time I see an injustice in boxing. I can't say that I enjoy the business, but it's addictive. And I don't want to be pushed out by the bad guys. I won't let the bastards beat me. If I quit, I want it to be when I'm on top. Maybe then I'll decide that I don't want to be a big fish swimming around in a sewage tank."

DiBella was born and raised in New York City and wants to build something in his hometown. Thus, one of his ventures has been a series called Broadway Boxing. One might think that it's easy to promote the sweet science in New York. It's not. To the contrary, the cost of renting a site, hotel rates, and other expenses make it exceedingly difficult to promote at a profit in The Big Apple. But Broadway Boxing is making its mark and has become an important part of New York's fistic renaissance.

DiBella has eleven fighters from New York under contract: Jaidon Codrington, Paulie Malignaggi, Sechew Powell, Curtis Stevens, Yuri Foreman, Jeffrey Resto, Raymond Joval, Dmitriy Salita, Emanual Clottey, Joshua Clottey, and Chris Smith. These fighters have been the centerpiece of twelve Broadway Boxing shows to date, and there are plans for five more before the end of the year. HD-Net pays the television production costs and carries each initial telecast. MSG Network televises the reruns.

"Broadway Boxing was a risk," DiBella acknowledges. "It was an investment in the future when I started. There was no guaranteed revenue, and I lost a few bucks in the beginning. Then I lost a few bucks less. Now I'm making a little money on each show."

"There are very few platforms in boxing to build new talent," DiBella says, explaining the rationale behind the series. "By and large, you're dependent on the TV networks and sites to build and establish the value of your fighters. I'm trying to build a boxing company and this gives me a chance to showcase my young fighters."

And each Broadway Boxing card features an added attraction: the crowd. For better or worse (and sometimes it's both), sports fans today are part of the show. Crowds can influence officials and the performance of athletes. In worst-case scenarios, such as last year's basketball game between the Detroit Pistons and Indiana Pacers, out-of-control violence results.

Most of DiBella's Broadway Boxing shows have been contested at the 1,400-seat Manhattan Center. Each fighter brings his own constituency. On a typical night, one section is filled with residents of Bedford-Stuyvesant wearing dark-blue doo-rags, cheering for Curtis Stevens. Next to them, Orthodox Jews with yarmulkes wait for Dmitriy Salita to do battle. There are Polish flags, Irish flags, and a contingent from the South Bronx with colors of its own. The fans are loud and passionate, but their energies are focussed on the ring. There's no ugliness between them.

But Broadway Boxing is just one component of DiBella's business. He has been the lead promoter for 29 shows since officially becoming a promoter in January 2002. And a number of his fighters are moving from "prospect" to "contender" status.

In that regard, 2005 began on a down note when Jose Navarro challenged Katsushige Kawashima for the WBC 115-pound crown. Navarro cut Kawashima above the right eye and dominated the fight. After round six, the ring doctor visited the champion's corner to determine if he was fit to continue. At fight's end, Kawashima was drenched in his own blood. Judge William Boodhoo of Canada scored the bout 120-109 for Navarro. But Gelasio Perez of Mexico (115-114) and Noparat Sricharoen of Thailand (115-113) gave the nod to Kawashima. Navarro outlanded Kawashima 530 to 252.

"I haven't even written 2005 on a piece of paper yet," DiBella said hours after the fight, "and the filth of this business has already sullied the year. Jose did everything but knock Kawashima out, and he was robbed. The damage done by a decision like this to a kid like Jose is immeasurable, emotionally and financially. Decisions like this, which are condoned and sometimes encouraged by the world sanctioning organizations, are destroying the sport."

Later that month. DiBella suffered another setback when Kofi Jantuah challenged Kassim Ouma for the IBF 154-pound crown and failed to rise to the occasion. In March, Raymond Joval came up short against Fernando Vargas.

But there have been positive developments as well. Ike Quartey returned to the ring in January after a five-year absence and knocked out Clint McNeil. Then he decisioned Verno Phillips. And earlier this year, DiBella closed a deal to become president and general partner of the Norwich Navigators, a San Francisco Giants affiliate in the AA Eastern League.

"Buying a baseball team is an effort to balance my existence," DiBella explains. "All of the infighting and ugliness in boxing is wearing me down. In fact, the biggest problem boxing has today is that the people who run the sport think their competition is each other. The Major League Baseball owners don't think that way. The NFL owners don't think that way. They understand that their real competition is other sports. Besides," DiBella adds, "I love baseball."

And then there's the matter of a fight scheduled for July 16th: Bernard

Hopkins versus Jermain Taylor (DiBella's flagship fighter) for the undisputed middleweight championship of the world.

Hopkins and DiBella despise one another. After they split, Bernard sought to justify his conduct by claiming that DiBella (while a television executive) took a $50,000 bribe to put the fighter on HBO. When the allegations continued, DiBella sued for libel and won. In addition, the judge who presided over the case ruled that Hopkins's attorneys had engaged in "multiple layers of improper conduct in an effort to mislead the court and jury" and referred the matter to the court's committee on grievances.

The libel judgment is eating away at Hopkins's insides. And Bernard's conduct has done similar damage to DiBella. Last year, they crossed paths at the Boxing Writers Association of America awards dinner in New York.

"Suck my cock," Hopkins offered.

"Like they used to do in prison?" DiBella countered.

Then, at the May 3, 2005, kick-off press conference for Hopkins-Taylor, Bernard told the assembled media, "This fight means a lot to me. I got a chance to beat Jermain Taylor and also foreclose on Lou DiBella's company, because his company relies on Jermain Taylor's success. When I beat Jermain Taylor, I shut down Lou DiBella's company, so I get two knockouts in one night."

Thereafter, for emphasis, Hopkins turned to DiBella (who was seated next to the lectern) and repeatedly tapped him on the back. After the third tap, DiBella told him, "Do me a favor and don't touch me."

"He's gonna sue," Hopkins mockingly told his audience.

DiBella held his temper, barely. "Bernard is a great fighter," he said afterward. "But he's a vile human being. And outside the ring, Bernard doesn't have the courage to do things man-to-man. When he turned on me, when he turned on Bouie Fisher, he smiled and then he stabbed us in the back. That's the mark of a moral coward. But July 16th isn't about Bernard and myself. It's one hundred percent about Jermain Taylor's quest to establish himself as the best middleweight in the world."

On one level, that's true. But it's also true that it would be immensely satisfying to Hopkins to beat DiBella's flagship fighter and exponentially more painful for him to lose to Taylor than to anyone else. And DiBella has a comparable emotional investment.

Meanwhile, Jermain Taylor says simply, "Whatever is between those two is between those two. But I will say one thing. The night Bernard beat Felix Trinidad, I saw Lou crying. That's how happy he was. I hope he's crying tears of joy again after I fight Bernard Hopkins." ❑

# ROUND 3

# ISSUES AND ANSWERS

*Some people ask why boxing should be regulated when other sports aren't and why boxers aren't allowed to decide for themselves whether or not they're fit to fight. This column was an attempt to answer those questions.*

# THE THRESHOLD ISSUE

On March 13, 2004, Joe Mesi fought Vassiliy Jirov in Las Vegas. Mesi won, but was hit so hard and so often that his brain bled in three places.

On May 17, 2004, former heavyweight champion Riddick Bowe was released from prison after serving 17 months for kidnapping his first wife and their children. At Bowe's sentencing, his lawyer called the boxer's actions a misguided attempt to reunite his family and asked the court for leniency on grounds that Bowe's judgment had been impaired due to brain damage caused by boxing.

On November 13, 2004, the legendary Evander Holyfield lost eleven of twelve rounds to a journeyman fighter named Larry Donald. Holyfield has won two of his last nine fights and has three victories in the past seven years.

Mesi and Holyfield are currently under national medical suspension thanks to action taken by state athletic commissions in Nevada and New York. Bowe would not be allowed to fight in either of those states but, due to the chaotic condition of boxing regulation, he has been licensed to fight in California.

This article is not about whether Mesi, Holyfield, and Bowe are fit to fight. There's an issue of broader significance that's not limited to any one boxer: "Should a fighter who is at increased risk of physical injury due to brain damage, diminished physical skills, or any other impairment be allowed to fight?"

Critics of boxing maintain that there's hypocrisy in refusing to let fighters fight once they're found to be suffering from a deteriorating physical condition. After all, boxing at its core involves punching people in the head. It accepts the premise that, on occasion, a participant will die within the rules of the sport. Each time a fighter steps into the ring, he's risking physical injury and death.

Meanwhile, at the libertarian end of the spectrum, one finds boxing maven Charles Jay, who opines, "One of the things that makes me chuckle is the notion that there is always someone out there who knows what's best for me and knows it better than me. I've often marveled at the proposition that there are total strangers who might actually feel more of a proprietary interest in my wellbeing than I would. Don't preclude the fighter from making his own choices because you believe you know what's better for his life than he does."

In other words: It's my risk, my body, and my life.

But the argument in favor of precluding fighters at increased risk from entering the ring is a strong one.

First, boxing is regulated. Other sports aren't. That's because boxing is legalized assault. It consists of conduct that would be a crime had it not been legalized. But this assault is subject to restrictions imposed by the state. It can only take place under rules and regulations that dictate the length of each round, the conduct of fighters in the ring, and hundreds of other guidelines. One of these guidelines is that a boxer must prove his fitness in order to compete. A license to box is a privilege, not a right.

Second, one of the underpinnings of a civilized society is that, in certain instances, it protects people from themselves. That's why there are laws against certain forms of drug abuse and other "victimless" crimes. It's why passengers are required to wear seatbelts in automobiles and helmets while riding motorcycles. People aren't allowed to make all of the rules for themselves. Part of being a boxer is the belief that, if something horrible happens, it will happen to the other guy. But that's not the way life works. All professional athletes know they won't be able to compete past a certain point in their lives. And if that point comes sooner rather than later for a fighter, well, that's life.

And last, the rules and regulations of boxing exist for the protection of fighters, but they're also for the good of the sport. State athletic commissions don't exist only to protect fighters. They're also guardians of boxing. Letting physically-impaired fighters fight is bad for boxing. More than simply hurt the sport's image, it debases the sport.

In sum, it's not just the right; it's the obligation of a state athletic commission to deny a physically-impaired fighter a license to fight.

Muhammad Ali is a prime example. For years, Ali enobled boxing. But there came a time when he shouldn't have been licensed to fight anymore. He was slurring his words like Riddick Bowe. His skills deteriorated as have Evander Holyfield's. Ali's brain, like Joe Mesi's, had bounced around the inside of his skull too often. The last two fights of Ali's career (against Larry Holmes and Trevor Berbick) did nothing to enhance his legacy. Now, when people look at Ali, they say, "Boxing did this to him."

The regulators who allowed Ali to fight those last two fights failed to fulfill their obligation to him and they betrayed boxing.

At various times and in varying ways—in terms of personality, skill, and courage—Joe Mesi, Riddick Bowe, and Evander Holyfield have been likened to Muhammad Ali. It would be a shame if, from a medical standpoint, that comparison turned out to be right.❏

*The advocacy of proper medical care for fighters is an ongoing battle.*

# MEDICAL ISSUES AND THE AAPRP

Boxing is a mess. Imagine if every National Football League match-up and Major League Baseball game were contested under different rules with different officials and different governing standards depending on the state in which the game is played.

That's where the sweet science is today. And the chaos is most evident and most dangerous with regard to medical issues as they pertain to fighters. Now an organization called the American Association of Professional Ringside Physicians (AAPRP) is seeking a voice in the sport.

The AAPRP is largely the creation of Michael Schwartz. Schwartz was born in Brooklyn in 1961 and grew up on Long Island. He went to college at Stony Brook and medical school at the New York College of Osteopathic Medicine. He now lives in Connecticut and practices general internal medicine.

Schwartz was a boxing fan as a boy and fell in love with the sport during the Ali-Frazier-Foreman era. He began working amateur fight cards in the Nutmeg State in 1991. Soon after, he moved to the pros. In 1997, he founded the AAPRP.

"I'd been working in boxing for six years," Schwartz recalls. "And I realized that there was no real flow of information from one jurisdiction to another. I didn't even know my counterparts in New York. So I decided to create an organization that would develop medical protocols and guidelines aimed at ensuring the safety and protection of professional boxers."

Schwartz is both president and chairman of the AAPRP. In his words, all of the group's officers are "volunteers" and the first election will take place "on a date to be determined later this year." He says that he has spent $40,000 of his own money to found and guide the organization and devotes three to four hours a day to that task. He estimates that there are between 400 and 450 approved ring physicians in the United States and that three-quarters of them belong to the AAPRP.

Both Tim Leuckenhoff and Greg Sirb, the present and past presidents of the Association of Boxing Commissions (ABC), say that they regard the AAPRP as a trade association for doctors, not a quasi-governmental body. But that hasn't stopped the organization from aggressively promoting itself, and this promotion has rubbed some people the wrong way.

Critics claim that many of the awards bestowed by the AAPRP have been calculated to generate publicity and political favors. Boxing guru Charles Jay made that point two years ago when he sent an open letter to Schwartz questioning the choice of Tim Leuckenhoff as "administrator of the year" and the presentation of a special award for "outstanding contribution to boxing" to Senator John McCain.

"You and I both know the rationale behind your choices, don't we?" wrote Jay. "You want control of the nationwide medical databank that would be established if the United States Boxing Administration were to come into existence. You want to be empowered with controlling the process by which ringside physicians are certified and trained. You have heretofore been unsuccessful in those pursuits, and apparently you feel you can't get there without the approval of McCain's office and at least some cooperation with Lueckenhoff and the ABC. So let's be perfectly honest, shall we? The 'awards' you give out are, in essence, for the sake of political expediency, are they not? Yours is just one more organization that is engaged in the practice of selling yourselves out for the sake of politics."

More recently, the selection of Florida physician Allan Fields as 2004 "ringside physician of the year" was seen by some as motivated by a desire to sell tickets to the AAPRP's annual awards banquet, which was held in Fields's home state of Florida. And the designatation of Robert Cantu as "distinguished educator of the year" looked like an attempt by the AAPRP to insert itself into Joe Mesi's high-profile effort to lift the suspension imposed on him by the Nevada State Athletic Commission (NSAC). More on Mesi later in this article.

Schwartz defends his modus operandi, saying, "In boxing, you have to be aggressive to get things done." He's equally forceful in defending the AAPRP and the doctors it represents on a host of economic issues.

The AAPRP is a not-for-profit corporation. Schwartz says that the organization breaks even on its annual convention and that its only other source of income is a $125 annual membership fee. But many of the issues facing ring doctors today have economic roots, and some raise the spectre of conflicts of interest.

Being a ring doctor is not a ticket to wealth. In New York, the fee for fight night is based on the live gate and ranges from $500 down to $175. In California, there's a sliding pay scale based on the live gate plus the television license fee with a $400 cap and a minimum of $200. Payment in Nevada is keyed to fight-night responsibilities and the magnitude of the fight. The lead doctor on a big fight in Nevada gets $750 and the number-two doctor receives $650. Doctors who work in back in the dressing rooms get less. For small shows, the minimum is $200.

Then there's the issue of medical malpractice insurance. In some jurisdictions, ring doctors work fights as an agent of the state and are covered by the state athletic commission. But in other jurisdictions, the doctors are present on fight night as private physicians and are thus vulnerable. Some doctors are affiliated with hospitals that incorporate ring duties into their insurance policies. But other doctors have no such protection, and more and more individual medical malpractice insurance policies are specifically excluding coverage for sports supervision.

Thus, Schwartz says, "It's not about the money." But then he adds, "Right now, the average pay for a ring doctor is a few hundred dollars a night. If you compare that to what judges get for a major fight; they're flown in from around the world, put up in nice hotels, and paid thousands of dollars for writing down tens and nines and a few eights on a piece of paper. The small pay for ring doctors reflects a lack of respect and, for that reason, it bothers me. Referees and judges and sanctioning-body officials all have a role to play. But there are times when the only thing that prevents someone from dying is us."

However, some ring doctors find ways to augment their income from boxing. In New York, where annual physicals are required, ring doctors are paid $75 for each physical they perform on a fighter. A "full physical" lasts roughly twenty minutes. So if a ring doctor performs four physicals at a weigh-in, he receives $300. That's not much, but it's better than nothing. And in a few states, pre-fight testing (as opposed to physicals) offers a bonanza for doctors.

Post-fight treatment can also be profitable. Ron Scott Stevens (chairman of the New York State Athletic Commission) declares, "Our policy in New York is that, on fight night, the ring doctor works for the commission-designated fee and nothing more. If a fighter is stitched up in the dressing room by a commission doctor, it has to be done for free."

But most jurisdictions adhere to a different set of rules. "The responsibility of the ringside physician is to stabilize, not to treat," says Schwartz. "If a fighter breaks his leg, it's not our job to put him in a cast. And if he's cut, it's not our responsibility to suture him up." And Dean Lohuis (acting executive director of the California State Athletic Commission) explains, "In California, the ring doctor is required to walk the fighter back to the dressing room and give a preliminary diagnosis. Then, absent the need for emergency treatment, his responsibility to the state and the fighter ends."

Lohuis might have added, "And the opportunity to make extra money begins."

There are times when a ring doctor approaches a fighter's camp or the promoter after a bout and says, "Your guy needs stitches. I can suture him up for a hundred dollars or you can send him to the hospital and it will cost you four hundred." It's natural for a fighter to want to be sewn up in the dressing room immediately after a fight. Going to the hospital means sitting around an emergency room for three or four hours. So a bargain is struck.

Insurance reimbursement also factors into the process. Promoters in the United States are responsible for purchasing medical insurance for fighters. The required amount varies from a high of $50,000 in California and Nevada to a low of $2,500 in several states.

From the insurance company's point of view, the best of all possible worlds occurs in states where ring doctors perform aftercare in their role as state employees and there's no extra charge. The least desirable situation from a financial perspective occurs in states like Nevada, where fighters are routinely sent to the hospital. Hospital bills are expensive and insurance payouts are higher as a result. The middle ground occurs when the ring doctor handles aftercare himself and the insurance company is billed for it.

For years, Joe Gagliardi was one of the primary agents for the sale of fight-night medical insurance in the United States. "Four or five years ago," says Gagliardi, "we had a problem in California, where some of the doctors were double-dipping. They were getting paid by the promoter or a fighter's manager and the insurance company. We attacked that and cleaned it up pretty well. But you still have a situation where ring doctors in some states submit a lot of charges for insurance coverage for services that ring doctors in other states perform without charge within their official duties."

Why don't the insurance companies complain about this practice?

Because, if they do, more ring doctors will send fighters to the hospital and insurance payouts will increase.

Michael Schwartz defends additional fight-related compensation for ring doctors as long as it's above-board and legal. "Ring physicians are paid so little for what they do," he says, "that you can't ask them to do more without compensation."

But there's an issue here that goes beyond the amount of payment. Unlike doctors in other sports, ring physicians are neutral officials with the authority to directly influence the outcome of contests. And some ring physicians have conflicts of interest that carry the potential to undermine their judgment. They treat fighters as private patients and, on occasion, even work as a second in a fighter's corner. And quite frankly, a manager or promoter might be concerned that, if they don't give pre- or-post-fight business to a particular ring doctor, that doctor might rule against them during the course of a fight.

Tim Leuckenhoff states, "As far as I'm concerned, either you're a ring physician working for the state or you treat fighters as private patients. You can't do both."

That's not a bad rule to follow. As neutral officials, ring physicians should be subject to the same scrutiny and standards as referees and judges.

Let's take an example. Perlman Hicks is a ring doctor in California and the plastic surgeon who did a brilliant job of suturing up Vitali Klitschko after his loss against Lennox Lewis. When Klitschko fought Danny Williams in Las Vegas last year, his promoter (K2 Promotions) hired Hicks at Vitali's request and brought him to Las Vegas as a precautionary measure in case Klitschko was cut. Should Hicks now work a Klitschko fight (or any K2 card) in California? No matter how honorable he is, one can argue that there would be an inherent conflict of interest.

There's considerable debate in boxing circles over medical economics. Clearly, not everyone agrees with the AAPRP on these issues. But having said that, it's just as clear that there are areas where the AAPRP can perform a valuable service. For example, the AAPRP can improve standards for ringside care by acting as a teaching organization.

"We're all individuals," says Schwartz. "We all do things a little bit differently. But certain things should be standardized in terms of how ring doctors respond during a fight. The most important thing is planning and following the procedures you've planned for each eventuality. It's not enough to be a good doctor. You can't just take a doctor from the local emergency room and put him in the corner for a fight. It's about recognizing little things during the course of a fight; tiny details so, if you see something you don't like, you act on it. And it's about acting in an appropriate way during those horrible moments when it appears as though a fighter might be badly hurt."

Many state athletic commissions don't have adequate training programs for ring doctors. And even in states that do, things sometimes go awry. Schwartz points to the December 4, 2004, fight between Sam Peter and Jeremy Williams as an example. That fight was seen by a national television audience on Showtime, and much has been made of the devastating one-punch knockout scored by Peter. But, except for a column by Elisa Harrison, there has been little exploration of what went on in the ring afterward.

"The outcome of the fight was ugly and very scary," Harrison wrote. "Williams got caught flush with one of the most devastating and powerful left hooks I've ever witnessed. He went down hard and was unconscious for what seemed like an eternity. I have some serious concerns over what transpired next."

What transpired next, according to the Showtime tape and reports from observers at ringside, was that Williams started seizing. Normally, a person loses muscle tone when he is unconscious. Immediately after the knockout, Williams had tonic extension of his arms (extreme muscle rigidity) followed by tonic-clonic movements (rhythmic shaking) of his arms and legs. Then, about two minutes later, there was another series of tonic-clonic movements. This is indicative of a seizure.

Referee Toby Gibson stopped the fight at the count of "four" and called the ring doctor (Jeff Davidson) into the ring. Normally, the first thing done under these circumstances is to remove the fallen fighter's mouthpiece to secure an airway. However, both Gibson and Davidson were unable to do so; perhaps because they were unfamiliar with type of mouthpiece that Williams was wearing; one that has to be removed from the back. Finally, two minutes and 52 seconds after the knockout, after Williams regained consciousness and offered assistance, the mouthpiece was removed.

Three minutes and 45 seconds after the knockout, a voice (probably that of Steve Brown, the number-two physician at ringside) was heard on Showtime saying, "Can we get a little oxygen in here?" The referee asked Davidson, "Do you want to bring him [Williams] back down [to the canvas]?" Davidson answered, "No, we're going to get him out of here." Then, as someone with oxygen came closer, Davidson instructed, "No, no, no."

Four minutes after knockout, with Williams still sitting on the canvas, Davidson queried, "Jeremy, do you want to walk or do you want to sit for a minute?"

"Let me sit for a minute," Williams told him.

Eleven-and-a-half minutes after the knockdown, with Williams still sitting on a stool in the ring, Davidson granted an interview to Showtime and advised its viewers that Jeremy "obviously suffered a concussion."

Several days ago, when asked by this writer if Williams had also suffered seizures in the ring, Davidson responded, "That's a good question. There were a lot of people in the ring who shouldn't have been there, so I couldn't see his whole body. There were people who said afterward that his arms and legs were shaking; but I was focussing on his head, which is where the A-B-C's [airway-breathing-circulation] are.

And none of the A-B-C's failed him."

Marc Ratner (executive director of the Nevada State Athletic Commission) was at ringside for Peter versus Williams. "Dr. Davidson is an excellent emergency room physician," says Ratner. "He sees head trauma injuries like that, and worse, all the time. From a medical standpoint, I'm confident that everything was done properly."

But Michael Schwartz is less certain. "If I was at ringside," says Schwartz, "I'd have been in the ring with a neurologist within five seconds. One of us would have stabilized the neck, removed the mouthpiece, and secured an airway. The neurologist would have done a quick check of pupilary response. And once the seizures began, without question, we would have administered oxygen. There's no downside to administering oxygen. Absolutely, oxygen should have been administered here. Within five minutes, we would have had the fighter in a neck collar and on a flat board and been carrying him to a stretcher."

"Look," Schwartz continues. "As far as I'm concerned, if a fighter is seizing or unconscious for thirty seconds—and here it was both—the EMTs are on the way. You don't know what damage has been done or is occurring in the brain. So you don't wait around to see if, well, maybe he's a little better; let's wait and see. And in my opinion, a fighter who has been unconscious and suffered seizures should not walk out of the ring. I know it's embarrassing for a fighter to be carried out of the ring on a stretcher with the crowd watching and photographers taking pictures. But the downside to not taking every precaution is that the fighter could die. Most of the time, he's okay. But if things go wrong, the fighter could die. Just because a fighter is alive and well after a knockout doesn't mean that he has been cared for properly. And the ring doctor had no business being interviewed on television until he was done with the entire process and the fighter was safely in his dressing room or on the way to the hospital."

Fortunately, Jeremy Williams appears to have recovered well from the knockout. "I'm fine now," he said in mid-January. "I went to my own doctor for a follow-up exam and all the tests came back okay. Everyone at the Nevada Commission was nice to me. They followed up with telephone calls to see if I was all right, and I can't complain about the treatment I got because everything worked out fine."

But then Williams added an interesting thought. "I'm a trained medic," he noted. "I took some courses two years ago. I love medicine; it amazes me. After boxing, I plan on being a paramedic. And from what I know, maybe they should have given me oxygen and immobilized my head and neck in the ring. If something more had been done in the ring for me for precautionary reasons, I wouldn't have had a problem with it."

Also, there's one very disturbing element to Williams's aftercare. Six weeks after the fight, he said that no one had told him he'd suffered seizures in the ring.

Williams plans on fighting again. "All my boxing people say 'keep boxing,'" he reports. "And I want to be a champion, so I'm going down to cruiserweight. Right now, I'm working on getting my weight down. I won't spar for a while; but when it's time, I'll be in the ring again. Obviously, losing a fight in that manner is the worst way to lose. But I'm going to be the best cruiserweight champion ever."

Following the knockout, Williams was suspended by the Nevada State Athletic Commission for sixty days with the requirement that he get the approval of a neurologist before resuming his ring career. Had the suspension simply been for sixty days, it would terminate automatically. However, because of the neurological requirement, it can only be lifted by an affirmative act of the NSAC. One hopes that the commission will examine the matter carefully before acting.

Michael Schwartz makes the point that the case of Jeremy Williams emphasizes the need for uniform procedures and standards of treatment. For example, he asks, "If the ring doctor in charge couldn't see that the fighter was seizing, why wasn't someone else in place to immediately bring it to his attention?"

And keep in mind, from a medical standpoint, the Nevada State Athletic Commission is one of the best-run commissions in the country. Watching Roy Jones stretched out on the canvas after his brutal knockout loss at the hands of Glencoffe Johnson in Tennessee, many people wished that the drama was unfolding in Nevada so Jones would be properly cared for.

The AAPRP can also make a significant contribution to boxing by pressing for a national medical databank. An advocacy group for ring physicians shouldn't control the system. But as Greg Sirb notes, "Boxing desperately needs a national medical databank for fighters. Right now," Sirb elaborates, "there's a different database for each state and Native American jurisdiction, and it's total chaos. Fighters come in and say they've had a particular test and it's, 'When did you take it?' 'I don't know.' 'Where did you take it?' 'I'm not sure; maybe California.' So you try to track it down, but the commission office in California is closed or whoever is in charge of their medical records is out for the week. You should be able to press a button on a computer and get what you need instead of making dozens of telephone calls for each fight card. And a national medical databank would cut down on phony medicals, which are still a problem."

The AAPRP also has the potential to become a force for good by lobbying in favor of uniform pre-fight testing and one set of criteria regarding which fighters should, and should not, be allowed to fight.

Pre-fight medical testing is expensive and nobody wants to pay for it, but it has to be done. And right now, the variation in requirements from state to state is a disgrace. For example, New York's pre-fight medical requirements include a physical examination, an MRI, an EKG, a dilated-eye exam, and tests for AIDS, hepatitis B, and hepatitis C. But some states require only a general physical examination.

"I hear all sorts of excuses from some commissions as to why proper pre-fight testing can't be done," Schwartz says. "It's too expensive. They can't afford it. It would require an act of the state legislature or a change in their regulatory code. In my view, pre-fight medical tests should be paid for by a federal commission and there should be approved medical centers in each state where fighters can go for the tests. And say what you want, without a strong federal commission dictating minimum medical requirements, standardized pre-fight testing will never happen."

As for which fighters should be allowed to step into the ring, Schwartz observes, "Right now, each state has a different set of standards, and it's a problem. Riddick Bowe is allowed to fight in some jurisdictions and not in others. As a kid, I used to love going to the annual 'Old-Timers' game at Yankee Stadium. The problem with old-timers competing in boxing is that someone can die. If Riddick Bowe applied for a license to fight in a jurisdiction where I was in charge, I'd turn him down. And I applaud the stand that the New York State Athletic Commission took with regard to Evander Holyfield. It would be great if the ABC found a way to standardize these things, but it hasn't and it won't. The only way to do it is through a federal commission with teeth."

There are many examples of the vagaries of fate regarding the state-by-state variation in medical standards. But none is more telling than the case of Joe Mesi.

As virtually everyone in boxing now knows, Mesi suffered at least one subdural hematoma (bleeding on the surface of his brain) as a consequence of his March 13, 2004, fight against Vassiliy Jirov in Las Vegas. After the bout, he complained of a headache and said he couldn't remember the last two rounds of the fight. Then, at the post-fight press conference, he declared, "I got hit on the back of the head. The back of my head is killing me. The last two rounds were a wash. I don't have any recollection of the last round-and-a-half."

"After a fight," says Michael Schwartz, "if a kid has a headache, we watch him a bit. Then, if the headache is preoccupying him or if he has a headache and can't remember what happened during the fight, we get him scanned."

That didn't happen with Joe Mesi. Jeff Davidson, who was the doctor assigned to Mesi's dressing room, recalls, "I was present in Joe's dressing room after the fight. At no time did he indicate that he wanted to go to the emergency room or give any indication that he needed to go. I asked if he was experiencing any problems. He said he was hurt on the spot of his head where he got hit, but he never complained of a headache, nausea, dizziness, neck pain, eye problems. All I can tell you is what he told me when we were together in that room. I can only say that I spoke to Joe Mesi and his camp for twenty minutes plus, and he had none of those symptoms."

If Mesi had been sent to the hospital for an MRI on fight night, the subdural hematoma would have been discovered and treated immediately and a lot of the subterfuge that followed would never have occurred. Be that as it may, Stuart Campbell (the attorney who represents Mesi in his dealings with the Nevada commission) says that he has no criticism of the way commission doctors handled the situation on fight night. However, Campbell has been at odds with the NSAC on other issues.

Section 467.017(3) of the Nevada Administrative Code states, "The commission will not issue or renew a license to engage in unarmed combat to an applicant who has suffered a cerebral hemorrhage." In addition, Section 467.562 (1) of the code declares, "A licensee who is determined by the examining physician to be unfit to compete must be suspended until it is shown that he is fit for further competition."

Mesi has been indefinitely suspended by the NSAC pursuant to these provisions. At first, his representatives denied that he had suffered a cerebral hematoma. Then, after the results of five post-fight MRIs were leaked to the media, Team Mesi acknowledged that there had been "a little bleed." Meanwhile, the Mesi camp refused to comply with a commission demand that it produce all medical documents generated subsequent to the Jirov fight, a list of all doctors with whom Mesi consulted, and an affidavit stating that the submission was complete.

In most instances, when a fighter is suspended by one state, he's free to fight in another jurisdiction. The one type of suspension that, under the Muhammad Ali Boxing Reform Act, must be honored by all ABC jurisdictions is a medical suspension. Thus, with the Nevada commission holding firm, the Mesi camp relented and sent what it says are all of the required documents to the NSAC. In all likelihood, the commission's Medical Advisory Board will hold a hearing in late February and make a recommendation regarding whether or not Mesi should be licensed to fight. Then the five members of the commission will vote on the matter.

In addition to exploring various legal theories and gathering medical evidence, the Mesi camp has mounted a massive publicity campaign on its fighter's behalf. On January 11, 2005, the City of Buffalo Common Council passed a resolution supporting Mesi's efforts to have his suspension lifted. There was a column written by Joe for the *Buffalo News*, an article in *ESPN Magazine* featuring a visit by Joe to his mother's grave, a televised segment on *Outside The Lines*, and more.

In all likelihood, if the Nevada commission refuses to lift Mesi's suspension, a lawsuit will be filed. A related case is already in the New York courts, where Mesi is suing the Physicians Imaging Center of Western New York, two doctors at the center, and the New York State Athletic Commission, alleging that the center improperly released the results of five MRIs to the New York commission without Mesi's consent and that the NYSAC improperly disseminated those records to the media. This, according to the complaint, led to Mesi being damaged by way of "public scorn, humiliation, emotional suffering, financial loss in the nature of decreased endorsement opportunities and/or available purses, suspension of the ability to keep and maintain a boxing license, and other derivative damages."

Even if the law was broken by the release of Mesi's medical records, the legal damages appear to be minimal. Once records are submitted to the Nevada State Athletic Commission and are the subject of a hearing, they become a matter of public record under Nevada law. So the truth would have come out anyway—unless, of course, it was improperly concealed.

"It's not that we were denied an opportunity to conceal," Donald Chiari (Mesi's attorney) said shortly after the lawsuit was filed. "We were denied the opportunity to present a complete picture. We believe that, because of what happened, not only from the leakage of the information but also what the media did with that information, it has added extra pressure on the [Nevada] commission with respect to any decision they make. You have a situation where medical records were leaked out and disseminated before the Mesis had an opportunity to fully explore the medical condition. We believe that ultimately tainted the public, the media, and maybe even the way the Nevada commission will rule on this case."

Nevada's chief deputy attorney general Keith Kizer is overseeing certain aspects of the Mesi matter for the NSAC. "Right now," says Kizer, "as far as we're concerned, it's a medical issue, not a legal one."

Either way, the case of Joe Mesi demonstrates the need for uniform medical standards. If Mesi had been injured in any state other than Nevada (or New York), he'd probably be back in the ring by now. In fact, one of the things the Mesi camp has suggested is that the Nevada commission refuse to license Joe but lift his suspension so he would be free to fight elsewhere.

After all, it's not unheard of for a fighter to suffer a subdural hematoma and fight again. Stephan Johnson is believed to have suffered one in an April 14, 1999, loss to Fitz Vanderpool in Toronto and then returned to score victories over Otilio Villarreal and Calvin Moody. Of course, in his third fight back, Johnson was knocked out by Paul Vaden on November 20, 1999, and died several days later without regaining consciousness.

And then there's light-heavyweight Robert Muhammad, who suffered a subdural hematoma after being knocked out by Marlon Hayes in September 1999. Muhammad was suspended for 18 months but was then allowed to return to the ring. He has lost 21 of his last 22 fights in North Carolina, South Carolina, Florida, Mississippi, and Georgia.

Michael Schwartz is ambivalent about allowing Joe Mesi to return to the ring. The fact that the AAPRP honored Robert Cantu as a "distinguished educator" at its most recent convention was seen by some as endorsing the fighter's position, given the fact that Cantu has been retained by Mesi to testify as an expert witness before the Nevada commission. Still, Schwartz has reservations. "To make a decision," he says, "I'd need more information. But based on what I know today, I probably wouldn't let Joe Mesi fight. You don't want to end a young man's career and take away his ability to earn a living. But either you have standards as to when fighters should be medically allowed to fight or you don't."

The issue, like so many others in boxing, boils down to whether fighters are guided by high standards of medical care or the lowest common denominator. When boxing is run right, it's a scary sport. When it's run wrong, the risks become unacceptable.

Meanwhile, despite the imperfection of his creation, Michael Schwartz has done a huge amount of work forming an organization that never existed before. If ring doctors can fix their own little part of the boxing world, they will have made a significant contribution to the sport.❑

*The case of Marco Antonio Barrera was another matter that focussed attention on the Nevada State Athletic Commission and medical issues.*

# A PASS-FAIL EXAM FOR NEVADA

The Nevada State Athletic Commission is at a crossroads. In the past, the NSAC has been in the forefront of setting medical standards for boxing. It has instituted mandatory MRI testing for fighters. Its medical director (Dr. Margaret Goodman) is the equal of any ringside physician in the world. And the commission has dealt appropriately with important test cases involving boxers like Joe Mesi, Terry Norris, and Augie Sanchez.

But over the past year, there have been signs that normal NSAC medical procedures are being circumvented by a minority of commission members. More specifically, it appears as though ring physicians have been assigned and several fighters have been removed from the suspension list to placate certain promoters.

Now Marco Antonio Barrera is scheduled to fight Erik Morales in Las Vegas on November 27th. Barrera-Morales III is notable for two reasons. First, it's the third installment of a classic trilogy between two superb boxers. And second, Barrera's return to the fight capital of the world will force the Nevada State Athletic Commission to deal with some thorny issues.

One year ago, on October 23, 2003, it was revealed that Marco Antonio Barrera had undergone brain surgery in Mexico City in 1997. The surgery, known as a craniotomy, was related to a congenital defect; not a fight-related injury. Barrera's skull was opened and a group of small malformed blood vessels were removed.

When the above information was made public, Barrera was in training for a November 15, 2003, fight against Manny Pacquiao in San Antonio. His promoter at the time was (and still is) Golden Boy Promotions. On October 24th, Richard Schaefer and Stephen Espinoza (respectively, the CEO and attorney for Golden Boy) issued a statement that read, "Marco's former promoter and manager were fully aware of the procedure. They were each provided with copies of Marco's medical records with the understanding that they would disclose the information to the appropriate parties, including the relevant boxing commissions. When Marco very recently learned that the information had not been timely disclosed, he immediately acted to remedy the situation."

Four days later, Schaefer elaborated on that statement and explained, "About six weeks ago, I got a telephone call telling me about it. Right away, I asked Marco, and he was very up-front with me. He told me everything about his condition and said that, all along, his manager and promoter knew about it. Then we informed the Nevada commission and asked for their guidance and made certain that the commission in Texas knew about it. It should not have taken six years for this to come out."

Thereafter, as part of the process of being licensed to fight in Texas, Barrera underwent a neurological examination by Dr. Andres H. Keichian. In a November 3, 2003, letter to the Texas State Athletic Commission, Dr. Keichian wrote, "The prognosis of this condition in Mr. Barrera is excellent. Based on his clinical history and neurological evaluation, I believe that Mr. Barrera is fit to participate in combative sports. He's completely cleared. We did a special three-dimensional CT-scan of the cranial bone. When the bone does not completely enclose the craniotomy area, then you've got a problem. This is completely closed now. His cavernous angioma; all that is is a dilated blood vessel. This is a dilated vein that had no pressure in it and has been taken away."

Barrera was knocked out by Pacquiao in the eleventh round. He has fought once since then: on June 19th of this year, when he prevailed on a tenth-round stoppage of Paulie Ayala in Los Angeles.

That brings us to the present and Barrera-Morales III.

The first issue to be resolved is whether or not Barrera is fit to fight. Nevada's chief deputy attorney general Keith Kizer (who represents the NSAC) says that the medical advisory board of the Nevada State Athletic Commission will meet to study the matter on October 26th. The board will then either recommend that Barrera be licensed to fight or ask for additional information and testing.

Barrera's situation is different from that of a boxer on the decline in that he is not impaired as a fighter. Nor is it clear that he is significantly more likely than other fighters to suffer bleeding in the brain. Rather, he is at increased risk, the degree of which is hard to quantify. He is also an intelligent man who understands the issues involved.

The danger to Barrera is that, after surgery of this nature, small blood vessels grow around metal implants that have been inserted in the brain to protect the area where the intrusion occurred. If an implant shifts, the vessels tear. In other words, if Barrera is hit with a punch in a way that causes an implant to shift, there is an increased likelihood of bleeding in the brain.

If Barrera were a four-round preliminary fighter, the NSAC probably wouldn't let him fight. But the reality of boxing is that, often in making medical decisions, financial considerations are weighed. A heavyweight championship bout in which a combatant is hurt is allowed to proceed longer than a undercard fight. Also, Barrera has fought eighteen times since his surgery with no apparent ill-effects. This, too, has to be weighed in the decision-making process.

On November 4th, the five-member Nevada State Athletic Commission will meet in open session to act upon the recommendation of its medical advisory board. Barrera is expected to attend that meeting. Most likely, he will be found medically fit to fight.

But there's an issue beyond medical fitness that the NSAC must face: "What action, if any, should it take with regard to the withholding of information and the making of false statements to the commission?"

As previously noted, Barrera has fought eighteen times since his surgery. Ten of these eighteen bouts were in Nevada. In each instance, medical questionnaires were filled out (apparently falsely), signed, and submitted to the commission. Additional questions were asked and answered (again, apparently falsely) at pre-fight physicals.

There is no indication that anyone at the Nevada State Athletic Commission was aware of Barrera's surgery at the time he fought in Nevada. Nor does there appear to have been wrongdoing on the part of his present promoter (Golden Boy Promotions). But someone is to blame.

If Barrera is called to testify, he will probably repeat what Richard Schaefer and Stephen Espinoza have said publicly: that his former promoter and manager were fully aware of the surgery and that they were each provided with copies of his medical records with the understanding that they would disclose the information to the appropriate parties, including the relevant boxing commissions.

At that point, if the NSAC wants to sweep the matter under the rug, it can end its inquiry with the declaration that "only Barrera's license is at issue here; not those of his former manager and former promoter."

But that would be an embarrassment.

Let's spell out what's at stake. The case of Marco Antonio Barrera goes to the heart of the integrity of the process. Someone committed a crime in Nevada. Now is the time for the Nevada State Athletic Commission to conduct a full hearing with testimony under oath from Barrera, his former manager, and his former promoter. Any licensee, past or present, who violated the law should be held accountable.

The manner in which the Nevada State Athletic Commission handles this matter will send a clear signal regarding whether or not the state respects its own high medical standards. If the NSAC doesn't take its own rules and regulations seriously, no one else will either.❑

*This article opened a Pandora's Box in Nevada.*

# FIGHTER SAFETY AND THE
# NEVADA STATE ATHLETIC COMMISSION

Every now and then, a chain of events reveals rot within a respected institution.

In recent years, the Nevada State Athletic Commission has been wrestling with a series of high-profile medical incidents. Through it all, Flip Homansky has been the commission's leading proponent of proper medical care for fighters. Homansky was appointed to the commission five years ago. Prior to that, he served as a ringside physician for two decades.

Homansky pushed for mandatory MRI testing and was in the forefront of the development of the NSAC's steroid and HIV testing policies. His medical expertise combined with his advocacy of good medical care makes him ideally suited for a commission that is dedicated to high medical standards. It also makes him a liability to those who think that properly caring for fighters costs too much and interferes with matchmaking.

Boxing is systemically corrupt. When something in the sweet science doesn't look right, most likely it isn't. Right now, something doesn't look right in Nevada.

On November 4, 2005, Nevada governor Kenny Guinn announced the removal of Homansky from the NSAC. His replacement, Theodore "T.J." Day, is chairman of a Reno-based private-investment firm. Over the years, Day has been a generous contributor to the Republican Party and its candidates. The *Las Vegas Sun* has called him one of "the top individual soft money donors in Nevada."

It's possible that Day will turn out to be a marvelous commissioner who learns the ins and outs of boxing and fights resolutely for high medical standards. However, this is not the time to remove one of the most knowledgeable ring doctors in the United States from the Nevada State Athletic Commission.

From 1933 through 2004, there were ten ring fatalities in Nevada. That's a relatively low number. But since May of this year, four fighters have left the ring in Las Vegas with bleeding in their brain. Leopoldo Gonzalez and William Abelyan survived. Martin Sanchez and Leavander Johnson didn't.

Sanchez was a 26-year-old club fighter from Mexico with 18 wins and 8 losses. He had gone past six rounds only twice in his career. On one of those occasions, he'd been knocked out in round seven. On the other, he lost a unanimous decision to a 2-6-2 fighter.

On July 1, 2005, Sanchez fought Rustam Nugaev at The Orleans in a scheduled ten-round bout. It was his first fight out of Mexico. Sanchez won the early rounds. Then, a minute into round four, he took a blow to the back of the head, turned, walked to a neutral corner, and knelt down, holding the back of his head. There was no count. Referee Kenny Bayless told him, "You got to fight; let's go." After ten seconds on the canvas, Sanchez rose but he was no longer the same fighter. His movement slowed and his punches lost their snap. For the rest of the fight, he took a beating. In round nine, he stopped throwing punches. Finally, two minutes into the round, a left hook put him into the ropes and down for the count.

After the fight, Sanchez sat on his stool for a long time. He did not go to ring center to embrace his opponent. When he finally stood up, it was only for a moment and then he sat down on his stool again. Dr. William Berliner (the lead physician for the night) examined Sanchez in the ring and concluded that he was fine. Chris Tognoni (the commission inspector assigned to the fighter) said later that he was concerned as Sanchez walked to his dressing room because his cornermen seemed to be giving him more than the normal assistance. Promoter Jeff Grmoja later said that Sanchez complained his legs had gone numb. Dr. Jeff Davidson (the #2 physician) then went to the dressing room, examined Sanchez, ordered that he be given a CT-scan, and returned to ringside to watch the final fight. Soon after, Chuck Anzolone (another inspector) noticed that Sanchez was experiencing further loss of control of his legs and called Davidson back to the dressing room. By the time Davidson got there, Sanchez was seizing and his pupils were enlarged. Davidson sent him to him Valley Hospital. Sanchez underwent emergency brain surgery and died the following morning.

In the aftermath of the Sanchez tragedy, NSAC chairman Raymond "Skip" Avansino asked chief deputy attorney general Keith Kizer to "review" the facts surrounding the death. Avansino was very clear and precise in asking "for a review, not an investigation."

On September 6th, Kizer presented his findings at a commission meeting. "As I see this," he said in conclusion, "I don't have any recommendation. I don't see any way to improve." Avansino thanked Kizer for doing "a commendable job" and commissioner Tony Alamo Jr. weighed in with the declaration, "We did everything right, and unfortunately this poor man passed away."

The primary responsibility of the Nevada State Athletic Commission is not to protect itself. It's to properly regulate the sport of boxing. When someone riding on a municipal transit system is killed in an accident, the government agency that operates the system conducts a full and honest inquiry into the cause of death. That's the best way to improve operating procedures and employee performance.

Keith Kizer is a capable attorney, but one wonders whether his "review" assignment was to search out the truth regardless of consequences. To some, his report to the NSAC seemed like a brief prepared by defense counsel on behalf of the commission and its personnel, not a serious look at the facts.

For starters, Sanchez's NSAC medical forms were not fully filled out and were never signed by the fighter. There are also questions regarding actions taken and not taken during and immediately following the fight.

Dr. Berliner acknowledged at the September 6th meeting that neither he nor Dr. Davidson (who was assigned to Sanchez's corner) saw any need to examine the fighter between rounds. Given Sanchez's strange behavior after he was hit on the back of the head in round four and the subsequent deterioration of the fighter's skills, that judgment is open to question. Moreover, since neither Berliner nor Davidson speaks Spanish, did either one of them really know what Sanchez was saying in the ring after the fight?

There are also issues regarding the timeline for Sanchez complaining about numbness in his legs, his appearing unfocused and disoriented, his seizing, and being transported to the hospital. Who was told, when were they told, and what were they told? After the decision was made that Sanchez should have a CT-scan, was he at any time not attended to by a paramedic or NSAC physician? And why was Sanchez sent to Valley Hospital instead of a level-1 trauma center such as the University Medical Center or Sunrise Hospital?

The above questions are asked with the benefit of hindsight. But another issue raised (and quickly buried) at the September 6th commission meeting has been a problem in Nevada and elsewhere for a long time.

It's a dirty little secret in boxing that some Mexican fighters are exploited by a system that allows them to step into a boxing ring without the medical safeguards required by law. Sanchez supposedly was given an MRI and other tests in Tijuana on June 29th on his way from Mexico City to Las Vegas.

Maybe he was. But there's a lot of talk these days about phony medicals for fighters who come to the United States from Mexico. Thus, at the September 6th NSAC meeting, Flip Homansky declared, "The data from Mexico is very difficult to substantiate. There are mills where one can get a result for an MRI without having taken one. The data that comes from Mexico is at times very suspect."

There are three lawyers on the Nevada State Athletic Commission. Once Homansky made his comment, one might have expected a follow-up question to Keith Kizer along the lines of, "Have you examined the integrity of the pre-fight medicals on Martin Sanchez that were forwarded to the commission?"

Except the question wasn't asked. Instead, Tony Alamo Jr. proclaimed, "It's a slippery slope when we start dictating which diagnostic center is worthy." Then the commission moved on to other matters.

Homansky's comments with regard to phony medicals made it clear that he would not sit silently through medical charades in the months ahead. As he himself said, "Every ring death is a blow to the sport. But the greater tragedy is if we don't try to understand what happened and how to prevent it from happening again."

Then came another trauma. On September 17th, IBF lightweight champion Leavander Johnson fought Jesus Chavez in the opening bout of HBO's pay-per-view telecast of a fight card featuring Marco Antonio Barrera versus Robbie Peden at the MGM Grand. Johnson took a beating. On two occasions during the fight, ring doctor Margaret Goodman visited his corner and found him alert with no sign of neurological damage. After the tenth round, she told referee Tony Weeks to keep a close eye on the fighter and not let him take too much more punishment.

Thirty-eight seconds into round eleven, Weeks stopped the fight. Again, Dr. Goodman examined Johnson and found him alert with no sign of neurological damage. On the way back to his dressing room, Johnson began dragging his leg. Goodman was told and instructed Al Capanna (a neurosurgeon) to go to the dressing room and care for the fighter. Capanna immediately accompanied Johnson to the University Medical Center in an ambulance. Forty minutes after first showing neurological symptoms, Johnson was in surgery for treatment of a subdural hematoma. He died five days later.

One can draw distinctions between the deaths of Martin Sanchez and Leavander Johnson. Dr. Goodman examined Johnson twice between rounds. After the fight, Johnson was alert and responsive and did not linger on his stool. Unlike Sanchez, Johnson spoke English so there was no problem in communication between the fighter and ring doctor.

Johnson was not left without a doctor at any time after showing neurological symptoms and he was taken to a level-1 trauma center. Also, there is no question regarding the integrity of Johnson's pre-fight medical tests.

Thus, Jim Lampley, who was HBO's blow-by-blow commentator for Johnson-Chavez, declares, "Some ring tragedies are avoidable; others aren't. If you can't live with Leavander Johnson's death, you ban boxing."

Still, both Martin Sanchez and Leavander Johnson are dead. And on September 23rd, after consulting with Governor Guinn, Avansino announced the formation of an advisory committee on boxer health and safety to review the NSAC's medical guidelines and recommend changes to better protect fighters in the ring.

The committee consists of three former NSAC chairmen (Sig Rogich, Luther Mack, and James Nave), state assemblyman Harvey Munford, and Dr. Charles Ruggeroli (a cardiologist). Rogich has been designated as chairman. The committee's findings are due on or before April 1, 2006.

Meanwhile, in some quarters, there is skepticism. "If the committee is about how to improve fighter safety," asks Allan Scotto, "why is it being chaired by a public relations expert? Why bring back three former commissioners? If they were going to do something about fighter safety, why didn't they do it when they had the power to do it? A cardiologist? With all due respect, when was the last time a fighter died of a heart attack in the ring? Since fighters are dying of subdural hematomas, why is a top-notch neurologist conspicuously excluded from this committee?"

Scotto might have added that Flip Homansky, who would have been an extraordinary asset to the committee, was by-passed in the selection process.

When the committee gets down to brass tacks, it must start with the underlying reality that boxers hurt each other on purpose. Except in rare instances, a fighter doesn't want to seriously injure his opponent. But he does want to knock him unconscious or cut him badly enough that the fight is stopped. Everything that takes place in a boxing ring is based on that premise.

Nevada has several outstanding ring doctors, foremost among them, Margaret Goodman. Goodman has worked fights for eleven years. In May 2004, she was designated as the NSAC's chief ringside physician. That job, when done properly, involves a Herculean effort. Goodman has a private practice as a neurologist but she was available to the commission seven days a week. She was constantly on the phone, reviewing medical reports, studying tapes of fighters, drafting letters, reviewing suspension lists, and talking with commission officials in the performance of a job that wasn't even her livelihood.

However, Goodman found herself fighting an uphill battle and too often was denied the authority to properly care for fighters. On July 26, 2005, she resigned in frustration as chief ringside physician because of the failure of the commission to enforce its own medical rules and regulations. It's fitting that, in her last fight as chief ringside physician, she intervened after ten rounds to stop Wayne McCullough from taking further punishment at the hands of Oscar Larios in a July 16th championship bout.

"I think we need to re-evaluate the system from top to bottom," Goodman said recently. "Maybe we can't find the answer, but it's something that has to be done and done very quickly. We need to re-evaluate the entire way we approach the testing and treatment of boxers. These kids trust their lives to us, and we're failing them."

Discussions with medical personnel and others in the sweet science make it clear that the NSAC advisory committee on boxer health and safety should address the following issues:

(1) Some of Nevada's ring doctors are inadequately trained and have questionable judgment. It's not enough to simply be a doctor and show up on the night of a fight.

(2) The NSAC critiques the performance of referees and judges after each fight. Shouldn't it do the same with ring doctors? For example, there is a widespread perception that, when a fighter is unconscious and seizing in the ring, he should be given oxygen. Yet Jeremy Williams was unconscious for almost three minutes and suffered two seizures in the ring after he was knocked out by Samuel Peter last December, and oxygen wasn't administered. "What's particularly upsetting about that," says Dr. Goodman, "is that I was instructed to not sit down with the doctor in question and discuss the situation with him afterward. So what happens the next time a fighter is unconscious and seizing on the canvas?"

(3) Too often, medical suspensions in Nevada are adjusted to accommodate a particular manager or promoter.

(4) There is a mentality in Nevada and elsewhere that "the show must go on." That's true of both club fights and major bouts. There are a lot of reasons (most of them economic) for allowing a mega-fight to proceed even though problems arise at a fighter's pre-fight physical. But other than Tommy Morrison testing positive for HIV in Las Vegas and Henry Akinwande testing positive for hepatitis in New York, how many times has a major fight been called off by a state athletic commission for medical reasons? Or

phrased differently, if Vitali Klitschko hadn't pulled out of his bout against Hasim Rahman, does anyone seriously think that an NSAC doctor would have told him, "Gee, you have a problem with your knee. You can't fight on Saturday night." At a minimum, let's have an honest dialogue on this issue.

(5) At least one NSAC doctor regularly treats and writes prescriptions for unarmed combatants in Nevada in violation of state law.

(6) Certain medical tests are sometimes not given to "protected" fighters in Nevada.

(7) Required pre- and post-fight NSAC medical forms are often not filled out properly or signed by the fighter.

(8) The NSAC does nothing to regulate gyms. That means Al Cole, who has been placed on administrative suspension by the New York State Athletic Commission because of his deteriorating skills, can work as a sparring partner in Nevada and get punched in the head on a regular basis by Samuel Peter.

(9) The NSAC often licenses unfit fighters and allows mismatches to take place. These fights might not lead directly to death, but they're responsible for much of the longterm brain damage sustained by fighters. The October 28th bout between Tye Fields and Bruce Seldon is an example of a fight that should not have happened. Seldon was stopped in the first round by Mike Tyson in 1996, courtesy of what some observers thought was a phantom punch. He returned to the ring in 2004 and hadn't fought since being knocked out by Gerald Nobles seventeen months ago. Seldon weighed 219 pounds when he fought Tyson. For Fields, he tipped the scales at 262. He was knocked out in the second round, after which Jesse Reid (Fields's trainer) said that Seldon "quit like a dog." John Bailey, a NSAC commissioner, expressed dissatisfaction with Seldon's effort and declared, "He won't fight here again as far as I'm concerned." Bailey also said that it was "a close call" as to whether Seldon should receive his $10,000 purse. That's hypocrisy. Seldon did exactly what he was expected to do.

(10) A significant percentage of fighters who compete in Nevada speak only Spanish. If the ring doctor doesn't speak Spanish, there should be a translator in the corner and in the dressing room afterward. And that doesn't mean a trainer or manager who will say that the fighter is "fine" whether he is or not.

(11) The NSAC accepts out-of-state medicals that it has reason to believe are phony. This is part and parcel of a larger problem in

that the commission knowingly accepts false bout agreements and other false documents that are filed by promoters. Under Nevada law, a person who knowingly procures or offers a false document for filing in any public office is guilty of a category C felony punishable by a minimum of one year and a maximum of five years in prison.

(12) The NSAC has failed to thoroughly examine several serious medical incidents, when a real inquiry might have led to greater understanding by the physicians involved and improved medical protocols for the commission.

It's very difficult for a state athletic commission to properly handle all of the medical issues that arise in boxing. Part of the problem lies with the fighters and their camps. When a fighter undergoes his pre-fight physical, he rarely acknowledges injuries sustained in sparring or otherwise. Also, there are many unanswered questions with regard to what causes a subdural hematoma and other forms of brain damage. Clearly, it's not just the force of the blow. If it were, fighters like Mike Tyson and George Foreman would have a string of fatalities on their record.

Also, it should be noted that Nevada is not alone in being plagued by the above-referenced issues. But the Nevada State Athletic Commission is uniquely suited to find answers to these and other questions and properly regulate the medical aspects of boxing. Unlike most states, Nevada derives a huge amount of revenue from boxing. The resources are there to do the job right. But as Greg Sirb (past president of the Association of Boxing Commissions and director of the Pennsylvania Athletic Commission) recently observed, "Pennsylvania regulates a sport; Nevada regulates a business." To that, one can add the thoughts of Kevin Iole, who wrote last month in the *Las Vegas Review Journal*, "For years, the state's elected officials have ignored the issue of boxer safety."

As if to prove Iole's point, Governor Guinn made his contribution to the debate last week when he removed Flip Homansky from the Nevada State Athletic Commission. It's unlikely that Dr. Homansky's replacement will push as aggressively (and it certainly won't be as knowledgeably) for the enforcement of rules and regulations and new medical initiatives to protect fighters. But that's what happens in an environment where some people are more concerned with power politics than they are with health and safety.

There have to be standards; even in boxing and even in Nevada.□

*ESPN has the power and infrastructure to become a major player in boxing. So what happens next?*

# THE FUTURE OF BOXING AT ESPN

Late last year (2004), ESPN and Main Events announced a ten-month partnership that called for Main Events to promote seven regular *Friday Night Fights* telecasts, three fight cards on "special" dates, and two pay-per-view shows.

The deal is central to a two-part ESPN strategy. Part one is to maintain its *Friday Night Fights* franchise. As such, boxing will be seen weekly on ESPN2 from January through August of 2005 with occasional nights off for events such as the women's NCAA basketball championship tournament. Then, in deference to college football, the sweet science will disappear from the screen until January 2006. ESPN is also planning a ten-fight Tuesday night package for summer 2005.

Part two of the strategy is potentially more significant. ESPN views its deal with Main Events as an investment in building a pay-per-view boxing program. The network will start with two PPV shows this year. The ten "free" Main Events cards are intended to build a fan base for the pay-per-view telecasts.

ESPN is the sleeping giant in boxing. One reason the sport has failed to attract corporate support (i.e. advertising for broadcast television) is its unsavory image. But another is the make-up of its fans. Young men and women between the ages of 18 and 34 are a key advertising demographic. But boxing attracts mostly male viewers over the age of 40.

ESPN is hoping that it can do for boxing what it did for Extreme Sports. The theory is, if television can turn poker into a significant viewing attraction, it should be able to the same for fisticuffs.

Can ESPN make boxing "cool"? For starters, it has a direct pipeline to young sports fans, many of whom don't think an event is important unless they've seen it on *SportsCenter*. But more to the point, ESPN has:

- Basic cable with a wide reach—Right now, ESPN and ESPN2 are in 86,000,000 homes. By contrast, HBO is in 28,000,000 homes and Showtime is in 14,000,000.
- Additional cable channels in the form of ESPN News, ESPN

Desportes, and ESPN Classic.
- A sophisticated international distribution network.
- A national radio network, ESPN Radio, with more than 500 affiliates.
- A major print outlet, *ESPN The Magazine*.
- A go-to sports website, ESPN.com.

As a subsidiary of Disney, ESPN also has synergy with ABC, a broadcast television network.

HBO and Showtime have most of the same elements in place. TimeWarner and Viacom (their respective parent corporations) are diversified entertainment conglomerates. But sports is a small part of what HBO and Showtime are about. ESPN, by contrast, has sports in its DNA. It's a network with a dedicated mandate for sports.

In sum, ESPN has the potential to become a dominant player in boxing. HBO Sports president Ross Greenburg acknowledges as much when he says, "ESPN has a lot of marketing muscle. They'll be a force if they want to."

A rising tide lifts all boats. Thus, a major commitment to boxing by ESPN is potentially the best thing that could happen to the sport. HBO and Showtime preach to the converted with their boxing telecasts. ESPN has the power to create new fans.

However, early indications are that things might not go smoothly. One reason for that is the feast or famine license-fee structure that ESPN has implemented.

ESPN is paying a huge amount of money to Main Events. Network executives won't reveal the price tag for the twelve-fight package. But reliable sources say there's a $6,000,000 floor, and the rumor-mill has license fees running higher. Either way, one would expect ESPN to get competitive fights between world-class boxers for its investment. Instead, there have been too many match-ups between shot fighters and Main Events "stars."

The key fighters in the ESPN-Main Events package when it was announced last October were Rocky Juarez, Juan Diaz, Dominick Guinn, and Kermit Cintron. Juarez, Diaz, and Guinn (along with Jeff Lacy, Francisco Bojado, and Malik Scott) were part of a deal that was struck between Main Events and Showtime after the 2000 Olympics. That deal turned out so poorly for Showtime that the network walked away from it when it could.

To date, the Main Events shows on ESPN have been:

- November 5, 2004—Juan Diaz versus Julian Lorcy (a shot

fighter) and Jorge Lacierva versus Armando Guerrero (Guerrero, the house fighter, got a gift draw).

• December 3, 2004—Rocky Juarez versus Guty Espadas (a shot fighter) and Dominick Guinn versus Sergei Lyakovich (Guinn barely extended himself and lost).

• January 21, 2005—Juan Diaz versus Billy Irwin (a shot fighter) and Calvin Brock versus Clifford Etienne (a shot fighter).

• February 18, 2005—Antonio Margarito versus Sebastian Lujan (a ten-round infomercial for ESPN's upcoming pay-per-view tele-cast; more on that later) and Joshua Clottey versus Steven Martinez (a two-round "no contest" terminated by an accidental head butt).

• March 4, 2005—Rocky Juarez versus Juan Carlos Ramirez (0 wins in 3 world title fights) and Jorge Lacierva versus Cruz Carbajal (this time, Lacierva's corner threw in the towel after six rounds).

Kudos to Main Events for getting the deal. The promoter pulled off another (albeit less profitable) coup when it entered into a contract with NBC for three shows in 2003 and five in 2004. But there's an uncomfortable suspicion in some circles that ESPN could have gotten twice the product for half the price.

The key people at ESPN in structuring, approving, and implementing boxing programming are John Wildhack (senior vice president, programming), Jim Noel (vice president, business affairs and programming), Matt Murphy (senior vice president, broadband and interactive sales), Radame Rodriguez (sports director for boxing), and Doug Loughery (a program planner with primary responsibility for green-lighting specific match-ups).

Murphy and Noel say that they talked with many people in the industry before finalizing their deal with Main Events but that ESPN didn't negotiate with other prospective promoters. "We sat down with a clean slate in our discussions with Main Events," says Murphy. "And we recognized quickly that they shared a similar vision. Main Events was willing to be flexible, and together we created a new business model."

"The plan," Noel adds, "is for *Friday Night Fights* to build awareness of the new generation of stars that we expect to emerge in the sport. What comes next flows from there."

But are Rocky Juarez, Juan Diaz, Kermit Cintron, and Dominick Guinn really the new generation of stars? Juarez isn't the next Julio Cesar Chavez; Diaz isn't the next Pernell Whitaker; Cintron isn't the next Oscar De La Hoya; and Guinn isn't the next Evander Holyfield.

"This is a shortterm deal," says Main Events CEO Kathy Duva. "It ends in August. If we don't deliver what ESPN wants, they won't make another deal with us, so we have every intention of giving them good value and good fights."

Still, it's a truism in boxing that promoters react to television executives who have money the way a shark responds to blood. And Main Events has taken a gargantuan-sized bite out of ESPN's boxing budget. The result is that, while Main Events is being well-compensated, ESPN is paying a woefully inadequate $15,000 license fee for most of its other *Friday Night Fights* cards. And as a consequence, there are times when ESPN accepts horrible fights.

The February 4, 2005, show is a case in point. The first of two co-featured bouts that night was Dale Brown versus Shelby Gross. Brown is a competent cruiserweight. Gross, a former toughman competitor, isn't. The first words that ESPN commentator Teddy Atlas spoke on the telecast were, "We have a responsibility here to bring the most competitive fights to our fans. And we also have the responsibility—and I was hired for that—to tell the truth when we don't think that's happening. I don't think that's happening right now. I do not think this is the most competitive match we can put out there."

Atlas is one of the best things that ESPN has going for it. And as Brown versus Gross unfolded, his candor served viewers well. "Right now," Atlas acknowledged, "although I'm trying my best not to use this word—'carrying'—there, I used it; I get the feeling that Brown is playing a bit with an overmatched opponent. I don't see full force on all those punches by Brown. Watch! Just watch and see if Brown is following through on punches or maybe he's taking something off the fastball."

Finally, at the bell ending round three, Brown knocked Gross down. "You know what," Atlas exclaimed. "I got to say this. It was almost like Brown did it by accident."

The commentary continued at the start of round four: "If Brown wants this to be the last round, this will be the last round. It's totally in the hands of Brown. I respect the heart of Gross, but I recognize the incompetence."

There were two knockdowns in round four. In round five, Atlas observed, "Brown's throwing hard punches now. I would be shocked if this fight goes beyond this round."

Two seconds later, a left hook put Gross down for the fourth time.

"Those were the first punches that I really saw thrown with bad intentions," Atlas noted.

Seconds later, there was a fifth-knockdown and the fight was over.

The issue here isn't whether or not Dale Brown carried Shelby Gross.

It's why ESPN chose to televise the bout to begin with. What is the logic behind establishing a pool of at least $6,000,000 for twelve shows and then starving everyone else with a $15,000 license fee?

The weekly *Friday Night Fights* cards are the lifeblood of boxing at ESPN. They're also where the initial pool of buyers for ESPN's pay-per-view telecasts will come from. In today's market, ESPN could take $6,000,000 and televise forty shows with world-class fighters in competitive fights. And the irony of it is that the first four Main Events telecasts have drawn lower ratings than ESPN's other fights during the same period. The Main Events shows have been Juan Diaz versus Julian Lorcy (.38 rating), Rocky Juarez versus Guty Espadas (.59), Juan Diaz versus Billy Irwin (.59), and Antonio Margarito versus Sebastian Lujan (.58). That's a .54 average.

The non-Main-Events shows have been Teddy Reid versus Eddie Sanchez (.55), Edner Cherry versus Ricky Quiles (.61), Laila Ali versus Cassandra Geigger (.79), and Terry Smith versus Fernely Feliz (.71). That's an average .67 rating.

All of this, of course, is a lead-in to the April 23, 2005, pay-per-view telecast that ESPN is planning with Main Events. The first thing to be said about that show is that it features four interesting fights: Antonio Margarito versus Kermit Cintron for the WBO 147-pound title; Juan Diaz against Ebo Elder for the WBA 135-pound title; Shane Mosley at welterweight versus David Estrada; and a heavyweight match-up between Jameel McCline and Calvin Brock.

ESPN won't make a prediction regarding the number of buys it expects. But Jim Noel says, "The Main Events deal has a longterm strategy of building storylines that we believe will pay off in the pay-per-view arena." And Matt Murphy promises, "When we do these fights, we're going to put all of the resources of ESPN behind them.

But will that be enough for success?

ESPN's pay-per-view programming to date has consisted largely of two college sports packages: *Game Plan* (football) and *Full Court* (basketball). Neither of these endeavors is anything like pay-per-view boxing. Moreover, a word of caution is in order for anyone who thinks that pay-per-view boxing is a pot of gold within easy reach. It's not. Sometimes a lot of revenue is generated; but most of it goes to local cable-system operators, the fighters, and promoters. There's a reason that Showtime has largely abandoned the pay-per-view boxing business.

Also, the prevailing logic in boxing is that a strong undercard might sell tickets on site, but does little to engender pay-per-view buys. For that, a strong main event is necessary. Antonio Margarito versus Kermit Cintron is a very good fight, but it's not a strong pay-per-view main event. And keep in mind, Margarito-Cintron is for the WBO welter-weight title. The real welterweight champion is Zab Judah. Diaz-Elder is for the WBA lightweight belt. But the best 135-pound fighters in the world are Diego Corrales and Jose Luis Castillo.

Nor is ESPN a magic bullet for engendering pay-per-view buys. People won't shell out big bucks for a fight just because it's promoted on *SportsCenter*. HBO buys ads and gets editorial coverage for fights on *SportsCenter*. Weigh-ins for major bouts are timed for live coverage on ESPN. Over the years, there have been tremendous promotional plans for pay-per-view fights that have fared poorly. That's because good marketing can make a big fight bigger, but it can't make a small fight big.

Pay-per-view buys are engendered city by city, market by market, publicity event by publicity event. When Don King promotes a pay-per-view card, he's on the telephone with dozens of radio stations every day in the days leading up to the fight. Who will work the phones for ESPN's April 23rd pay-per-view telecast?

Mark Taffet (HBO's pay-per-view boxing expert and probably the most knowledgeable person in the business) tells a tale that's instructive. When HBO launched TVKO, its first pay-per-view show featured Evander Holyfield against George Foreman. That fight, on April 19, 1991, engendered 1,400,000 buys. Three weeks later, TVKO televised its second show: a middleweight championship bout pitting Michael Nunn against James Toney. HBO knew that there would be a substantial decline in buys, but even the most pessimistic prognosticators were stunned. Nunn-Toney did a meager 19,000 buys.

The lesson that TVKO learned was simple. Fight fans can be very discriminating when asked to pay for a product. In Taffet's words, "Pay-per-view can be a very unforgiving business. A handful of fights are major attractions. Most aren't. There are fights that are worth the consumer's time, and there are events that are worthy of the consumer's money. The difference at the cash register, as we learned, is not subtle."

When ESPN decided that it wanted to be a player in the National Football League, it went out and bought an NFL package. It did the same thing with Major League Baseball and every other sport it has coveted. If the network wants to become a major player in boxing, it will.

But April 23rd could be a humbling experience for ESPN with regard to its ability (or lack thereof) to drive pay-per-view buys. Right now, the network is spending a lot of money on boxing. Whether it's doing so wisely or not is another matter. ❑

*On occasion, I've been critical of Bob Arum. But he deserves credit where credit is due.*

# NOBODY DOES IT BETTER:
# BOB ARUM AND BUILDING A FIGHTER

Building a boxing superstar is a long arduous process with no easy road to success. Bill Cayton built fighters brilliantly from a manager's perch; most notably, Mike Tyson. Main Events shepherded Evander Holyfield's rise to glory. Lou DiBella is trying to do the same with Jermain Taylor. But nobody has built superstars from scratch more consistently than Bob Arum.

Arum's latest project is WBO junior-welterweight champion Miguel Cotto. A native of Puerto Rico, Cotto turned pro four years ago. He has 23 wins, no losses, and 19 knockouts. This Saturday (June 11, 2005), Cotto will step into the ring at Madison Square Garden to face Mohammad Abdullaev, who defeated him in the first round of the 2000 Olympics en route to 141-pound gold medal.

June 11th is one of the foundation stones in Arum's plan to make Cotto a mega-attraction. The fight will take place hours before New York's Puerto Rican Day Parade. There will be a large pro-Cotto crowd at the Garden. If all goes as planned, the electric atmosphere will be apparent to those watching on television. That, in turn, will create more Cotto fans. For some promoters, this would be the event of a lifetime. For Arum, it's par for the course.

Arum was born on December 8, 1931, in the Crown Heights section of Brooklyn. He graduated from New York University in 1953 and Harvard Law School in 1956. Six years later, he was working as an attorney in the tax division of the United States Attorney's Office in Manhattan when Floyd Patterson defended his title against Sonny Liston. Arum was given the assignment of impounding revenue from the fight's closed-circuit television outlets. He had never seen a fight before, but he could count and the numbers impressed him.

Arum left government service in 1965 and was introduced to Muhammad Ali by football great Jim Brown. Before long, he was promoting Ali's fights under the promotional banner of Main Bouts.

Thereafter, he mastered the complexities of closed-circuit television, which was the forerunner of pay-per-view. At one time or another, he has promoted Ali, George Foreman, Joe Frazier, Larry Holmes, Marvin Hagler, Roberto Duran, Thomas Hearns, Ray Leonard, Alexis Arguello, Carlos Monzon, James Toney, Erik Morales, Floyd Mayweather Jr., Bernard Hopkins, and Oscar De La Hoya.

Arum says that his essential strength as a promoter is that he's a good administrator. But his abilities go beyond that. He's a savvy businessman; he's smart; he knows what he's doing in boxing. And he's a real promoter, not just a middle-man money manager.

Building a superstar starts with talent. It's essential to have a special fighter and to know what the fighter is ready for at all points in his career. That means the foundation of building a fighter is matchmaking.

Arum has always had good matchmakers. It's no accident that, during their rise to prominence, Cotto and other Top Rank stars have shared the common denominator of fighting smaller opponents with credible names who were a bit past their prime.

Arum is also good at turning big fights into bigger events. Years ago, fighters were built for a national audience. Now superstars are built largely for boxing fans with disposable income who buy shows on pay-per-view. The key here is planning.

"One of Bob's strengths as a promoter is his insistence on having a longterm plan for his flagship fighters," says HBO senior vice president Mark Taffet. "Bob rarely comes in to discuss just one fight. It's always a 12-to-24-month plan with each fight serving as a building block to the next one. Everything is a progression. And Bob's fighters don't call out other fighters. They wait for other fighters to come to them."

Former HBO Sports president Seth Abraham concurs, noting, "Bob comes in, and he has looked at the competition in his fighter's weight class and also the weight classes above and below. He has analyzed the natural constituency for his fighter as the starting point for building a fan base. He always has a roadmap. "Also," adds Abraham, "most promoters promote the same way every time. Bob was the most innovative promoter I dealt with in all my years in boxing."

Once Arum has a plan, he assembles the pieces well. He has the money to finance what has to be done and the staff to implement it. Putting Miguel Cotto in Madison Square Garden the night before the Puerto Rican Day Parade might seem like a no-brainer. But Arum did it where another promoter might have failed.

It's harder to build fighters today than in the past because the broadcast networks have abandoned boxing. But for decades, Arum has employed longterm relationships with cable networks to benefit his promotional empire. *Top Rank Boxing*, which ran on ESPN from 1980 through 1995, was the longest-running weekly boxing series in television history. In recent years, Arum's ties to Telemundo and Univision have helped him develop Hispanic fighters.

Moreover, as Richard Schaefer (chief executive officer of Golden Boy Promotions) acknowledges, "Bob knows how to leverage his credibility with the cable networks and the rest of the media as well as anyone in the sport. If Bob says a fighter is a potential superstar, the television networks will take at long look at him."

HBO needs stars; they're at the heart of its programming philosophy. So when Arum comes calling, HBO is often willing to assist him. And strength perpetuates strength. That means Arum can use existing stars to get media exposure for his stars of the future. Almazbek Raiymkulov (now being marketed as "Kid Diamond") is a case in point. Raiymkulov (a 28-year-old lightweight from Kyrgyzstan with a 20-0 record) is fighting Joel Casamayor on HBO's featured undercard bout just prior to Cotto-Abdullaev.

Also, Arum is as good as anyone at the political maneuvering that goes on between promoters and the world sanctioning organizations. He has mastered the art of lobbying compliant state athletic commissions. And he uses every edge possible to extract concessions in television negotiations. He's stubborn, and some say ruthless, in pursuit of his goals. Larry Merchant, whom Arum tried to have fired by HBO, calls him "a brilliant scorpion."

Arum's promotional masterpiece, of course, was Oscar De La Hoya. De La Hoya was ideal clay for a sculptor. Good-looking, charismatic, an Olympic gold-medalist, bilingual, articulate, willing to play the PR game, and a great fighter. But from a commercial point of view, Arum molded the clay perfectly, putting Oscar on display in Los Angeles, Las Vegas, San Antonio, El Paso, Atlantic City, and Madison Square Garden. He promoted him as well as the job could be done; although as Mark Taffet recounts, there were moments of drama.

"We were taping the promos for De La Hoya versus Felix Trinidad in the Valley of Fire, which is in the Nevada desert," Taffet recalls. "It was eleven in the morning. The temperature had already reached 110 degrees. There were snakes slithering around on the ground. Bob had a headdress draped over his head to protect him from the sun. And he was screaming at us, 'This is the dumbest idea in the history of boxing. You're total morons. By two o'clock, we'll all be dead.'"

But Arum stayed through the whole shoot because he wanted to make sure the promo was done right. And in the end, De la Hoya versus Trinidad generated $70,000,000 in pay-per-view revenue stemming from 1,400,000 buys.

Meanwhile, rival promoter Dan Goossen says admiringly, "I've always felt that the greatest job Bob did with a fighter wasn't with De La Hoya. It was the way he built Michael Carbajal. Anyone could have made a star out of Oscar. Did Bob do it well? Absolutely. But Carbajal was a sweet kid without much charisma and a junior-flyweight at a time when no one had ever heard of junior-flyweights. And look what Bob did with him."

Not every fighter that Arum touches turns to gold. Philadelphia middleweight Anthony Thompson seems to be fizzling rather than sizzling. It's hard to promote Floyd Mayweather Jr. as a mega-attraction because, as talented as Floyd is, he has a Tysonesque rap sheet without Tyson's aura of menace and destruction. And in the end, fighters don't necessarily show loyalty to the people who built them. Tyson left Cayton; Holyfield left Main Events; and ultimately, De La Hoya left Arum.

Erik Morales is now Arum's flagship fighter, but more superstars will come his way. Most promoters are beating the bushes for the next great heavyweight; or in Don King's case, heavyweights with a pulse. Since his days with Ali, Arum has flirted with the heavyweight division. Last year, he explored a multi-fight deal with Mike Tyson and might do so again. But in all likelihood, his greatest success will continue to come in the lighter weight divisions. That's where his magic works best.

2005 has been penciled in as the breakout year for Miguel Cotto. He won't be able to make 140 pounds much longer, but there are big fights waiting for him at 147. Floyd Mayweather Jr. and Arturo Gatti could go up in weight. Zab Judah, Shane Mosley, and Antonio Margarito are possibilities. And then there's Oscar. De La Hoya versus Cotto would bring some interesting emotions to the surface.

Let's not forget, though, it remains to be seen whether Cotto has the talent to meet the demands of stardom. At the end of the day, all a promoter can do is give his fighter an opportunity to live up to the hype. The fighter has to deliver.

Meanwhile, tucked away on the undercard of Cotto-Abdullaev is a young man named John Duddy. Duddy is a 25-year-old Irishman who lives in New York. He's handsome and articulate with movie-star charisma. He's also undefeated with nine knockouts in nine pro fights. To round out the storyline, the man who would have been his uncle (had he lived long enough to see John born) was shot to death by the British Army on "Bloody Sunday" in 1972 during a protest march in Derry, Ireland.

Does anyone see a plan?❑

*This ran on Secondsout.com. It's more of a political piece than a boxing article. But Jack Newfield fought long and hard for boxing reform. And as one of his friends wrote to me after the article went online, "Jack would have especially loved it that this was published on a boxing website."*

# JACK NEWFIELD AND GEORGE BUSH

The second inauguration of George W. Bush seems like a good time to remember Jack Newfield, who died of cancer last month.

Jack hated hypocrisy and injustice. The three public arenas of his life were journalism, politics, and boxing. Obviously, there's an abundance of the vices that he abhorred in each. But Jack fought the good fight, and the people he worked with and wrote about were well-represented at his funeral service. Looking around the chapel, I couldn't help but think that many of the mourners seemed considerably older than they had just a week earlier. I thought about how Jack, the columnist, might have covered his own funeral. And my mind turned to our last conversation.

It was on the telephone not long after the November presidential election. "I'm weak; you talk," Jack instructed.

So I did. And the gist of what I said follows.

For many Americans, myself included, the reelection of George Bush feels like 9/11 all over again. It's like a death in the family. Our rulers have retained power by distorting the truth and twisting reality into a grotesque fantasy.

Contrary to some, we don't find George Bush charming as a person. We think he's a smug arrogant little man and we dislike him intensely. But our feelings go far beyond the personal. We're appalled and devastated by how he and his administration are changing our country.

We're horrified at what our government is doing around the world in our name. George Bush deceitfully led the United States into a disastrous unwinnable war in Iraq. Saddam Hussein was a malevolent dictator. But most of us are more worried about North Korea building a nuclear arsenal, the sale of nuclear weapons by remnants of the old Soviet Army, and the sharing of nuclear technology by Pakistan. That's where the greatest nuclear peril lies.

The past was far more confused, the present is far more complex, and the future is far more contingent than people care to realize. But now we have George Bush reducing our soldiers to props by prancing around the deck of an aircraft carrier in a *Top Gun* outfit and carrying a plastic turkey into a mess hall in Baghdad on Thanksgiving Day. We have the prison abuses at Abu Gharib and 380 tons of missing explosives that are being used to cause a never-ending stream of American casualties.

There's nothing brave about middle-aged politicians who have never seen combat sending other people's children to die in battle. Yet this administration attacks the courage and patriotism of any member of the opposition party who questions the war. And the truth is, as the war goes on, our government will be unable to recruit enough soldiers to fight it. Because like Dick Cheney in the Vietnam era, when it comes to fighting in Iraq, most of the people who voted for the war have "other priorities."

What happens when tours of duty can no longer be extended and Donald Rumsfeld runs out of troops? Will George Bush seek to reinstate the military draft? If he does, the Republican Party will lose the youth vote big-time and protests on college campuses will make the Vietnam era look like a church social.

The war, of course, is being fought in the name of combatting terrorism. That leads to another question. Fifteen of the September 11th hijackers were from Saudi Arabia and none were from Iraq. The money to finance 9/11 came from Saudi Arabia, not Iraq. So why did we invade Iraq instead of Saudi Arabia? At the heart of it, of course, is oil. This administration wants access to Iraqi oil in case the flow from Saudi Arabia is interrupted. And as the war goes on, companies like Halliburton are making a nice profit.

Meanwhile, the states that suffered the most grievous losses on 9/11 (New York and New Jersey) voted overwhelmingly for John Kerry. So did our nation's two primary terrorist targets (New York and Washington). Guess which presidential candidate the people whose lives are really on the line thought would do a better job of fighting terrorism?

In terms of economic policy, this is the most reckless administration in the history of America.

The annual budget deficit was reduced to zero under Bill Clinton. When George Bush took office, the ten-year budget projection showed a surplus of six trillion dollars. The Bush Administration has given us an annual budget deficit of $450 billion, and a large part of that is because of irresponsible tax cuts that are skewed in favor of the rich.

Forty percent of the last tax cut went to the richest one percent of the American population. This administration believes in taxing the wages of working people but not income from capital gains or inherited wealth. Many of us who oppose Mr. Bush are well off financially. It would be easy for us to sit back and say, "Okay, we'll inherit more money from our parents and leave more to our children; and when the tax code is further revised, we'll accumulate even more wealth." But we don't want economic inequity to be the hallmark of our society.

At times, it seems as though the Bush Administration has allowed a white-collar-crime lobby to take over America. The lawyers at most major corporations function primarily as defense counsel for senior management. Retirement funds have vanished in a wave of securities fraud.

Meanwhile, the Internal Revenue Service estimates that the federal government loses almost $300 billion dollars to tax evasion each year. Off-shore accounts amount to $70 billion of that total. Yet the Bush Administration hasn't bothered to prosecute 65,000 Americans who have been identified as using offshore accounts to evade taxes. Honest taxpayers are footing the bill for this travesty, just as they pay the bill for sham tax shelters that make profits disappear on paper for tax purposes but don't affect the bottom line that corporations show to investors.

Double the budget for the IRS. Give additional funding to special units empowered to investigate tax shelters and go after off-shore tax havens. Audit all returns of taxpayers with an annual gross income in excess of one million dollars. I guarantee you that each of these steps will be cost-effective. Instead, George Bush has proposed reductions in funding for the IRS.

The Bush Administration, as a matter of course, gives phony economic statistics to Congress to gain the passage of legislation that it supports. It has gutted environmental safeguards in favor of corporate economic interests. In a world where lawyers charge $500 an hour and CEOs are paid millions of dollars annually, it has steadfastly opposed an increase in the minimum wage, which is now $5.15 an hour.

A wage of $5.15 an hour translates into $206 for a forty-hour work week. That's $10,712 a year for loading crates onto a truck. George Bush says that raising the minimum wage would be "bad for the economy."

Whose economy?

Now Mr. Bush wants to hand Wall Street a bonanza in the form of "privatizing" Social Security. It's true that allowing Americans to invest a portion of our Social Security accounts in the stock market will enable some of us to receive more in our "golden years." But what happens to those who invest in Enron?

Then there are the "social" issues.

Many of us don't want assault weapons in our midst and are appalled by the Bush Administration's obeisance to the gun lobby.

We believe that whether or not a woman has an abortion should be decided by the woman (often in conjunction with her family and doctor); not by the government. George Bush has shown no respect for "the sanctity of human life" in his governance. We think that, on the issue of abortion, he's a phony.

We're tired of political ideologues who are so busy trying to abolish abortion, curb stem-cell research, and boost the profits of large American drug companies that they failed to secure an adequate supply of flu vaccine for the American people.

We view decent affordable health care for all Americans as a "moral" issue. The next time Dick Cheney has chest pains, let him go to the emergency room at a public health clinic and experience first-hand what this administration has wrought. Of course, in Washington, D.C., unless Mr. Cheney pulls rank, he can probably get a pizza delivered to his home faster than he can get an ambulance to take him to the hospital if he has a heart attack.

The tearing down by the Bush Administration of the wall between church and state also troubles us.

After the 2004 election, there was a much-quoted statement from a woman who voted for George Bush. "I'm so happy," she said. "It feels like we've elected Jesus as president."

Guess what, lady. Jesus didn't want to be president. And more to the point: Would Jesus have invaded Iraq? Would Jesus favor tax breaks for the rich over the working middle-class?

The Bush administration has done more than any other administration in history to turn religious institutions into a political lobbying force, and we resent it. More Americans now say that they believe in the Virgin Birth than in evolution. We respect the Bible, but we don't believe that the Bible should be imposed on our society as the literal word of God.

After all, the Bible countenances slavery. Chapter 25, Verse 44, Leviticus: "Both thy bondsmen and thy bondsmaids which thou shalt have shall be of the heathen that are about you. Of them shall ye buy bondsmen and bondsmaids."

And then there's the Biblical view of marriage. A Constitutional amendment codifying marriage on the basis of the Bible would state the following:

(1) Marriage in the United States shall consist of a union between a man and one or more women (Genesis 29:17-28, II Samuel 3:2-5).

(2) Marriage shall not impede a man's right to take concubines in addition to his wife or wives (II Samuel 5:13, I Kings 11:3, II Chronicles 11:21).

(3) A marriage shall be considered valid only if the wife is a virgin. If the wife is not a virgin, she shall be executed (Deuteronomy 22:13-21).

(4) The marriage of a believer and a non-believer is forbidden (Genesis 24:3, Numbers 25:1-9, Ezra 9:12, Nehemiah 10:30).

(5) If a married man dies without children, his brother shall marry his widow. If the brother refuses to marry the widow or deliberately does not give her children, he shall pay a fine of one shoe and be otherwise punished in a manner to be determined by law (Genesis 38:6-10, Deuteronomy 25:5-10).

(6) Divorce shall not be allowed (Deuteronomy 22:19, Mark 10:9).

George Bush talked a lot during the 2004 presidential campaign about the sanctity of marriage in the context of gay marriage. He used gay Americans as a wedge issue in the same way that Richard Nixon exploited antipathy toward black Americans in 1968. But we didn't hear much from Mr. Bush about TV reality shows where some bozo bachelor chooses a bride from sixteen contestants who are hoping to parlay their selection into a centerfold spread for an adult magazine. Maybe that's because the leader in "reality" television of this kind is FOX (a virtual house organ for the Republican party).

Meanwhile, it should be noted that the state with the lowest divorce rate in the country is Massachusetts (5.7 divorces per 1,000 married people), which is the only state that allows for same-sex marriages.

Nothing is more appalling to those of us who oppose George Bush than the fact that millions of Americans voted for him in the belief that he somehow epitomizes good moral values.

Moral values are about more than the lavish profession of a belief in Christ. We believe that there is no sense of decency or honor in the Bush administration and that it's morally rotten to the core.

The voices of "conservatism" who are filtering our values today include a drug addict who has been divorced three times (Rush Limbaugh), a sexual predator (Bill O'Reilly), and a compulsive gambler (William Bennett a.k.a. the author of *The Book of Virtues*).

Rudolph Giuliani (a hero to Republicans when it's mutually beneficial) had a much-publicized extra-marital affair with his former communications director, Cristyne Lategano. Then he embarked upon an even more public extra-marital affair with Judith Nathan before advising his wife by way of a television interview that he wanted a divorce. This is known in some circles as "thinking with your cock." And as we know from Bill Clinton's impeachment hearings, Republicans don't like it (unless of course, the cock belongs to one of their own).

Do we smell hypocrisy here? We sure do.

George Bush pledges to "leave no child behind," but millions of children are being left behind. He promises "clean air." We get dirty air. He says "clean water." We get dirty water.

So let's talk about core values.

Honesty is a core value. Without honesty, there can be no trust and the bonds that hold society together fall apart.

Rewarding hard work over accumulated wealth is a core value.

Caring for the weak, the poor, and the elderly is a core value, as is educating our children properly,

Eradicating discrimination on the basis of race, religion, and sexual orientation is a core value.

George Bush has done none of these things. Rather, his administration has been largely about about serving those in power. And there's a horrible sense that, from Tom DeLay's forced Congressional redistricting in Texas to the ugly "Swift Boat Veterans For Truth" attacks on John Kerry, Mr. Bush and his cronies will do anything to maintain power.

Meanwhile, many of us are crying because we love our country. We fear that irrevocable damage is being done to our most cherished institutions and to the human community.

Jack Newfield and I were on the telephone for about twenty minutes during our last conversation. We talked about how people want to trust their leaders; how the Democrats, for the most part, have been a lousy party in opposition; and the parallels between the alienation that many of us feel today and the sense of alienation that black Americans have experienced over the decades. We talked about twists of fate and how easily the course of history is altered. If John Kennedy hadn't gone to Dallas . . . If Monica Lewinsky hadn't given Bill Clinton a blow job . . .

Then Jack strengthened a bit and started talking nuts and bolts. In recent years, the Republican juggernaut has had two distinct advantages: fundraising and campaigning in a way that frames the issues on its terms. In 2004, the Democratic Party was competitive in fundraising. Now it has to sharpen its message. 115,000,000 voters participated in the November presidential election. Democratic senatorial candidates received more votes than their Republican counterparts. If 60,000 Ohioans had changed their choice at the top of the ballot, John Kerry would be the next President of the United States.

"So much for an overwhelming Bush mandate," Jack said.

And that's how our conversation ended, save for one final exchange.

"After the election, some friends and I didn't know whether we should sit around feeling depressed or fight back," I told him. "We've decided to do both."

"Right on," Jack exhorted.

And then he spoke the last words he ever said to me: "Keep the faith."❏

*There was a time when people thought* The Contender *might save boxing. That time has long since passed.*

## THE CONTENDER ON THE ROPES

Ten months ago, I wrote an article about *The Contender* for Secondsout.com. I recounted the plans of the show's producers and closed with the words, "At some point, *The Contender* will become more than a game, and reality in its truest sense will intervene."

On February 14, 2005, reality intervened. Najai Turpin, a 23-year-old boxer from Philadelphia who had lost in the first round of *The Contender* competition, shot himself to death.

Prior to *The Contender*, Turpin had a professional record of 12 wins and 1 loss with 8 knockouts. By all accounts, he was a hard worker, a good person, and a quality fighter. Despite what he did in the ring, there was a gentleness about him. A lot of people who come from where he came from have hard insides. They have to in order to survive. Najai had a personality that bordered on sunny and innocent. He was also very quiet and kept a lot inside.

TV "reality" shows put a great deal of stress on their participants. High-pressure situations are constructed to entertain the viewing public. Contestants live in a fishbowl, where every mistake and embarrassing moment are magnified.

Also, unlike most reality shows, *The Contender* has the potential to impact enormously on the real jobs of its contestants. If a truck-driver goes to the South Pacific for some *Survivor* fun and games, his old life is there for him when the show is over. Fighters who appear on *The Contender* will benefit from the attendant publicity. But they're precluded by contract from plying their trade outside the confines of the show for almost a year. And even then, they're bound to the show's promotional entity.

Because of these and other pressures, both *The Contender* and *The Next Great Champ* (its rival on FOX) administered psychological tests to prospective fighters in the form of written questions and a personal interview. In each instance, the television network and the program's insurer required it. The tests were administered by an outside group and sought to determine the fighters' ability to deal with stress, anger

223

management skills, and their predisposition to depression and other forms of mental illness.

In the case of *The Next Great Champ*, close to three dozen candidates were tested. One insider recalls, "There were a couple of guys who we liked a lot who we lost because of the psychological testing."

As the selection process for *The Contender* narrowed, each of the fighters vying to be among the sixteen finalists was similarly tested to determine how suited he was to cope with the emotional rigors of a television reality show. The *Contender* test was graded on a scale of 1 to 6. Most of the fighters chosen as finalists scored a 6. Najai Turpin finished last out of the sixteen fighters chosen. His score was 3.

"They knew going in that there was a problem with Najai," says one person familiar with the test results. "I don't know how far the word spread internally. I'm sure there were a lot of people who didn't know about the results; and obviously, no one thought that Najai would commit suicide. But the tests showed that he was a fragile guy."

*The Contender* has five equity participants with varying degrees of input into the show. They are Mark Burnett (who's best known for having created *Survivor* and *The Apprentice*), movie executive Jeffrey Katzenberg, show business veteran Jeff Wald, Sylvester Stallone, and Sugar Ray Leonard. NBC is paying a higher price per episode for *The Contender* than has ever been paid for a TV reality show. It has backed the project with a huge promotional budget. And there are other revenue streams as well.

According to a February 10, 2005, article in *The Hollywood Reporter* and information gathered from other sources, Contender Partners LLC will reap the benefit of:

(1) A license fee from NBC of close to $2,000,000 per episode.

(2) The right to sell six commercial spots per episode. NBC sold these spots to Contender Partners LLC at a discount with the understanding that they could be resold at a profit.

(3) All product integration fees, including stock warrants to purchase up to five percent of the stock in Everlast Worldwide Inc. at $2.75 per share. Everlast is the exclusive supplier of boxing equipment, active-wear, and shoes for the show and is featured prominently in every episode. The warrants were worth several hundred thousand dollars at the time the deal was made but have increased in value as Everlast stock has risen. As of the close of business on March 24, 2005, the stock was selling at $10.09 per share. If *The Contender* returns to NBC for a second season with at least ten new episodes, Contender Partners LLC. will receive

warrants for an additional five-percent stake in Everlast. The same is true for a third season, which could give them a total equity interest of fifteen percent in the company.

(4) A significant portion of ticket-sale revenue from the grand finale, which will be contested live in Las Vegas at Caesars Palace.

(5) Future promotional rights to all of the fighters in the show. The fighters still alive are Anthony Bonsante, Jesse Brinkley, Brent Cooper, Miguel Espino, Juan De La Rosa, Jeff Fraza, Joey Gilbert, Alfonso Gomez Jr., Ahmed Kaddour, Jimmy Lange, Peter Manfredo Jr., Sergio Mora, Jonathan Reid, Tarick Salmaci, and Ishe Smith.

(6) Various other commercial rights to the name, story, and likeness of each fighter; for example, the right to make a feature film about Najai Turpin.

Each episode of *The Contender* to date has had a common structure. The fighters have been divided into two teams (East and West). The teams compete in a "challenge," and whichever team wins gets to determine the match-up for the fight shown at the end of the episode. In addition, there's a "reward" for whichever team was represented by the winner of the previous week's fight. And of course, there's a lot of personal interaction between the fighters, their families, and the camera. That plays to Burnett's strength, which is getting viewers emotionally involved with the characters on his shows.

Some boxing fans like *The Contender*. Others find it silly and boring. The challenge in the first episode involved fighters carrying logs up a hill. In Episode #2, they ran around the Rose Bowl, picking up pieces of a cloth puzzle. In Episode #3, it was "Contender Dodge Ball." Episode #4 saw the fighters pulling a 5,000-pound Toyota Tundra along a dry river bed, picking up Everlast heavy-bags with letters on them, and, at the finish line, assembling the bags so they spelled out the word "Contender." The most obvious purpose of this exercise was product placement for Everlast and Toyota.

The "challenges" are reminiscent of "trash-sport" television from the 1970s. For those too young to remember, in one episode of ABC's *Superstars* televised in 1973, Joe Frazier found himself in a 50-yard freestyle swimming race that gave new meaning to the phrase "down goes Frazier."

"You think he's kidding," Jim McKay cried as Frazier thrashed around in the water and began to sink. "He is not kidding."

The "rewards" given to fighters on *The Contender* are as inspiring as the "challenges." In Episode #2, viewers were supposed to get excited about watching George Foreman eat hamburgers with the "west" team. The "east" team wasn't invited because Peter Manfredo Jr. had lost the fight that ended Episode #1.

Other rewards to date have been an "awesome" dinner with Sugar Ray Leonard at an "exclusive" restaurant and a shopping spree for suits with Tommy Gallagher serving as a fashion consultant. Getting fashion tips from Tommy Gallagher is like getting advice on business ethics from the folks who ran Enron. Given the fact that the clothing store's outdoor signage was prominently displayed, one assumes that an exchange of goods for services was involved.

A more serious criticism of *The Contender* has been that it's phony. Boxing, in the ring, is the most basic and honest of all sports. But *The Contender* is contrived on its face.

Reality in boxing is Don King handing Hasim Rahman a duffel bag filled with cash to lure him away from Cedric Kushner. Reality in boxing is Gatti-Ward and Mike Tyson biting off part of Evander Holyfield's ear. Reality in boxing is Dan Goossen on the telephone day after day at five o'clock in morning, talking with people in Mongolia to arrange a fight for Lakva Sim. In the real world of boxing, sixteen fighters don't live together in a beautiful training center and do everything that they're told to do when they're told to do it.

The rebuttal to this criticism is that a reality show isn't a documentary. A reality show takes people and puts them in situations they wouldn't normally be in and entertains viewers by showing them how the participants react. But the bottom line is, when you mix fantasy with reality, you get fantasy.

Contracts and gag clauses give the producers of *The Contender* the right to filter out any whiff of reality that might interfere with their chosen storyline. The show doesn't tell its audience about the contractual requirement that the fighters are forbidden to bring a cell phone, pager, computer, credit card, or cash with them. There's an inherent phoniness in "intimate private" moments that are recorded when a husband and wife know that cameras are rolling. And let's not forget that the fighters and their loved ones have long since been asked to leave the wonderful *Contender* family housing and have returned to their previous surroundings.

Also, the fights that end each episode are flawed. For starters, they're contested in an unusually small ring—one that is smaller than the 18-by-18-foot minimum required by law in some states. Five rounds of boxing are reduced to five minutes of cut-and-paste action with a good portion of those five minutes devoted to camera shots of Stallone, Leonard, and others in the crowd. The bouts are accompanied by background music that builds to a crescendo and sound effects that exaggerate the power of punches. During the introduction of fighters and the fight scenes that follow, viewers hear loud roars from the crowd. But looking at the television screen, it's clear that the mouths of most crowd members are closed.

These failings haven't been lost on the general public. *The Contender* has done better than expected in England. But in the United States, it has been a ratings disappointment. *Survivor* and *The Apprentice* each averaged roughly 20,000,000 viewers per show. By contrast, *The Contender* started its run with 8,100,000 viewers and is now down around 6,700,000. That puts the show far behind its primary Sunday-night competition and looking very much like a fighter who's five rounds into a 15-round fight and just trying to survive.

Men don't like *The Contender* because it isn't real boxing. Women don't like it, period. Following Mike Tyson around for fifteen weeks would have been less expensive, garnered higher ratings, and been more interesting "reality" television. Also, the show's ratings can be expected to take another hit on April 3rd, when it loses sports fans to the season opener between the Yankees and Red Sox.

But there are issues regarding *The Contender* that go beyond whether or not it's compelling TV drama. The first of these issues deals with the fighters themselves. At the start of each episode, Sylvester Stallone tells them, "The only difference between you and the current world champions is that they got a shot and you didn't." But that's not quite true. *The Contender* features sixteen hard-working young men. However, at this stage of their respective careers, none of them are A-list fighters. Yes, they entered the tournament with impressive won-lost records. But those records were built against opponents who had won only forty percent of their fights.

Moreover, there's a significant size differential among the fighters. Some, like Sergio Mora, are natural 160-pounders. But Najai Turpin, who lost to Mora in the fourth episode, fought his last fight prior to the tournament at 150 pounds. Ishe Smith weighed in for his final pre-tournament bout at 146.

And the size differential could have been more lopsided. Paulie Malignaggi is a talented junior-welterweight with a 19 and 0 record. His last fight was at 139 pounds. Paulie has personality, style, and a big mouth. In other words, he's perfect for *The Contender*.

"They were begging me to do it," Malignaggi says. "They told me, 'Do it; it will be great for your career. If you don't win, you'll still be a star.' And I was tempted. I think they're good people and it was a fantastic opportunity. But in the end, the weight difference was just too much, so

I turned them down."

Malignaggi's promoter, Lou DiBella, takes a more cynical view. "It was, 'Paulie, we love you' and 'Paulie, you're great,'" DiBella recalls. "But it was clear that they didn't care about Paulie because, if you love a highly-skilled light-punching 140-pound fighter, you don't try to put him in the ring with guys who weigh 160."

Chucky Tschorniawsky is another 140-pounder who was courted by *The Contender*. He's a charismatic club fighter whose personal life has been filled with drama. "You're from Philadelphia; you're the real Rocky; you can do it," Chucky T was told. But Tschorniawsky declined, so *The Contender* made do with another Philadephia fighter: Najai Turpin.

Also, returning to the fights that end each episode of *The Contender*, there's no way to know what they were really like because the producers only show viewers what they want to show them. Each fight is edited in a way that makes it impossible for viewers to know who really won. And the contracts for *The Contender* require that each fighter waive his right to challenge any decision rendered against him in the tournament, including his right to challenge a decision under the Rules and Regulations of the California State Athletic Commission.

The judges' scores aren't announced on *The Contender*, but they are released by the California commission several days after a bout is televised. These scores are instructive. On television, Ishe Smith versus Ahmed Kaddour looked like a down-to-the-wire barn-burner. But in reality, the bout was scored 50-45, 50-45, 49-46. Jesse Brinkley ousted Jonathan Reid by the same margin. Meanwhile, Alfonso Gomez's victory over Peter Manfredo was presented as a back-and-forth struggle that was up for grabs in the final round. But the judges scored it 50-45, 49-46, 48-47.

Thus, promoter Dan Goossen declares, "The fights are phony on their face. You've got a phony soundtrack. You've got make-believe trainers. We know who the producers want us to think won each fight but not who really won. There's no accountability regarding the judges or any way to tell if the decisions are fair or not."

There are also questions regarding the extent to which the California State Athletic Commission bent its rules and regulations to accommodate *The Contender*. The commission chose to bypass the requirement of federal law that fight results be promptly reported. That's understandable given the nature of a TV reality show. But in Episode #1, Alfonso Gomez Jr. suffered an ugly cut on his right eyelid that required sutures. How long would Gomez have been suspended under normal circumstances?

"The cut was a concern," acknowledges Dean Lohuis (executive officer of the California State Athletic Commission). "It was deep enough that Gomez was placed on 60-day suspension with the understanding that he could be cleared to fight earlier by a physician. They had fights every three days," Lohuis continues. "Gomez was cut on August 18, 2004, and cleared to fight again on September 15th."

It would be instructive if a public accounting were made of all compensation paid directly or indirectly to CSAC physicians by *The Contender*.

Next, there's the criticism that *The Contender* has failed to explain to a national television audience what it takes from a physical point of view to be a fighter; the skills involved and what it feels like to be punched in the face or body by a pro. To the contrary, it has trivialized the demands of the job with glimpses of Sylvester Stallone working out in the ring. Stallone is an actor, who wrote and starred in one of the best boxing movies ever. He is not, nor has he ever been, a professional fighter.

Also, Mark Burnett's genius as a producer is his understanding of everyday people, both as participants and viewers of television reality shows. But professional boxers aren't everyday people. There's something very different inside them. There has to be, given what they do.

Here, the thoughts of Tokunbo Olajide are instructive. Olajide is a promising junior-middleweight with a 20 and 2 record and 17 knockouts. He's also a talented musician (trumpet and piano), immensely likeable, articulate, and thoughtful.

"Tommy [Gallagher] was the first to tell me about *The Contender*," Olajide remembers. "I told him, 'It's not me; I'm not interested.' Boxing isn't a game, and I didn't want to be part of a game show. Then Gary Shaw [Olajide's promoter] said it would be good for my career and I'd be perfect for it, so I agreed to do a screen test at the New York Hilton. *The Contender* people called me the day after the test and said they'd love to have me on the show. Then they sent me the contracts. I read them. And it was 'no way, no how.' The contract was like indentured servitude, and it was demeaning. I could see right away that they'd have me doing clown stuff."

"I look at the show, and it's ridiculous," Olajide continues. "It has nothing to do with what a boxer's life is like. It's a circus with professional fighters playing silly games for other people's amusement. Team dodgeball? Come on. It's the reality show formula: copy, cut, and paste. And it's obvious that they're oblivious to the fighters' dignity. This isn't an attempt to make boxing better. It's about making money. The bottom line for the show, the only line for the show, is how many people watch it."

The people behind *The Contender* take issue with that view. They've talked openly about their desire to restructure boxing for the betterment of fighters and the sport. They plan to stay in the business through a promotional entity that includes contracts with *The Contender* fighters among its assets. And they've ruffled a few feathers with their plans for the future.

"Mark Burnett and Jeffrey Katzenberg are talking like they spent the last twenty years at Gleason's Gym instead of Spago," says Showtime's Jay Larkin.

"In our reality business," adds Dan Goossen, "I'm used to other promoters trying to talk to my fighters behind my back and lure them away if they can. But for people to make a grandstand show of saying that they'll be doing things the right way and then doing things the same old way is very discouraging."

Success in other areas of business doesn't necessarily translate into success in boxing. Sylvester Stallone tried his hand at real boxing promotion in the early 1980s. His debut card was Sean O'Grady versus Pete Ranzany in Las Vegas in 1982. The experiment didn't last long. Sugar Ray Leonard also promoted fights for a while. Last year, Sugar Ray Leonard Promotions closed its doors.

But whatever comes next, let's hope that *The Contender* does right by the fifteen remaining fighters when the show's run is over. And let's hope that it does right by boxing too. In other words, no "people's championships." Boxing already has too many phony titles.

Meanwhile, on the streets of Philadelphia, Najai Turpin has become a symbol of "reality" in its truest sense. Based on what is publicly known, it would be irresponsible to say that *The Contender* contributed to his death. But it's pushing the envelope to say (as those involved with the show have done), that his participation in the show and the restrictions that *The Contender* placed on his life afterward had no bearing whatsoever on the tragedy.

Percy "Buster" Custus is part of the fabric of boxing in Philadelphia. He has been training fighters for twenty years. Custus started training Najai when Najai was twelve years old and became the proverbial father figure in the young man's life.

"I'm not blaming anyone," Custus says. "Najai did what he did, but I'll tell you a few things. When they wanted Najai on the show, they were calling me three and four times a day. But once they got him out there, they blocked the phones and he couldn't even call me unless he got their permission to use the phone in their office. I think they let him call me once; that's all. Under the contract he signed, he wasn't allowed to talk about the fight afterward, so that was something he had to keep inside. And under the contract, he wasn't allowed to fight again until the show ends. That's a long time for a young man to stay away from something he loves. Fighters want to fight. Sugar Ray Leonard came out of retirement three times because he wanted to fight. Boxing made Najai happy. And *The Contender* people wouldn't let Najai fight for eight months after he lost. There's no way to know what that did to his mind."

"And another thing," Custus continues. "Someone who was out there for *The Contender* told me that Najai won his fight. He said, 'Man, I don't know what's going on. Najai whipped his ass.' Now, I don't know if that's right or not. I'm not saying Najai won the fight because I don't know. But it would be interesting to see a tape of that fight. It would be interesting to see tapes of all their fights. I try to be positive about things. I try to look for the best in everyone, including *The Contender* people. But I know one thing. I'd never send another one of my guys to them."

At the end of Episode #4, Sugar Ray Leonard appeared on camera and informed viewers of what he called "the heartbreaking news that Najai Turpin had passed away." *The Contender* is a reality show. Why not tell viewers the truth? That Najai Turpin put a bullet in his head.

"The show was never the problem," Najai's brother, Diediera said recently. "Boxing and all of that was never the problem. It was a personal problem."

That might be so. But Najai's death is part of a high-stakes game. There were a lot of publicists for NBC and *The Contender* at his funeral. And one wonders what happened to the article that *Sports Illustrated* was planning on *The Contender*. It was known in boxing circles that Franz Lidz, a conscientious researcher and talented writer, was putting considerable time and effort into a feature story. Then, according to a reliable source, a call was made from NBC to TimeWarner (*SI's* parent company), complaining about some of the questions that Lidz was asking. The article never ran. And, oh yes. NBC televised a *Sports Illustrated* swimsuit-model-search reality show earlier this year.

It should also be mentioned that Dean Lohuis was at ringside for all of *The Contender* fights, including Sergio Mora versus Najai Turpin, which each judge scored 49-46 in Mora's favor. Lohuis's notes on that fight read as follows: "Non-stop action. Every round competitive. Very close bout. Phone-booth war. Both gave it everything they had. Scores do not do justice to Turpin's effort."

*The Contender* still represents an enormous opportunity for fifteen of the sixteen young men who were chosen to participate as fighters. It has made them far more marketable than they were before. "I told them 'no,' and that was the right decision for me," says Paulie Malignaggi. "But I think the show is great. I look forward to watching it each week. I was talking to Ishe Smith a few days ago. Ishe fought on Showtime, he fought on ESPN, and no one knew who he was. Now, wherever he goes, people recognize him. I think *The Contender* is great for boxing."

But a contrary view is expressed by those who think that, with all the money and talent involved, *The Contender* should have been something more. And to its most severe critics, *The Contender* epitomizes words spoken by Marlon Brando in *On The Waterfront*: "You don't understand. I could've had class. I could've been a contender. I could've been somebody, instead of a bum, which is what I am."❏

*After several fighters involved with the show contacted me, I revisited* The Contender.

# MORE TROUBLE FOR *THE CONTENDER*

On the morning of February 14, 2005, at 3:00 a.m., Angela Chapple's telephone rang. The caller was Najai Turpin.

Angela and Najai met in 1996 during a summer youth program that they attended after ninth grade. Two years later, they began dating. Angela is now a computer technician. Najai became a professional boxer and also worked as a cook at Bottom of the Sea Restaurant in Philadelphia to support the daughter that they had together two years ago.

Najai's life was in a downward spiral and had been since he'd travelled to California several times the previous year. The first trip was in July 2004. He'd impressed representatives of NBC's TV reality show *The Contender* at an audition in Philadelphia and was invited to Los Angeles for further testing. He hoped to be one of sixteen fighters chosen to appear on the show, but there was a snag. The candidates were subjected to extensive psychological testing.

Representatives of *The Contender* refuse to discuss the matter, but the best available information is that a written psychological test was administered to the fighters on Thursday, July 15th, and that psychological-profiling interviews were conducted on July 16th and 17th. One fighter selected for the show says that the personal interview lasted well over an hour and was conducted by a man and a woman. The written portion of the examination took longer. "One of the things they asked me," he recalls, "was if I got depressed or ever considered killing myself."

"Najai came back to Philadelphia after they did the testing," Angela remembers. "He told me, 'I didn't make it because the doctor said I'm manic-depressive.'"

That evaluation had a foundation. It's unclear how much the people who evaluated Najai for *The Contender* knew about his personal history. But five years earlier, at age eighteen, he had attempted suicide by swallowing 47 Tylenol pills and a bottle of vodka after his mother died.

The statement that Najai made to Angela is similar to what he told Percy "Buster" Custus. Custus runs an inner-city gym in Philadelphia and began training Najai eleven years ago. When Najai filled out an application for *The Contender*, there were spaces for "mother" and "father." Next to his mother's name, he wrote "deceased." He made no entry at all for "father." Then, beneath his mother's name, he wrote in "Percy Custus" as his "stepfather."

"After the testing," says Custus, "Najai told me, 'Mr. Buster, they won't take me. This guy out there said I was manic-depressive.'"

"I didn't know what that meant at the time," Custus acknowledges. "I thought it meant you got depressed sometimes and had highs and lows, but that it's something you work through."

Then a representative of *The Contender* telephoned and said that Najai had been selected to be one of sixteen fighters on the show.

But *The Contender* experience was very different from what Najai expected. The tone was set by a written directive entitled "Rules For First Week At Hotel" that instructed the fighters "There is absolutely no talking between contestants." Note that they were referred to as "contestants" (as on a television game show), not "boxers" or "fighters."

The fighters were further advised "No one is to leave the hotel room without permission and an escort" and "all phone calls to home will be made from the production office in the hotel."

Angela later recalled, "Whenever Najai called me from the office, before we could talk, there was a voice on the phone that said everything in our conversation was being taped. It was like he was in a prison cell."

Each fighter who appeared on *The Contender* was required to sign a non-disclosure agreement stipulating that any breach of confidentiality would subject the fighter to the "imposition of liquidated damages of up to $5,000,000."

Nonetheless, on condition of anonymity, several fighters who appeared on the show have begun to talk. One says that there came a time when they began to understand how much money was passing into the hands of the show's producers and talked about organizing a strike. "There was a time when some of us were upset at the way things were going," says another. "But we decided as a group that we all knew what we were signing up for when we signed the contracts and we should stand by what we signed."

Other fighters went AWOL during production, including one who departed on an unauthorized overnight trip to Las Vegas.

*The Contender* experience was particularly painful for Najai, who was rooming with Ahmed Kaddour. The TV people liked Ahmed. He was good-looking, wore flashy clothes, had a sexy girlfriend, and shot his mouth off. Najai didn't like him and, at one point, there was a physical altercation between them away from the ring.

There was also grumbling that black fighters were under-represented on the show and that some of the decisions made by the show's producers were motivated by inappropriate racial considerations. One person familiar with the situation says that Najai was subjected to racial taunts and told by another fighter, "All you niggers fold when you get hit on the chin."

By that time, Najai wanted nothing more to do with *The Contender*.

The rules for participants forbade the fighters from communicating with the outside world on their own. Cell phones, pagers, and email devices were prohibited. To enforce the rules, the fighters were subject to personal searches at any time. But some of the fighters found a way up to the roof, where no cameras or microphones were present. And one of them had managed to smuggle in a cell phone.

"Najai called me from the roof," says Angela. "He said, 'It's awful here. I feel like I'm in jail. I want to come home.' But he was afraid to come home because he was afraid that *The Contender* people would sue him for breach of contract."

"Najai was so distraught at times that your heart broke for him," says another fighter who appeared on *The Contender*. "Mostly, he kept to himself. Juan [de la Rosa] was the only person he really talked with."

Najai returned to Philadelphia at the close of *The Contender* taping. In October, Angela and their daughter moved in with him. But despite the fact that he was home, his unhappiness lingered.

Part of the problem was that boxing, which had been an anchor in Najai's life for more than a decade, had been taken away from him. In the past, he'd fought regularly; first as an amateur, then fourteen professional fights in three years. But after losing a decision to Sergio Mora in August, Najai's career had been put on hold. The contract he'd signed gave *The Contender* the right to control his ring life through May 24, 2009. Under no circumstances would he be allowed to fight again prior to May 24, 2005. And thereafter, *The Contender* could limit him to two fights per year.

"After Najai got back from California," says Angela, "he started drinking. That wasn't like him. And he started going to the gym less because he wasn't allowed to fight. *The Contender* was still controlling his life."

Meanwhile, one of *The Contender* fighters recalls, "After the show, Najai cut himself off from the rest of us. Some of us tried to call him; and for a while, he wouldn't even take the calls. If a guy won't talk to you, what can you do?"

On Tuesday, February 8th, Najai agreed to go with Percy Custus to a training camp in the Pocono Mountains to work with Custus and several of his fighters. Angela went to her mother's home with their daughter so there would be someone to assist with childcare. Unbeknownst to her, Najai returned to Philadelphia two nights later and stayed at home alone for three days. In the wee small hours of Valentine's Day, he telephoned her and said that he was outside her mother's house in his car.

Angela went downstairs and got in the car. It was cold. Najai turned on the heat so she'd be more comfortable.

"What would you do if I killed myself?" he asked her.

"Don't talk like that. We went through that once."

"Would you take care of my daughter?"

"I always do."

Najai reached down with his left hand, pulled out a gun, and shot himself in the head.

●●●

Last month, in an article entitled *The Contender on the Ropes* that was posted on this website, I reviewed the history of *The Contender* and discussed many of the issues surrounding the show. In summarizing the first four episodes, I noted, "Some boxing fans like *The Contender*. Others find it silly and boring."

Five weeks later, "silly and boring" seem to be carrying the day.

Fighters don't carry logs up a hill in 90-degree weather the day before a fight. That's not how real boxing works, but it happens on *The Contender*. A fighter doesn't leave his living quarters and go someplace to visit with his wife and children the night before a big fight. That's not how real boxing works, but it happens on *The Contender*. A fighter's team doesn't leave him alone in the dressing room before and after a fight and make him walk to the ring alone. But that's what happens on *The Contender*.

Week after week, it's the same show, from the controlled scenes of fighters talking on the telephone with family members to the funeral dirge music that plays as the loser sits in his dressing room. There's excessive crying in every episode. Guys cry when they lose. They cry when they talk about their children. They cry when they reflect upon their mothers and fathers and other loved ones.

And despite being a "reality" show, there are times when *The Contender* departs from reality altogether. In Episode #8, Peter Manfredo Jr. was seen as the chief cornerman for Jimmy Lange, while Jeremy Williams served in a similar capacity for Joey Gilbert. In Episode #9,

Ahmed Kaddour and Alfonso Gomez were working the corners. Since these are supposed to be "real" fights, it would be nice to have a real trainer in each corner.

The show gets sillier and sillier. Recent "challenges" have included:

- Hauling Everlast medicine balls up the Sepulveda Dam and putting them in the back of a Toyota truck.
- Demolishing a cinderblock wall with sledgehammers and putting the blocks into the back of a Toyota Tundra. As the fighters were doing this, Ray Leonard said admiringly, "You guys are animals, man," and Tommy Gallagher shouted, "Don't scratch the Toyotas."
- Navigating an "urban obstacle course" that required the fighters to "run through the Toyota traffic jam" (I'm not making that up; Ray Leonard actually instructed the fighters to "run through the Toyota traffic jam"); jump over some hurdles with advertising on them; throw tires in a dumpster; empty the tires out of the dumpster; take the keys out of a Toyota; use the keys to unlock a lock; and climb to the top of a truck with advertising for Bally's on it.
- Running around an obstacle course while wearing Everlast boxing gloves, picking up Everlast medicine balls, and throwing the medicine balls in a basket.
- Pulling harness-racing carts around Santa Anita Race Track. This was one of the most demeaning moments for professional fighters ever on network television. Anthony Bonsante pulled a hamstring muscle during this idiocy, demonstrating from a technical point of view why fighters shouldn't be treated like racehorses.

The "rewards" are comparable. After Peter Manfredo Jr. won a mulligan over Miguel Espino, the East team was invited to sit in the audience for *The Tonight Show* and shake hands with Jay Leno. Afterward, Manfredo said, "It was awesome to shake his hand," while Joey Gilbert declared angrily, "It really sucks, losing this reward." That came one week after the West team played poker with Antonio Tarver, who was described as "the only man to ever knock out Roy Jones." Apparently, the masterminds behind *The Contender* have never heard of Glencoffe Johnson. And let's not forget Episode #8, when the seven remaining fighters [Ahmed Kaddour had not yet returned] were flown to Caesars Palace, where they kissed cocktail waitresses and ate grapes in an infomercial for Caesars. They also drew cards to see who would win a Toyota Tundra. Sergio Mora emerged victorious and ran to the vehicle to the accompaniment of music that sounded like the soundtrack from *The Ten Commandments*.

These shortcomings have not been lost on the public. From a financial point of view, *The Contender* has turned into Jack Dempsey versus Tommy Gibbons, with NBC playing the role of Shelby, Montana, to *The Contender's* Doc Kearns.

Ratings have been a disaster. NBC was told to expect 15,000,000 viewers per episode, but the number keep decreasing and is now hovering around 5,000,000. The network has done everything possible to right the sinking ship, including putting additional money into a wave of radio ads and preempting *Dateline* for an hour-long *Contender* rerun special on Easter night. But *The Contender* is running on wishful thinking.

One industry insider says that NBC has already decided against bringing the show back for a second season on network television. But it wouldn't be good business to brand *The Contender* a failure before it finishes its run, so the public execution will have to wait. If there's a second season for the show, most likely it will be on cable.

Meanwhile, the finger-pointing has begun, with some in *The Contender* camp complaining that NBC's decision to run the initial three episodes on three different nights during the first week undermined its success. But the scheduling was designed to offer *The Contender* to the widest possible audience. The fundamental problem is the show itself.

Anyone who has ever been around boxing knows that fighters are the most quotable athletes in the world. But *The Contender* is so contrived and so antiseptic that not one memorable quote has come out of the show.

Also, reality shows thrive on diversity. As far as viewers are concerned, there must be something for everyone. But all of the participants on *The Contender* are professional fighters. They're all portrayed as having the same motivation ("I'm doing this for my family; I want to be a champion"). They react the same to winning; they react the same to losing. It's repetitious and boring.

There is one area, however, where *The Contender* realistically reflects professional boxing. The promoters have made every dollar possible off the fighters. Best estimates are that the show's producers have taken in gross receipts in the neighborhood of $40,000,000. That's roughly equal to the annual boxing budgets of Showtime and ESPN combined.

There's also concern in some circles about the way several of the fighters have been portrayed on the show. For example, in Episode #6, Anthony Bonsante was trashed for betraying his teammates by turning his back on an agreement to fight Jimmy Lange and calling out Brent Cooper instead. This led to Bonsante being branded a "back-stabber" and a "coward." But the fighters have to fight whomever the producers of the show tell them to fight. That's made clear by the promotional contract, which states, "All bouts hereunder shall be against opponents on dates and at sites to be designated by Promoter in its sole and absolute discretion."

Likewise, it was unfair to criticize Juan De La Rosa for withdrawing from the competition because of a badly-cut eyelid, sprained wrist, and swollen knuckles. De La Rosa is a young man who, prior to *The Contender*, had only three fights in his entire career. If De La Rosa had fought on in the tournament, his eye might have wound up looking like David Reid's.

And most recently, the tape of Ishe Smith's loss to Sergio Mora was edited in a way that made Smith look foolish in the ring. It's unfair to do that to any fighter. Also, several people who were on-site say that Ishe left the ring shouting he'd been "robbed" and pushed a TV camera away from him. That didn't make the final cut.

Mora-Smith was a split decision: 50-45, 49-46, 46-49. "Sergio was badly hurt at the end of the last round," says one of the fighters who was there. "Thirty seconds more, and Ishe would have had him. So how do you score all five rounds for Sergio? The truth is, none of us wins five out of five rounds against Ishe. There's no way you can score that fight a shut-out for Sergio, but one of the judges did. If that fight had been in Vegas, Ishe probably would have won. But I don't think *The Contender* tried to fix the decisions," the fighter continues. "I think it's a question of California judges doing funny things for California fighters all through the show. I can't blame *The Contender* for something that happens all the time on ESPN."

Still, some of the fighters have begun to question other aspects of the tournament process. Among other things, they're skeptical about the "vote" by which Peter Mandredo Jr. was brought back into the fold after losing to Alfonso Gomez.

"Why would we vote Manfredo back?" asks one fighter. "Manfredo had a bad fight against Gomez, but we all knew he was tougher than, say, Jonathan Reid. We're fighting for a million dollars. Don't tell me that a majority of us voted to bring back Manfredo. It's the TV people that voted to bring back Manfredo."

But another fighter says, "I voted for Peter, and nobody tried to influence my vote. My reasoning was, we could vote back Jonathan but that would give someone else an easy fight. So bring back Peter. He was bruised from fighting Alfonso. And whatever happened in his next fight, he was going to bruise the other guy and come out more bruised himself."

Nonetheless, questions linger; including questions about the fighters themselves. They're championship-caliber fighters. Right? After all, Sylvester Stallone tells them, "The only difference between you and the current world champions is that they got a shot and you didn't."

Wrong.

Let's take Brent Cooper as an example. Cooper, fans of *The Contender* will remember, is the nice young man who told viewers, "My relationship with Jesus is outstanding. The Lord put me here to be The Contender. I don't think God brought me here to lose."

Cooper took a beating during the first two rounds of his fight against Anthony Bonsante. At that point, his girlfriend ran to the corner and told him, "I love you." Properly motivated, Brent was knocked out 38 seconds into the third round.

Cooper entered the tournament with a record of 20 wins, 2 losses, and 2 draws. But sixteen of Cooper's wins came against opponents who had never won a fight in their entire career at the time he fought them. As for the other four victories, one was against Lester Yarbrough (who is now on a 36-fight losing streak). One was against Bob Walker (who won two fights in his entire career). The other two were against Jerome Hill (whose record is currently 1 win and 48 losses).

Worse, one of Cooper's losses was against Robert Muhammad, who has lost 21 of his last 22 bouts and is continuing to fight after being treated for a subdural hematoma. Cooper's other loss was at the hands of Reggie Strickland, who has been defeated the staggering total of 272 times. Cooper's draws were against Rashawn Gore (in the only fight of Gore's career) and Strickland. That's right. Cooper couldn't beat Reggie Strickland in two tries.

As for the future, *The Contender* finale is slated for May 24, 2005 in Las Vegas. There will be six fights divided into morning and early-evening sessions. The "championship" bout is scheduled for seven rounds; each of the other fights for five. The Nevada State Athletic Commission has granted permission for an extra round to decide each fight in the event of a draw. However, it refused to grant a waiver that would have allowed the fights to take place in a 17-foot-square ring.

All of the pre-taped *Contender* bouts have been fought in a smaller-than-regulation enclosure. But fighting in a miniature ring so there will be more punches is like playing basketball with nine-foot baskets so there will be more dunks. Professional fights should be contested in a real boxing ring; in this case, a 20-by-20-foot enclosure.

It's unclear what will happen to the 15 remaining fighters once the tournament is over. The promotional contracts they signed purport to bind them to *The Contender* well into the future. But one prominent boxing attorney said recently, "It's a slave contract. Any good lawyer could get them out of it."

Also, the Muhammad Ali Boxing Reform Act has a section entitled "Disclosures to the Boxer" that declares, "A promoter shall not be entitled to receive any compensation directly or indirectly in connection with a boxing match until it provides to the boxer it promotes the amounts of any compensation or consideration that a promoter has contracted to receive from such match."

Several of *The Contender* fighters say that this required disclosure has not been made in a timely manner. However, at the same time, they agree with one of their own who declares, "It was tough at times. The producers were learning what it's like to be around boxers, and we were learning the television business. They made mistakes, and we made mistakes. But on balance, they were good to us. Usually, when we complained about something, they tried to make it better. The good outweighed the bad. I'd say they treated us well."

Thus, the biggest legal headache facing *The Contender* might relate to Najai Turpin. After his death, representatives of the show established a trust fund to provide for his daughter. They've refused to state publicly how much they contributed, but reliable sources put the amount at $100,000. Public donations have increased the fund to $200,000.

In addition, *The Contender* paid for Najai's funeral, although Percy Custus complains, "They ran these guys like Stallone out here to carry the casket, and then they refused to pay for the headstone. We had to ask them and ask them until finally, I guess, someone there decided it would look bad if they didn't pay for that too."

Complicating matters is the fact that Angela is expecting her second child, a boy, in late-September.

Prior to appearing on *The Contender*, each fighter was required to sign a contract providing that neither he nor his estate could sue the show, NBC, or various classes of employees, licensees, successors in interest, or assignees for wrongdoing even if such wrongdoing was the direct cause of the fighter's injury or death. But legal experts say that this prohibition would be invalid if *The Contender* engaged in certain types of wrongdoing.

Also, Najai wasn't the custodial parent for his daughter. Angela was. And Angela says, "As far as I know, I only signed one thing. The TV people came to Najai's home to tape with us. Right before they left, they asked me to sign a paper that they said was a confidentiality agreement and also would allow them to show tapes of me and my daughter on the show. They asked me to sign it right then, and I did. I never had a chance to show it to a lawyer."

Thus, Najai's daughter might have a claim against *The Contender* and some of its participants independent of his estate. And it's impossible to inadvertently waive the rights of an unborn child.

In the end, Najai Turpin bears the ultimate responsibility for his own death. He's the one who pulled the trigger. And doing it in front of Angela made it a particularly horrible act. But just as clearly, Najai must have been suffering terribly to do what he did. And something was very wrong with his emotional balance.

"Let's be honest about this," says one person who works for *The Contender*. "The man is sleeping in the closet. You have his psychological test results. If I'm running the show, if I care about him at all, I'm going to give him all the emotional support I can, and I'm going to keep giving it to him when the taping is done and he goes back to Philadelphia. We say over and over that the key to our success is to make viewers care about the fighters as people. And with Najai, it might look to some people like we didn't care about him at all."

In order for *The Contender* to be held liable for damages, there would have to be a judicial finding of wrongdoing on its part AND a causal connection between that wrongdoing and Najai's death.

Did the people who evaluated Najai's psychological profile on behalf of *The Contender* find him to be manic-depressive or in some other way more vulnerable to the pressures of a TV reality show than the other fighters? Did they include him in the show knowing that he had a psychological condition that put him at greater risk than the other fighters? How much did Najai's experience in California and being precluded from boxing afterward contribute to his mental slide?

The records of Najai's psychological-profile testing could be very interesting to a plaintiff's lawyer. So might the thousands of hours of Najai and others on unedited tapes. In the event of a lawsuit, there would also be depositions, including extensive questioning of the fifteen remaining fighters. In the event that liability is found to exist, most likely the damages would be considerable. *The Contender's* own promotional material emphasized the bright future that Najai had in the ring. Two children have lost their father. The punitive damages could be enormous.

Meanwhile, Angela hasn't decided yet what course of action she wants to take. She's balancing her desire for privacy, the need to provide financially for her children, the hope to get on with her life, and myriad other considerations. But several new developments trouble her.

"In seven years, I never once saw Najai's father," Angela says. "Buster was the closest thing that Najai had to a father. The first time I saw Najai's father was after Najai died, but he's here now. Najai didn't have a will, and now some of his family—I won't say all of them—are doing and saying things that aren't right."

"I've heard a lot of ugliness since Najai died," Angela continues. "I've heard stories that the baby's not his. I've heard stories that we were breaking up. And in my mind, that's a spin *The Contender* people are putting on things. None of it is true. Najai and I were planning together for the future. We were going to move to Delaware. *The Contender* people told me they want a DNA test for the baby that's coming in September. That won't be a problem. Najai is the father. There's no chance of anyone else."

Then Angela smiles. "Najai always wanted a junior," she says.❏

*As* The Contender's *marketing blitzkrieg continued, an honest update seemed in order.*

# KEEPING AN EYE ON *THE CONTENDER*

When boxing fans last saw *The Contender*, the TV reality show conjured up images of the *Titanic* after the iceberg. One week before its May 24, 2004, grand finale, NBC announced that it was canceling the series. Then, for good measure, the network put *The Contender* championship fight between Sergio Mora and Peter Manfredo up against the finals of *American Idol*.

*The Contender* asked several HBO luminaries to work the finals, but the request was declined. Ultimately, blow-by-blow chores were handled by Al Trautwig with color commentary from Sylvester Stallone and Ray Leonard. The latter two shilled for a rematch throughout the telecast, and Stallone called Mora-Manfredo a "candidate for fight of the year." Possibly, he'd never heard of Castillo-Corrales.

*American Idol* outdrew *The Contender* finale by 19,000,000 million viewers. More humiliating was the fact that *The Contender* finished 2,000,000 viewers behind *Rob and Amber Get Married*. Shortly thereafter, Mark Burnett and company announced that their next fight card (featuring the four *Contender* semi-finalists) would be held on July 5th. Like so much else about the series, that too was more wishful thinking than reality.

This history is relevant because the rebirth of *The Contender* has been announced. Mora and Manfredo will meet again at the Staples Center on October 15th with an undercard featuring Alfonso Gomez versus Jeff Fraza, Anthony Bonsante against Jesse Brinkley, and Jonathan Reid versus Miguel Espino. ESPN will air the fights live and televise a full second season of *The Contender* starting in April 2006.

The decision by *The Contender* to have its participants fight each other again and again is like the inbreeding of royal families in Europe centuries ago. It breeds insanity. It's also worth noting that *The Contender* is a perfect example of how television creates boxing promoters. Without NBC, there would have been no *Contender* promotional company. Now ESPN is keeping The Tournament of Contenders LLC alive.

That raises a host of questions. Will ESPN promote *The Contender* at the expense of its own *ESPN2 Friday Night Fights* (which occupy a different column on the organizational chart)? And will the network that goes ballistic when fighters wear temporary advertising tattoos look the other way when linked to *The Contender*'s product-placement money-machine?

Last season, according to Nielsen's rankings, *The Contender* had more product placements than any other show on network television. There were 6,085 "brand occurrences" as compared to 3,102 for the runner-up, *American Idol*.

There's also an issue as to whether ESPN can breathe real life into *The Contender*. Yes, ESPN is powerful and, yes, ESPN is the biggest name in sports media. But let's not forget, ESPN is the same network that last year was going to make a household name out of Juan Diaz.

In truth (or perhaps one should say "in reality"), *The Contender* has problems. Let's start with the fighters themselves and the relationships between them. Peter Manfredo and Sergio Mora were popular with the other participants. So were Jonathan Reid, Juan De La Rosa, and Jimmy Lange. And Alfonso Gomez was the de facto mayor of the village. "If I was going to war," one of *The Contender* fighters said recently, "I'd want Alfonso by my side. He's loyal; he'll fight for what he believes in. He's the type of guy who would risk his life for the group and, if things went wrong, take a bullet and tell you in his dying breath to look after his parents. To me, Alfonso is the heart and soul of *The Contender*."

But some of *The Contender* fighters dislike each other intensely. Jesse Brinkley and Ishe Smith were frequently at each other's throats on camera and off. Anthony Bonsante and Joey Gilbert rubbed a lot of people the wrong way, and Ahmed Kaddour irritated just about everyone. Kaddour, in turn, was at war with Smith and told the *Las Vegas Review-Journal*, "If I saw him on the street today, I'd kill him. Well, I wouldn't kill him because I wouldn't want to waste my time. But I'd rip his lungs out. I hate the guy."

The stuff of rivalries? Not if the public doesn't care. And of greater concern to *The Contender* is the fact that Smith is now rattling the cage, loudly. Ishe is generally regarded as, pound-for-pound, the best of *The Contender* fighters. After winning his first bout against Kaddour, he lost a questionable split decision to Mora. He is not a happy camper.

*The Contender* contracts specifically preclude participants from giving interviews to the media without the show's prior authorization. Some of the fighters have circumvented this prohibition with off-the-record conversations. Smith has chosen to talk openly.

Ishe's grievances against *The Contender* fall into several categories. First, he believes that several of the show's producers played favorites throughout the taping and undermined the fairness of the process. In that regard, he is infuriated by the decision that went against him in his fight with Sergio Mora.

"I won that fight," Smith says. "You know there was something phony about the decision because one judge gave it to me 49-46 and another judge had it 50-45 for Mora. How can two judges score a fight that differently? How can one judge score every round for Sergio when I had him out on his feet at the end of the fight? They didn't show the crowd booing when the decision was announced. They didn't show the way Sergio staggered around the ring at the end of the fight. To this day, they won't let me see a tape of the whole fight. My own fight! If there's nothing to hide, show me the tape. Show everyone the tape. There's no way Sergio beat me, but the producers are protecting him. I've pleaded with them to let me fight Sergio again, and they say 'no way.' Instead, they wanted me to fight Jesse Brinkley in their next show at 165 pounds. That's not my weight. If they said 154, fine; but not 165. So I told them 'no,' and then they said, 'Well, bring your own opponent and you can fight him at 154 pounds but it will be an off-TV fight. The only way you get on TV is if you fight Jesse at 165.'"

"And that's the way it is," Smith continues. "Under the contract, as long as they pay me my minimum [$50,000 a fight for two fights a year], they can keep me from ever getting exposure or fighting a world-class fighter. They can keep me from ever testing myself to see if I can be a world champion. I don't want to fight five-round fights against bring-your-own opponents. I don't want to be a carnival act like Butterbean. I want an opportunity to be recognized as a great fighter. I want to be a world champion, not a make-believe *Contender* champion. How do I know if I can fight a Winky Wright when they won't let me fight more than five rounds? David Estrada just fought Shane Mosley. I beat David Estrada. These guys have no respect for fighters. They're playing with fighters' lives as a hobby and I don't want to be part of it anymore. I want to fight real fights. I want to be a real fighter, not a TV-reality-show guy. The people who are running *The Contender* don't know the difference."

Smith is now saying publicly what some other fighters have been saying privately. But Ishe has taken things a step further by filing for arbitration before the California State Athletic Commission. His case is expected to be heard in late August. If he wins, he'll be free and clear of *The Contender*. At this point, the outcome of the arbitration proceeding is uncertain. But Smith could prevail based on broad public-policy arguments or technical violations of state and federal law.

That would please Smith. "There were some good people involved with producing the show," he says. "I'm not complaining about all of them. But forget about the idea that the people running the show are all good guys who made a lot of money in other businesses and now they're trying to make a contribution to boxing. That's bullshit. These are rich guys who want to get richer and make their egos bigger by promoting fights. They told us, 'We're not like Don King; we're not like Bob Arum.' And they were right. They're worse than King and Arum. At least King and Arum get championship fights for their fighters. Now they're threatening to sue me if I give interviews like this. Not even King and Arum do that to their fighters."

Smith has his own agenda. But the question remains, "If these guys are such wonderful promoters, why do so many of their fighters want to leave them?" That in turn leads to the thoughts of a television executive for a rival network, who says, "The major print media abdicated its responsibility to report honestly on *The Contender* because the people in charge didn't want to lose NBC's advertising dollars. So what we got was a lot of puff pieces on Sylvester Stallone and Ray Leonard. No one was looking at how the development of these guys as fighters was being impaired. And no one was looking seriously at what happened to Najai Turpin."

Najai Turpin. There's that name again. Turpin was the Philadelphia fighter who committed suicide after appearing on *The Contender*. Smith says one of the show's producers told him that, while Najai's death was a tragedy, it might be "good for the show." And Ishe recently told BoxingTalk.com, "They have the blood of Najai Turpin on their hands. They drove this man to killing himself. I firmly in my heart believe that they played a big role in the excess stress on this man's life. They knew that Najai was an individual that could have a problem dealing with something like this. The producers knew that Najai had attempted suicide at least once before when his mother passed away. They thought him being a little unstable would be good for television."

Turpin left behind a two-year-old daughter named Anyae Chapple. Anyae's mother (Angela Chapple) was pregnant with Najai's second child, a boy, at the time of his death. The baby is expected in September. A lawsuit for wrongful death could follow.

Meanwhile, *The Contender* keeps rolling along, albeit with lowered expectations. Richard Schaefer (CEO of Golden Boy Promotions) recounts a moment when the show's producers were negotiating with Oscar De La Hoya to serve as their host. Ultimately, the deal fell apart and De La Hoya launched a TV reality show of his own. Schaefer says the deal-breaker was *The Contender*'s insistence that Golden Boy be folded into *The Contender*'s own promotional company. "We're the future of boxing," he says he was told.

There was a time when most people in the sweet science thought it would be good for boxing if the *The Contender* were to succeed. Now, a growing number think it would be better for the sport if *The Contender* failed. Still, as long as the show is on the air, one hopes for the best. And that leads to a letter I received from a reader after two recent articles I wrote were posted on SecondsOut.com.

"Dear Mr. Hauser," the letter read. "You've been awfully hard on *The Contender*. In a lot of instances, you had very good reasons. But I think it would be helpful if you offered some suggestions on how to make *The Contender* a better reality boxing show in the future."

Fair enough. *The Contender* could have worked. Here's how.

Suggestion #1: Using a TV-game-show format demeaned boxing and, in the end, made for bad television. Forget the "challenges." Pulling a harness-racing cart around Santa Anita Race Track has nothing to do with boxing and wastes valuable air time. Also, deep-six the "rewards." Viewers don't need to see Jackie Kallen (wearing an outfit reminiscent of the clothes Julia Roberts wore in early scenes from *Pretty Woman*) shopping with Sergio Mora in a product placement orgy on Rodeo Drive.

Suggestion #2: Show each fighter in his real home enviroment rather than in the antiseptic *Contender* and *Contender* family housing. Let viewers see where these guys really come from and what their lives are really like.

Suggestion #3: Have the fighters live the way real fighters live when they're training for a fight. And don't do silly things like leaving them alone in the dressing room before a fight. That's not the way boxing works. Follow the mantra, "Anything that compromises the real routines of the fighters compromises the show."

Suggestion #4: Cut the trite lines. Viewers got tired of hearing fighters say over and over, "I'm doing this to support my family." Most people who have jobs do it to support their family.

Suggestion #5: Bringing a fighter's young children to a fight to see their father beat up other people and get punched in the face is a frightening experience and, in the eyes of some, a form of child abuse. In the quarter-finals, Jesse Brinkley KO'd Anthony Bonsante in the fifth round in front of Bonsante's sobbing daughter. Enough said.

Suggestion #6: Stop telling us that these are championship-caliber fighters. Peter Manfredo Jr., who was constantly touted as one of the best middleweights in the world, proved to be a .500 fighter against good club-fight oppposition.

Suggestion #7: Don't try so hard to get likeable telegenic guys. Get guys with hard edges. And to quote Ishe Smith, "Stop trying to make

*The Contender* a 'white' show. Boxing isn't a white sport." Ishe might have gone over the line when he said that his website would soon feature a photo of himself picking cotton while wearing a Mark Burnett T-shirt. But the bottom line is that only four of sixteen fighters on *The Contender* were black. That's not a "real" boxing demographic.

Suggestion #8: Show us the fights. The grand finale was exciting. It wasn't world championship boxing. To the contrary, it was contested on the level of a good club fight. But Peter Manfredo and Sergio Mora showed some skills and fought with heart. It was enough to make viewers wish that, in previous weeks, *The Contender* had opted for more realism and less schlock. The way the episodes were cobbled together supports the view that the producers didn't really believe in boxing; that they felt the fights had to be altered because they weren't good enough to stand on their own. Thus, rounds were cut in half. The same punch was shown several times from different camera angles so that it looked like multiple blows. One person who was on-site for the fight between Jesse Brinkley and Anthony Bonsante says that Bonsante was only knocked down once despite the fact that, on television, he was shown being knocked down two times. There's a lesson to be learned in the fact that the most dramatic and satisfying viewing experience that *The Contender* offered the public was its only full-fledged start-to-finish "real" fight.

Suggestion #9: Adapt a format that doesn't involve compromising the health and safety of the fighters. Anthony Bonsante, we were told, fought a week after he tore his hamstring muscle. Alfonso Gomez went into his semi-final fight against Peter Manfredo with the skin around both eyes bruised and swollen. On September 21st, Jesse Brinkley suffered a cut on his left eyelid that required five stitches. California State Athletic Commission records show that Brinkley was suspended for sixty days after that fight. Then, remarkably, he was cleared by a commission doctor to fight Sergio Mora three days later and the cut opened up again.

That raises some troubling questions. It appears as though, when it came to *The Contender*, normal medical standards were not adhered to by the California commission. "These guys got away with all sorts of things because they were TV guys and they had money," says one journalist whose investigative report on the show was killed after a telephone call to his editor. Another source says that at least one California commission doctor was paid quite well by *The Contender* for extensive medical work he performed at the same time he was performing official duties for the commission. How well? The estimate is in the neighborhood of $100,000.

The California State Athletic Commission is now under new leadership. On June 12, 2005, Armando Garcia became its executive officer.

He is now responsible for managing the commission on a day-to-day basis, but what happens next is uncertain. *The Contender* has tentative plans to begin shooting its second season in California before the end of this year. However, on January 1, 2006, the commission will cease to exist and its responsibilities will be folded into the Department of Consumer Affairs, which will then establish an athletic bureau. Garcia may, or may not, be the new bureau chief.

*The Contender* announced to the world that it was going to reform boxing and do right by fighters. On the medical front, it appears to have fallen far short of that goal. Indeed, Ishe Smith complains that, while he and the other fighters were promised medical insurance, he's still paying the full amount for his own family policy.

Also, when it comes to fighter contracts, *The Contender* seems to have played an ugly game of bait-and-switch.

Tarick Salmaci was one of the fighters on *The Contender*. "It was a great experience for me," he says. "Whatever you write, I want people to know that I'm very grateful and happy that I was on the show."

Still, one thing sticks in Salmaci's craw. Like all of the fighters, he signed a contract that bound him to *The Contender* for a period of up to five years. In return, he was guaranteed at least two fights a year after the May 24th grand finale. Those fights were to be for a specified minimum purse. In Tarick's case, the minimum was $75,000 per fight. (Salmaci had a higher minimum than Ishe Smith by virtue of finishing higher in the Internet "fan favorite" voting.)

But there was a problem. *The Contender* contract was terminable at will by the promoter. Salmaci lost to Juan De La Rosa in the first round of *The Contender* tournament on September 9th of last year. Then, a week after the May 24, 2005, grand finale, he received two letters from *The Contender* on the same day. The first letter terminated his promotional contract. The second letter said he could continue fighting under *The Contender* banner if he signed a new contract that would cut his minimum payment to $10,000 a fight.

"If I was twenty-three years old, I might do it," says Salmaci. "But I'm not. I'm thirty-three. My future is now."

Nor is Salmaci alone in what happened to him. Ahmed Kaddour, Jimmy Lange, and Joey Gilbert were released under similar circumstances after refusing to accept a similar cut in pay. Meanwhile, at least six of the other *Contender* fighters are believed to have accepted the pay cut that was demanded of them.

So . . . Let's take a poll. Who still thinks that *The Contender* is going to clean up boxing?◻

*The proliferation of sanctioning bodies and weight classes has diluted championships in boxing. The issue of who controls the titles presents a problem of equal magnitude.*

# WHO OWNS THE TITLES?

On June 25, 2005, Carlos Maussa knocked out Vivian Harris to earn the right to be called the WBA junior-welterweight champion. Note that I didn't say Maussa won the WBA title (although, like others in the industry, I frequently use that terminology). That's because the title stayed with Main Events.

Main Events was Harris's promoter. In order to get a shot at the title, the Maussa camp had to give Main Events options on its fighter. Now Maussa is scheduled to fight Ricky Hatton in a November 26th title-unification bout. Vivian Harris will be watching on television and Main Events will make a nice profit.

The history of boxing is the history of promoters controlling titles. Tex Rickard, Jim Jacobs, James Norris, Bob Arum, and Don King are prime examples. The people at Main Events didn't break any law or do anything immoral. They simply availed themselves of the way the business is structured and the system works. The money a promoter puts into developing a fighter is like the money that goes into grooming a racehorse. Often, a fighter is simply the promoter's vehicle for capturing a title. And once a belt is won by the promoter, it isn't lost until (a) the promoter's contract with the champion expires; (b) the champion loses a purse-bid title fight to a mandatory challenger; or (c) the champion loses a title fight for which the promoter receives sufficiently lucrative trade-offs that he allows it to take place without requiring options on the challenger.

Defenders of the status quo make the following arguments:

(1) Promoters put a lot of time and money into developing fighters and are entitled to a generous return on their investment should one of them win a title.

(2) If a promoter has other fighters under contract, he has an obligation to to do the best job possible to secure title fights for them, which is best done by controlling championships. As Don

King reasons, "You can't help the loser if you don't have the winner."

(3) Without the current system of options, there would be fewer competitive title fights because promoters would be unwilling to put their champions in risky match-ups.

The promoters also say, "This is a matter of contract law and a business right."

But should it be that way? Opponents of the present system maintain:

(1) A promoter's interest should be in the fighter he has developed; not in the title and not in a fighter whose success is the result of another promoter's work.

(2) A champion puts far more time and effort into his career than anyone else and risks his title every time he steps into the ring. Why shouldn't his promoter take the same risk?

(3) Suppose, prior to the 2005 NBA Championship finals, Detroit Pistons general manager Joe Dumars had said that his team wouldn't defend its title against San Antonio unless it got options on Spurs superstar Tim Duncan? Absurd? Absolutely. But that's what happens in boxing. Too often, the public doesn't see the fights it wants to see (and fighters who want to fight each other can't) because of a promoter's refusal to proceed without options.

The current heavyweight title mess is a classic example. Don King controls three of the four belts and wants a fourth. Meanwhile, the public is stuck with an endless stream of unsatisying match-ups as promoters lobby the world sanctioning bodies to further protect their interests and mandatory challengers are manufactured to maintain the power of favored promoters.

All of this, of course, leads to the larger issue of the validity of today's titles. "The whole thing is a scam," says boxing historian Mike Silver. "Boxing fans are the dumbest fans in the world to accept it. The titles only have meaning because people say they do. The emperor has no clothes. The sanctioning bodies and their titles are fraudulent."

The sanctioning bodies, in turn, take the position, "They're our titles. We created them and we can do what we want with them. If you don't like it, start your own sanctioning organization."

That mantra was most recently on display in the IBF's treatment of Juan Manuel Marquez (the WBA-IBF featherweight champion) who, in August, was stripped of his belt by a ludicrous slight-of-hand. Marquez was ordered by the IBF to make a mandatory defense against Phafrakorb Rakkiatgym of Thailand. It was a fight that virtually no one wanted to see and no one wanted to promote. The bout went to a purse bid, and no promoter stepped forward with the required $50,000 minimum offering. The IBF then stripped Marquez of his title for failing to fulfill his mandatory obligation and ordered a box-off between Rakkiatgym and the next-highest-rated available challenger. That meant Marquez also lost his WBA "super-championship" belt because, having been stripped by the IBF, he was no longer a "unified" super-champion.

Where was Marquez's promoter in all of this? Top Rank declined to bid on the fight or lobby aggressively to protect Marquez's rights because it had only one option left on Marquez's services and was at odds with his manager, Nacho Beristain.

If there were a legitimate poll (and not just one person making rankings for *USA Today* or the many Internet-site efforts), the importance of titles would disappear and be replaced by the issue of "who's number one" in each weight division. But for the moment, boxing still relies on titles to spur interest in the sport and belts translate into dollars.

Meanwhile, champions lose their belts on a regular basis and promoters roll on without missing a beat. On a gut level, it's troubling. Titles are controlled by the world sanctioning organizations and promoters. They should belong to fighters and the public. But very few people in positions of power want the system to change, so it won't.□

*Shortly after this article was posted on Secondsout.com, it was presented by USA Boxing to AIBA and the International Olympic Committee.*

# OLYMPIC BOXING: SCORING THE FIGHTS

The Beijing Olympics are three years away. The London Games are seven years in the future. But reform comes slowly in the convoluted world of international sports, so now is the time to take a long hard look at how Olympic boxing is scored.

Beginning in 1960, Olympic boxing matches were scored by five judges. Each judge voted for a winner based on his separate scoring of each round. The boxer who prevailed on a majority of the judges' cards was declared the victor.

Unfortunately, as is often the case with Olympic officiating, incompetence and favoritism reigned. Then came a scandal that couldn't be ignored. At the 1988 Seoul Olympics, Roy Jones Jr. fought Park Si-Hun of South Korea in the gold-medal bout. Jones threw more punches than Park in every round. He landed more punches than Park in every round. And he landed at a higher connect rate than Park in every round. The numbers, provided by CompuBox, were as follows:

> Round 1:
> Jones: 20 of 85 = 24 percent
> Park: 3 of 38 = 8 percent
>
> Round 2:
> Jones: 30 of 98 = 31 percent
> Park: 15 of 71 = 21 percent
>
> Round 3:
> Jones: 36 of 120 = 30 percent
> Park: 14 of 79 = 18 percent
>
> Totals:
> Jones: 86 of 303 = 28 percent
> Park: 32 of 188 = 17 percent

But there was a problem. The judges, who were allowed a measure of subjectivity due to the rules in force at the time, declared Park the winner. Thereafter, seeking to regain a modicum of credibility, the International Olympic Committee turned to electronic scoring.

The scoring system currently in use at the Olympics was introduced at the 1989 World Championships and has been part of every Olympic boxing competition since then. Each of the five judges is given a computer console. The console has a blue button and a red button; one for each fighter. When a boxer lands a "scoring blow," each judge is supposed to press the button for that fighter.

A scoring blow is a punch that has (1) cleanly connected (2) with the knuckle surface of the glove (3) within the legal scoring area of the body (4) with the weight of the puncher's body or shoulder (5) while not infringing a rule (for example, a blow struck while holding doesn't count). In order to push his button, a judge must have been in position to see clearly that all of the above criteria have been met. At the end of the bout, the boxer with the most punches scored wins.

But here's the rub. For a punch to register, three of the five judges must press the same color button within a one-second time frame. And the system doesn't work.

Spectators watch a fight, and the scoring is at odds with what they see unfolding before their eyes. Boxers are throwing fifty punches a round; and at the end of the bout, the score is 9 to 7. It's obvious that scoring blows (a lot of them) aren't being recorded. Regardless of whether or not the right boxer wins, scores aren't being tabulated properly. It's like watching a soccer game, seeing Manchester United score four goals, and being told at the end of the match that the final score is 2 to 1.

The International Amateur Boxing Association oversees standards for Olympic judging and selection of the judges themselves. AIBA (the acronym has a transposition in letters because of translation from the French language) divides the world into five "continents": Europe, Asia, Africa, Oceana, and the Americas (which includes North and South America). Thirty-six judges are assigned to each Olympics. Three of these come from the host country. The other 33 are chosen by the governing boxing federation of each continent. For example, six positions were allocated to the Americas for the 2004 Athens Olympics.

AIBA rules require that Olympic judges attend mandatory electronic-scoring sessions and have worked at least one World Championship in addition to other international competitions. But judges have different motor-skill reaction times. And under the present system, one incompetent or corrupt judge can significantly influence the outcome of a fight.

As previously noted, in order to be counted, a blow must be acknowledged by three of the five judges (60 percent) within a one-second time frame. But if a judge is looking for a reason to discount the punches of a particular fighter, he can simply push his button late or not at all. In that instance, the required percentage jumps to 75% (three of the other four judges). Conversely, if a judge is inclined to push his button in favor of a particular fighter landing a punch, only two of the other four judges (50%) are needed for the blow to score.

The system is so absurd that there have been instances in Olympic competition in which all five judges scored a bout in favor of a given boxer. Yet because of the timing of their button-pushing, the other boxer was awarded the decision on points.

The IOC is aware of the problem. In August 2005, it announced that it had frozen $9,000,000 in payments that had been earmarked for AIBA. Giselle Davies (an IOC spokeswoman) explained, "It's due to general judging issues that have remained unresolved since the Athens Olympics." IOC president Jacques Rogge has declared that the funds will remain frozen until AIBA provides a "clear timeline and planned actions" for dealing with the problem.

The solution is a no-brainer. IOC and AIBA, take note. The concept of each judge registering each blow makes sense. But you've taken something simple and screwed it up,

The judges should continue to register blows. But their findings should be tabulated separately. That way, one judge's score won't impact on the scores of the other judges. At the end of a bout, whichever boxer prevails on a majority of the judges' cards wins.

In other words, "Punch-Stats" with each judge being held individually accountable for his scoring. Here, the thoughts of Bob Canobbio, who founded CompuBox with Logan Hobson in 1984, are instructive.

The CompuBox system utilizes a laptop computer with two keypads and two operators. Each keypad has four active keys; one each for jabs thrown, jabs connected, power punches thrown, and power punches connected. If a punch is blocked by an opponent's gloves or arms, it's registered as a miss. Each operator records the efforts of one fighter.

CompuBox was hired by NBC in 1988 to compute at the Seoul Olympics. Canobbio and Hobson were in Korea for a month, compiling statistics for every fight that involved an American, all other televised fights, and miscellaneous match-ups where one of the participants was perceived as a possible future opponent for an American. The Roy Jones fight was the culmination of their efforts.

"The current system of Olympic scoring doesn't work." says Canobbio. "The sixty-percent requirement is one reason. Another reason is that each judge is counting punches for both fighters. Even if you're just counting punches landed and not worrying about misses or the distinction between jabs and power punches, I'm not sure the eye is trained to accurately follow four gloves. We learned that at CompuBox twenty years ago. Also," Canobbio continues, "because of the way punches are counted, the fights are awful. Olympic boxers are taught to land one punch at a time rather than flurry because, no matter how many punches you land, the likelihood is that only one punch in a combination will be counted. That means Olympic boxing has started to look like fencing."

The CompuBox system is imperfect in that the distinction between "jabs" and "power punches" is often irrelevant. Not all "power punches" are damaging blows. But in Olympic scoring, all connects count the same so that flaw doesn't matter.

Meanwhile, Canobbio would be delighted to work with AIBA, train its judges, and license his computer program to them. "It would be good for boxing," he says. "And quite frankly, another reason I'd like to do it is because, right now, the Olympics are giving computerized punch-counting a bad name."

If the people who run AIBA are smart, they'll take Canobbio up on his offer. And they'll change the current system of scoring, because it's hurting the sport. Also, I should add, honest judges would help.❏

*Sam Kellerman's death was a horrible blow to everone who knew him.*

# THE OPEN WOUND

The horror of Sam Kellerman's murder is almost too great to grasp. We know these things happen, but not to us or to anyone in our family. Not if we live in a safe world and come from a comfortable upper-middle class home. But the reality of life is that no one is completely safe.

The initial report came in the form of a press release issued by the Los Angeles Police Department:

> "On Sunday, October 17, 2004, at about 7:45 p.m., officers from Hollywood Division responded to a radio call from a citizen who had found a dead body inside an apartment in the 1400 block of Vista Street. The citizen directed the officers to where the body was lying on the floor of the apartment. Paramedics from the Los Angeles City Fire Department responded to the location and pronounced the victim dead. Detectives from the Hollywood Area Homicide Unit responded and assumed responsibility for the investigation. The detectives learned that the victim was renting the apartment and had recently allowed a guest to stay with him. Since the discovery of the crime, the guest and the victim's car are missing. The car is a bluish-green 1993 Cadillac Seville with Texas license plate number J04GHX. The motive for the crime is under investigation. The victim has been identified as Sam Kellerman, 29 years of age."

Sam Kellerman was born on November 24, 1974. He grew up in Manhattan, attended Stuyvesant High School (a public school for academically-gifted students), and took courses at Columbia College. His older brother, Max, is wellknown in boxing circles for the years he spent as studio commentator on *ESPN2 Friday Night Fights*.

Max was fifteen months older than Sam. Two other brothers, Harry and Jack, turn 28 and 26 later this month. Their lives will never be whole again.

"To understand what Sam meant to me," Max says, "picture the smartest person you know. Next, think of the most talented person you know. Now think of someone you grew up with. And last, think of the person you're closest to in the world. For most people, that would mean naming three or four different people. For me, it was one. Sam and I were so close, sometimes it seemed as though we shared a consciousness."

Sam did many things in his brief career. He wrote a play called *The Man Who Hated Shakespeare* and hosted a public-access cable-television show. He worked at a publishing house and wrote rap lyrics that, in Max's words, "came at you like a machine-gun."

"He was a creative genius," Max recalls. "He was the best writer for his age I've ever read. I used to tell him, 'I'll always be able to get someone to pay me for talking, and you'll always be able to get someone to pay you for writing.' When it came to writing, I felt like Salieri to Sam's Mozart. Sam wanted to direct film, but I think he was fated to write and be in front of the camera. He was starting to get work as an actor. He was in several national commercials. And acting wasn't even what he did best. Sam was a sure thing. It was just a matter of time before he made it big."

James Butler was at the other end of the spectrum. Born in Harlem, 31 years old, Butler was once regarded as a ring prospect. Fighting as a super-middleweight, he won 18 of his first 19 fights, scoring 12 knock-outs in the process. The sole blot on his record was a four-round decision loss to Richard Grant in his third pro fight.

On November 23, 2001, Butler and Grant met in the ring again; this time at a fundraiser for the families of police officers and firefighters who had died on 9/11. The site was Roseland Ballroom in New York. Two months earlier, Butler had suffered his second loss as a pro in an IBF title fight against Sven Ottke.

Grant beat Butler again, this time on a ten-round decision. As the victor stood in the ring awaiting a post-fight television interview, Butler walked over and sucker-punched him.

It was a horrifying moment. Grant dropped to the canvas. Blood poured from his mouth. His jaw was fractured and he went into convulsions.

Butler was arrested on the spot. He later pled guilty to felony assault, served four months in prison, and was released on five year's probation. He resumed his ring career in February 2004, but the fire was gone.

Sam Kellerman had met Butler in the early 1990s. At the time, Butler was a promising amateur and Sam was training in the same gym with the intention of entering the novice division of the New York City Golden Gloves. Ultimately, Sam put his fistic aspirations aside without entering the ring for a fight. But a bond was forged.

The day before Butler went to prison for assaulting Richard Grant, Max Kellerman took him out to lunch at Sam's request. Then Butler went to Sam's apartment to hang out for the rest of the afternoon. Sam was one of the few people to visit him when he was in prison. In early autumn 2004, Sam was living in Los Angeles when Butler contacted him. He was in L.A., trying to get his career back on track. Could he stay with Sam for a few days? Sam said yes.

James Butler did the same thing to Sam Kellerman that he did to Richard Grant. He sucker-punched him. Only he did it with a hammer, and there was no one to stop him from continuing his deadly assault.

Max Kellerman is sitting on a sofa. He feels weak and his head aches. Sixteen weeks after his brother's death, he still gets nauseous when he talks about it.

"It was on a Friday [October 15, 2004]," Max says. "I was on my way to East Hampton with my wife, when I got a call from my brother Harry. Harry was worried. I remember his saying, 'Max, do you know anyone in L.A. who can check up on Sam? I called him on Tuesday and left a message on voice-mail and I haven't heard back from him. That's not like Sam.'"

Max takes a deep breath to steady himself.

"So I called Sam and got a phone company message saying that his phone had been disconnected. That turned out to be a screw-up by the phone company. It had no bearing at all on the murder. So all Friday afternoon, I was livid at the phone company, but I felt better about not being able to reach Sam. Still, it bothered me enough that, late in the day, I called a friend named Steve Schneider and asked him to check out Sam's house. Steve went over and reported back that the doors were locked, the blinds were down, and the car was gone. I knew Butler was staying with Sam. He'd been supposed to stay for a few days and had been there for two weeks. Sam had been taking him around to the gyms in L.A., trying to help him out. I thought maybe Sam had gone to Vegas with Butler to find a fight or some kind of situation for him. Then, on Sunday, Harry called again. 'Max, I emailed Sam and I still haven't heard back from him.'"

There's a long pause as Max fights to control his emotions.

"So I called Sam again. His phone service had been restored, and I left a message on voice-mail. 'Sam, it's Max. This is not good. I know your phone was disconnected, but people worry. Please call.' And as I spoke those words, there was a sickening thought in the back of my mind but I pushed it aside."

Max cradles his head in his hands.

"That night, I was watching the fourth game of the playoff series between the Yankees and Red Sox when Harry called again. He was more worried than before, so I called Steve Schneider and asked him to go over to Sam's house a second time. The car was still gone, the blinds were still down, the door was still locked. But when Steve had gone over on Friday, he'd left a note on the door, and the note was gone. Steve asked me if I wanted him to break into the house. I told him no. Then Steve's girlfriend crawled in through a window, and the world was forever changed."

The woman who entered Sam's apartment was confronted by a scene akin to the nether regions of hell. The room was dark. It was stifling hot and the stove burners were on. Sam's body was on the floor beneath a sheet. His computer was on. He had been bludgeoned to death by multiple blows to the back of his head. Physical evidence suggests that he'd been facing his computer monitor when he was struck down from behind. The murder weapon, a hammer, was found near his body.

According to the police, Sam was killed on Tuesday, October 12th. One day earlier, he had told a friend that he was kicking Butler out. "I'm not looking forward to telling him," Sam had said, "but I'm doing it tonight."

"The reason Sam hadn't kicked Butler out earlier," says Max, "was that he felt sorry for him. Everyone else had abandoned him, and Sam was an incredibly loyal person. Probably, Sam told Butler on Monday, 'Look, you have to go.' Then, on Tuesday, he said, 'Leave now.'"

Butler was arrested on Wednesday, October 20th. Two days later, he was charged with first-degree murder and arson. The punishment for first-degree murder in California is death, life imprisonment without the possibility of parole, or imprisonment for a term of 25 years to life. The arson count alleges that Butler set a fire in Sam's apartment between the time he killed him and the time when the body was found. Bail has been set at $1,250,000.

Nothing recounted above can come close to describing the pain that Sam Kellerman's family has endured.

"You grow up believing as a kid that the world is here for you," Max says. "And the fact that the world is still here and Sam isn't, that there are six billion people alive and Sam's not one of them, is unbearably hard to accept. Sam never gets to have a family, have a career, grow old. It isn't supposed to be that way. Luke Skywalker doesn't die in the first half of the movie."

"I feel like half a person now," Max continues. "For two or three weeks afterward, I couldn't function. I couldn't stop crying. You know how sometimes you have a nightmare and wake up and say to yourself,

'Thank God, it was only a nightmare.' Well, each day, I woke up into the nightmare. My first and last thought each day was Sam. I couldn't talk. I still haven't been able to write thank you notes for all the condolence letters I got; and those letters meant a lot to me. Now, for the most part, I don't cry unless I'm alone."

"How do I deal with it? I don't. Not really. There's medication, distraction, pain, compartmentalization. I'm on four different medications now. And I'm thinking all these crazy thoughts. It's like a struggle with my own sanity. Fifteen billion years from now, if time reverses, I'll see Sam again before the big crunch. Once you're dead, a million years is no different from a second. So Sam and I will be separated for fifty years or so. Then there will be nothing. And after that, billions of years later, I'll see him. Or I think about string theory and maybe, if I concentrate hard enough, I can get to a parallel universe and Sam will be there. But it's all a charade, mental gymnastics to make me feel better. The arrow of time goes forward. Sam exists now only in memory. I smile sometimes when I think of him. But we'll never see each other again, and that thought alone is enough to keep me crying for the rest of my life."

James Butler's next scheduled court appearance is a preliminary hearing set for March 14th. There has been relatively little interaction so far betweeen the criminal authorities and the Kellerman family.

"I'm not really interested," says Max. "Nothing that happens to Butler will bring Sam back. Butler is meaningless to me. I hate him. I don't care about his life. I wish he had never been born. He had murderous intent; he used a hammer. Why did he have to take a hammer and kill my brother? Why couldn't he have punched him in the face, beaten him up, put him in the hospital? Do anything, but don't put a hammer through the back of his head. My brother was the last person to help James Butler; and for that, he was killed."❑

# ROUND 4

# CURIOSITIES

*A boxing ring is a sparse stage that plays host to some of the greatest dramas imaginable.*

# IN THE RING

Most people have been on a baseball diamond and a basketball court. At least once in their life, they've walked across a football field. But relatively few people have ever set foot inside a boxing ring.

The ring is a fighter's office. Unlike most sports playing fields, it's a temporary structure. Four people can assemble a boxing ring in less than three hours, although promoters complain that workers being paid by the hour often take longer.

The basic components of a boxing ring are the same whether the site is Madison Square Garden, a glitzy Las Vegas hotel-casino, or a small union hall in Pennsylvania. Plywood boards roughly five feet long and three feet wide are set on top of a skeletal steel frame. Foam padding an inch to one-and-a-half inches thick is placed on top of the boards. Then a large piece of canvas is stretched over the padding. Steel ring-posts are set into each corner of the skeletal frame. Ropes covered with velour, vinyl, or leather are attached to the posts. The ropes can be tightened or loosened by turning one of eight turnbuckles. Corner cushions shield each turnbuckle and post.

Most sports have variations in playing conditions. Artificial turf versus natural grass is a universal divide. Baseball fields have different dimensions beyond the infield. There are dead spots on the parquet floor at the Fleet Center in Boston and patches of soft ice in many hockey arenas. There's more variation in boxing rings than meets the eye.

First, there's the matter of size. Most professional rings are between 18 and 22 feet squared inside the ropes. Punchers prefer a small ring. Stylists would rather do battle in a large one.

The "speed" of a boxing ring depends on the thickness of the foam padding, the tightness with which the plywood boards are wedged together, and how tautly the canvas is stretched. The "faster" the ring, the better it is for movement. A slow ring negates speed, much like heavily watering the basepaths in baseball cuts down on stealing. But the firmer (and faster) the canvas, the more likely it is that a fighter will be hurt if he's knocked down and his head slams against the canvas.

The more flexible the ring ropes, the better able a fighter is to lean his upper body back away from punches.

For decades, ring canvases were grayish-white. That changed in the 1970s to accommodate the demands of color television. Now most ring canvases are blue. They're tough enough to withstand the constant pounding of fighters' feet and the stiletto heels of roundcard girls.

When a fight is televised, the ring is well-lit. In most non-televised fights, the lighting is regular room light, which is often poor.

Entering a boxing ring has a feel that's different from walking onto any other surface where sports are contested. Climbing between the ropes is an awkward maneuver that requires bending, stretching, and stepping at the same time.

The canvas isn't a uniform hard surface. It has a spongy feel that takes a while in the gym to get used to. Moving on it isn't like walking on a regular floor.

Inside the ring, the fighters are alone under bright lights in the boldest relief possible. Everything is focused on one small square of illuminated canvas. Every eye in the arena is upon them.

A boxing ring looks different from the inside; particularly when it's shared with another man who is intent upon rendering you unconscious. There's no place to hide. Once a fighter climbs the stairs, he's roped in, unable to leave until his night's work is done. The outer reaches of the arena fade into darkness, but the fighters can hear the roar of partisans screaming for blood.

Ancient Rome, the Colosseum. *"Morituri te salutamus . . .* We who are about to die salute you."

The fighter blots out the crowd and focuses on his opponent. He is standing on Muhammad Ali's dance floor, Mike Tyson's killing field.

When a fight ends, the multitude pours into the ring. Often, the ring canvas, which was clean at the start of the evening, resembles a Jackson Pollock painting fashioned from mucous and blood. The promoter, each fighter's camp, and hangers-on jostle for position to be seen on television and stand at the victor's side. The boxing ring, which moments before was the site of glory and pain, no longer seems like hallowed ground.❑

*"How can you sit there and watch two people punch each other? Don't you understand the damage they're inflicting on each other's brain?" I'm asked that question a lot. This was my answer.*

# THE DISCONNECT

Boxing is the most basic and most easily understood of all sports. Virtually any person who ever lived in any place at any time could watch a fight for the first time and understand what the combatants were trying to do to one another.

But fans who attend fights on a regular basis tend to become hardened to the reality of what's going on.

I'm not talking about sitting in the mezzanine, watching tiny stick figures in action or viewing a fight on television (which cosmetizes the violence). I'm talking about sitting up close in the first few rows at ringside.

The first time I watched a fight from the press section, I sat transfixed. I could almost feel the punches. The combat was taking place within an enclosure, but I had a sense of violence akin to a street fight spilling out in front of me.

Now there's a disconnect. I can eat a hot dog while someone is getting beaten up before my eyes.

Cognitive dissonance is a phenomenon that refers to the psychological discomfort a person feels because of a discrepancy between what that person knows or believes to be appropriate behavior and new information that supports an opposing view. When such an inconsistency exists, "something's gotta give" to eliminate the conflict. In the case of a discrepancy between attitudes and behavior, usually the attitude changes to accommodate the behavior.

That's why I can now sit at ringside and enjoy a good fight or simply be bored by a bad one. It's why, on two occasions, I've watched a man be literally beaten to death a few feet away from me in the name of "sport" and gone back for more. But sometimes old attitudes surface.

A minority of boxing fans enjoy watching someone get beaten up. The rest of us wrestle with this issue from time to time. We ponder, not only how a fighter will feel the following morning, but also what the condition of his brain will be ten years from now. We're aware of the fact that a "good fight" means that two boxers have engaged in combat with a brutal ebb and flow and been punched in the head and hurt multiple times.

I remember a moment that occurred four years ago at Madison Square Garden, when Shane Mosley defended his WBC welterweight title against Antonio Diaz. Mosley was 35-0 with 33 knockouts. He was coming off a win over Oscar De La Hoya that put him at or near the top of most pound-for-pound rankings.

Mosley was too good for Diaz. He stopped him in six rounds. I sat there, watching him dismantle his opponent in the manner of a great performing artist at work. There was one punch: a perfect left hook that landed flush on Diaz's cheek and spun his head around, wobbling his knees and sending a shower of spray into the air. In that moment, I said to myself, "I don't know if I'll be able to watch people do things like this to one another forever."

Fourteen months later in the same arena, Mosley was on the receiving end of the punishment. Midway through round two, Vernon Forrest staggered him with an overhand right, backed him against the ropes, and followed with a barrage of six punches, all of which landed flush and put Shane on the canvas. He survived the round, but not before Forrest administered a fierce beating, culminating in a second knockdown just before the bell that ended the stanza.

Mosley showed enormous heart and courage that night and worked his way back into the fight. Then, in round ten, Forrest blasted him with a hellacious hook to the body.

An involuntary scream escaped Shane's lips. I'll always remember that scream.

Forrest followed with a right uppercut and an overhand right that sent Mosley's mouthpiece flying.

And right then, the man sitting next to me muttered, "Shit, there's blood in my coffee." ❑

*Boxing has the greatest history of any sport. This article reflected on that history.*

# FIGHTERS OF THE DECADE

A. J. Liebling once wrote of the importance of tradition in boxing with the words, "The sweet science is joined onto the past like a man's arm onto his shoulder."

With that in mind, I embarked recently upon a sentimental journey. More specifically, I decided to travel back in time and choose a "fighter of the decade" for each decade beginning with the 1880s.

Comparing fighters is difficult, particularly where only fragmentary film footage (or none at all) exists. But I've done my best and had fun doing it. Several historians and fight aficionados shared my journey. My thanks to Randy Roberts, Mike Silver, Steve Farhood, and Craig Hamilton for sharing their thoughts. Don't blame them for what follows. The final judgments are mine.

## 1880-1889

The choice here is easy. John L. Sullivan was America's first sports superstar. He began in boxing's bare-knuckle days and won the world heavyweight championship in 1882 by knocking out Paddy Ryan in nine rounds. Then, in one of boxing's most-storied encounters, he knocked out Jake Kilrain in 75 rounds in Richburg, Mississippi, on July 8, 1889, in the last bare-knuckle fight for the world heavyweight championship.

Sullivan was dominant throughout the decade. More than anyone else, he created modern boxing. At decade's end, he was undefeated and one of the most famous men in America.

## 1890-1899

There are two candidates in this decade: James J. Corbett and Bob Fitzsimmons. But Corbett's primary accomplishment was beating an old John L. Sullivan in 1892. He defended his title only once over the next four years (a 1894 stoppage of Charley Mitchell) before being knocked out by Fitzsimmons in 1897.

Meanwhile, Fitzsimmons won the world middleweight championship in 1891. Except for a loss on fouls to Tom Sharkey, he was undefeated over the next eight years. He beat Corbett. And for good measure, after losing his title to James Jeffries in 1899, Fitzsimmons went down in weight to campaign successfully as a light-heavyweight. In the next decade, he would knock out George Gardner to capture the world light-heavyweight crown, making him boxing's first champion in three different weight classes.

The nod here goes to Fitzsimmons.

## 1900-1909

This decade narrows down to James Jeffries, Joe Gans, and Stanley Ketchel.

Jeffries was a dominant champion. But his two best showings (winning the title from a much smaller Bob Fitzsimmons and defending it successfully against Tom Sharkey) were in 1899 and he retired in 1905. In the first decade of the twentieth century, Gans and Ketchel are more deserving of laurels.

Joe Gans was a boxer's boxer and set the standard for fighters in the lighter weight classes who followed in his wake. He captured the world lightweight title with a first-round knockout of Frank Erne in 1902 and, four years later, added the welterweight crown. He remained a champion until 1908, when he lost his lightweight title to Battling Nelson, eight years his junior, who he had beaten in a 1906 title defense. He had 87 fights in the decade and lost only five of them: to Erne (who he later defeated), to ring greats Terry McGovern and Sam Langford, and twice at the end of his career to Nelson.

Ketchel began fighting in 1903 and won the world middleweight title in 1908. He ducked no one, fighting Billy Papke four times, Philadelphia Jack O'Brien twice, and Sam Langford. He even went so far as to challenge Jack Johnson for the heavyweight crown in 1909. Films of the fight support the view that Johnson agreed to "carry" Ketchel and knocked him out with one punch when Stanley was more aggressive than his end of the bargain called for.

Ketchel was shot and killed in 1910 at age 24 while still middleweight champion, which added to his legend. But by that time, the decade was done, and his credentials don't measure up to those of Gans.

Joe Gans is the fighter of this decade.

## 1910-1919

Jack Johnson won the heavyweight championship by knocking out Tommy Burns on December 26, 1908. He began the new decade by brutalizing James Jeffries en route to a 15th-round stoppage on July 4, 1910. That was followed by triumphs over Fireman Jim Flynn, Jim Johnson, and Frank Moran.

On April 5, 1915, Johnson was defeated by Jess Willard in Havana. But he dominated the decade in and out of the ring and, in the process, challenged the core values of America.

## 1920-1929

This is the most difficult decade to evaluate with Benny Leonard, Mickey Walker, Harry Greb, Jack Dempsey, and Gene Tunney in contention.

Benny Leonard was a complete fighter. He turned pro at age fifteen and was stopped three times in his first twelve fights. Then, over a nine-year period, he fought 154 bouts without a loss (many of those bouts went the distance and were ruled "no decision"). Leonard entered the "Roaring 20s" as lightweight champion, having dethroned Freddie Welsh in 1917. He held the crown until retiring in 1925, giving him the longest lightweight title reign ever.

Mickey Walker won the welterweight crown by besting Jack Britton in 1922 and defended it successfully six times. Then he moved up in weight and captured the middleweight title from Tiger Flowers in 1926. But Walker is best remembered for his quixotic quests at higher weights. In 1925, weighing only 149-3/4 pounds, he challenged Mike McTigue for the light-heavyweight crown. And at the start of the next decade, he moved to the heavyweight ranks for a losing effort against Max Schmeling and a draw with future champion Jack Sharkey.

Harry Greb was tough as nails and a dirty fighter. He fought an astounding 294 times in his career. Included in these bouts was a fifteen-round decision over Gene Tunney on May 23, 1922, the only loss of Tunney's career. Greb won the world middleweight title on August 31, 1923, and successfully defended it six times, including a 1925 victory over Mickey Walker. Other victims included Tommy Gibbons and Tommy Loughran. Greb died in 1926 at age 32 after complications from surgery on his nose following an automobile accident.

Gene Tunney turned pro in 1915. He avenged his 1922 defeat at the hands of Greb with two 15-round-decision victories the following year. They also fought to "no decision" on two occasions in later years, although it's worth noting that Tunney was a bigger man.

Tunney, of course, is best known for his 1926 and 1927 triumphs over Jack Dempsey in two of the most-storied heavyweight championship fights ever. He lost only once in his 77-bout career and was the first man to retire as heavyweight champion and stay retired.

Dempsey, with Babe Ruth, ushered sports into a golden era. He won the heavyweight title by decimating Jess Willard on July 4, 1919, and provided boxing with some of its most memorable moments. His 1921 bout against Georges Carpentier engendered boxing's first million-dollar gate. In 1923, he and Luis Firpo enaged in the greatest heavy-weight championship slugfest ever, with Dempsey going down twice and Firpo hitting the canvas seven times before the Manassa Mauler prevailed in the second round.

Let's eliminate Walker first. He simply wasn't as good as Leonard or Greb. Then take Greb off the list because he was such a dirty fighter. That leaves Leonard, Dempsey, and Tunney. But this was a heavyweight era, so let's narrow the choice to Dempsey and Tunney.

Dempsey was a brutal puncher and a "crossover star" who fired the public imagination and changed the way fighters fight with his brawling assaults. But his greatest win and the fight that first fired the public imagination was against Willard in the previous decade. Also, Dempsey put the title on ice for much of his seven-year reign and refused to defend it at all during the three years prior to his meeting Tunney.

Tunney, in turn, refined the science of boxing and beat Dempsey twice. Still, Dempsey did more for the sport. And let's not forget: Tunney got Dempsey at the end of Dempsey's career and after a three-year lay-off. If Dempsey and Tunney had fought at their respective peaks, Dempsey might well have won.

Is is right to choose Dempsey over Tunney when Tunney beat Dempsey twice? Is a fighter's dominance in the ring the only standard by which a "fighter of the decade" should be chosen, or can a boxer's impact on the sport also be weighed?

Some rounds should be scored 10-10. The 1920s should be scored even. Jack Dempsey and Gene Tunney are my fighters of the decade.

## 1930-1939

Joe Louis defined the era. The choice is Joe Louis, right? Probably, but first, let's hear from a worthy challenger.

Henry Armstrong was "pound-for-pound" before the phrase was invented for Sugar Ray Robinson. Armstrong fought 27 fights in 1937 and won them all, 26 by knockout. He captured the featherweight crown that year by knocking out Petey Sarron. Then, over the next nine months, he added the welterweight championship with a lopsided deci-sion over Barney Ross and annexed the lightweight title with a victory over Lew Ambers. Armstrong held all three titles at the same time. And for good measure, he fought twelve title fights in 1939 and won eleven of them. His accomplishments were almost beyond comprehension.

Now for Joe Louis. The Brown Bomber changed the fabric of America. He was one of the greatest fighters in history, and possibly the most important fighter who ever lived. But Louis didn't have the inquisitors that Armstrong had and his ring opponents in the 1930s didn't compare with Armstrong's. Armstrong fought the best in every division he conquered. Louis fought some tough opponents on the way up. But once he was champion, setting aside his fabled 1938 rematch against 33-year-old Max Schmeling, he finished the decade with a succession of "bums of the month."

Still, this was an era when the heavyweight championship was the most coveted title in sports. And Louis-Schmeling II weighs heavily on the scale, both in terms of its societal impact and Louis's performance.

Boxing historian Randy Roberts asks plaintively, "How can you pick anyone over Joe Louis?"

You can't. Joe Louis is my fighter of the decade.

## 1940-1949

Joe Louis fought through the 1940s, but lost four years to the war and ultimately faded. Willie Pep turned pro in 1940 and, two years later, won the world featherweight championship at age twenty. Pep had 148 fights in the deacde and lost only twice (to Sammy Angott and Sandy Saddler).

But the 1940s belonged to Sugar Ray Robinson.

Robinson turned pro on October 4, 1940, with a second-round knockout of Joe Escheverria at Madison Square Garden. He had 103 fights in the decade and lost once, to Jake LaMotta. He beat LaMotta five times.

There's no such thing as perfection in boxing, but Robinson as a welterweight came close. He won the title in 1946 with a decision over Tommy Bell and kept it until the next decade when he moved up in weight and captured the middleweight crown. Without doubt, he's the fighter of the decade.

## 1950-1959

Sugar Ray Robinson began the 1950s with 27 more consecutive wins including his February 14, 1951, seizure of the middleweight crown from Jake LaMotta. His record for the decade was 41 and 5, which included winning and losing the middleweight title four times. Robinson's dramatic one-punch 1957 knockout of Gene Fullmer might have been the most perfect left hook ever thrown. But Sugar Ray as a middleweight was beatable. Rocky Marciano wasn't.

Marciano turned pro in 1947 and captured the heavyweight championship with a dramatic 13th-round knockout of Jersey Joe Walcott in 1952. He didn't have the inquisitors that some champions have had. Most of the men he fought had limited skills or were great fighters past their prime. But Marciano didn't duck anyone. The great young heavyweights just weren't there to fight. And when Rocky retired in 1956, his record stood at 49 fights with 49 wins and 43 knockouts.

Archie Moore, like Marciano, won his title in 1952. But Archie was 39 at the time. He had begun his career in 1935 and was denied a title shot for far too long. Given the opportunity, he made the most of it by dethroning Joey Maxim and holding the championship for the rest of the decade. But Moore was more interested in pursuing the heavyweight crown. Indeed, he was stopped by Marciano in nine rounds in the last fight of Rocky's career.

Give Moore credit for his accomplishments, but Rocky Marciano is the fighter of the 1950s.

## 1960-1969

The 1960s are "no contest" as Muhammad Ali used to say.

Cassius Marcellus Clay Jr., turned pro on October 29, 1960, with a six-round decision over Tunney Hunsaker. At decade's end, he was Muhammad Ali; a gleaming symbol, unbeaten and unconquerable in his prime.

Ali's record in the 1960s was 29-and-0 with 23 knockouts. The Ali of that era would have beaten any fighter ever.

## 1970-1979

Ali faded in the 1970s. There were glorious victories over George Foreman in Zaire and Joe Frazier in Manila. But two other fighters, Roberto Duran and Carlos Monzon, are more deserving of consideration for fighter of the decade honors.

Duran brought savagery and power to the 135-pound ranks and redefined what a lightweight could be. He won the championship in 1972 by knocking out Ken Buchanan at Madison Square Garden. Then he avenged his only loss of the decade (a decision defeat at the hands of Esteban De Jesus) by knocking De Jesus out twice. His record for the decade was 54-1 with a 13-0 mark in championship bouts.

Monzon captured middleweight honors with a November 7, 1970, stoppage of Nino Benvenuti. Victims in his fourteen successful title defenses included Emile Griffith, Benny Briscoe, and Jose Napoles. Monzon held the crown until his retirement in 1977, and his record for the decade was 26-0 including a 15-0 mark in title bouts.

It's a close call. But Monzon's toughest opponents were smaller men who were getting on in years when he fought them. And unlike Monzon, Duran was going strong at the end of the decade. Indeed, the following year, he would temporarily wrest the welterweight crown from Sugar Ray Leonard.

Roberto Duran is the fighter of the decade.

## 1980-1989

This is another tough choice with five nominees: Larry Holmes, Mike Tyson, Julio Cesar Chavez, Marvin Hagler, and Sugar Ray Leonard. It's a bit like comparing apples and oranges, but let's start with Holmes and Tyson (who we'll call the oranges).

Holmes began the decade as the undisputed unappreciated heavyweight champion of the world. On October 2, 1980, he brutalized Muhammad Ali en route to an eleventh-round knockout. Two years later, he stopped Gerry Cooney in the thirteenth-round of their Las Vegas mega-fight. And there were successful title defenses against Lorenzo Zanon, Leroy Jones, Scott LeDoux, Trevor Berbick, Leon Spinks, Renaldo Snipes, Randall Cobb, Lucien Rodriquez, Tim Witherspoon, Scott Frank, Marvis Frazier, James "Bonecrusher" Smith, David Bey, and Carl Williams. Then came decision losses to Michael Spinks in 1985 and 1986.

Meanwhile, just prior to Holmes losing his crown, Mike Tyson arrived on the scene. "Iron Mike" turned pro on March 6, 1985. Twenty months later, he was the WBC heavyweight champion by virtue of a second-round annihilation of Trevor Berbick.

Tyson consolidated the belts with victories over Bonecrusher Smith and Tony Tucker. Next, he destroyed Pinklon Thomas, Tyrell Biggs, Holmes, and Tony Tubbs. Then, on June 27, 1988, he disposed of Michael Spinks in 91 seconds. Knockouts of Frank Bruno and Carl Williams followed. At decade's end, Tyson had 37 wins in 37 fights with 33 knockouts. He was Godzilla and (people were sure) would reign for a thousand years.

Now for the "apples" (Chavez, Hagler, and Leonard).

Chavez turned pro on February 5, 1980. He had 68 fights in the decade and won all of them, including title-bout triumphs over Roger Mayweather, Rocky Lockridge, Juan Laporte, and Edwin Rosario. In the process, he won titles in the junior-lightweight, lightweight, and junior-welterweight divisions.

Hagler captured middleweight honors with a third-round stoppage of Alan Minter in 1980 and successfully defended the title twelve times. Included in that run was his extraordinary third-round knockout of Thomas Hearns. He lost his title to Sugar Ray Leonard on a disputed decision in 1987.

That brings us to Leonard. Ray began the 1980s with a successful defense of his WBC welterweight title against Davey "Boy" Green. Later that year, he lost and regained the crown in memorable fights with Roberto Duran. And in 1981, he emerged victorious from a titanic struggle with a 14th-round knockout of Thomas Hearns. Thereafter, Leonard fought sporadically, with one notable moment of glory. On April 6, 1987, he beat Hagler.

If my ballot had been cast on December 31, 1989, I probably would have voted for Tyson. But in retrospect, Mike didn't fight anyone who presented as great a challenge as Leonard's most formidable inquisitors: Duran, Hearns, and Hagler. Tyson was a steamroller, but he never climbed a mountain. How good was he? Probably not as great as most of us thought he was at the time.

Thus the question: Should a "fighter of the decade" be chosen based on how the candidates were regarded at the end of the decade or with historical perspective?

Looking back, Holmes was steady; Tyson was electrifying. Hagler lost to Leonard, and Chavez was better at front-running than coming from behind. The key determining factor here is that none of the others fought big fights on a par with Leonard. Sugar Ray fought and beat everyone. He's the fighter of the decade.

## 1990-1999

Four men deserve consideration in this decade: Evander Holyfield, Lennox Lewis, Pernell Whitaker, and Roy Jones Jr.

Holyfield captured the heavyweight title with a second-round knockout of James "Buster" Douglas on October 25, 1990. Over the course of the decade, he won the heavyweight championship three times, defeated Riddick Bowe in their classic second match-up, and won both a glorious victory and an ugly disqualification over Mike Tyson. But in the four title defenses of his first reign, he beat two men well past their prime (George Foreman and Larry Holmes), was life-and-death against Bert Cooper, and lost to Bowe. He also lost to Michael Moorer and Bowe again and failed to win either of two closely-contested bouts against Lennox Lewis. His overall record for the decade was 13 wins, 4 losses, and 1 draw.

Lewis was 29-1-1 for the decade. His sole defeat was a second-round knockout by Oliver McCall which resulted from one punch and a premature stoppage. The draw came against Holyfield and was hotly disputed. Lewis avenged both of those blemishes on his record. His other victims for the 1990s included Razor Ruddick, Tony Tucker, Frank Bruno, Tommy Morrison, Ray Mercer, and Andrew Golota. Lennox ended the millennium as boxing's last undisputed heavyweight champion, but his most dominant years came in the next decade.

Pernell Whitaker entered the 1990s as the WBC and IBF lightweight champion. He successfully defended his title six times before moving up in weight to beat Rafael Pineda for the IBF 140-pound belt. Then he journeyed to 147 pounds and decisioned Buddy McGirt twice. He also outclassed Julio Cesar Chavez in a 1993 WBC welterweight-championship bout, although the judges embarrassed themselves by calling it a draw. Whitaker had 24 fights in the decade and won all of them except for the draw against Chavez, a decision loss to Oscar De La Hoya, and lesser performances against Andrei Pestriaev and Felix Trinidad at the end of his career.

That brings us to Roy Jones Jr., who turned pro in 1989. He had 37 fights in the 1990s and won all of them, save for a ninth-round disqualification against Montell Griffin. In their rematch, Jones knocked Griffin out in one round. He dominated the middleweight, super-middleweight, and light-heavyweight divisions in a way that few boxers ever have. He totally outclassed some very good fighters, Bernard Hopkins and James Toney among them. And most telling, at the end of the decade, one could have asked a hundred professional fighters, "Pound-for-pound, who's the best fighter in the world?" Virtually all of them would have answered, "Roy Jones, Jr." Roy Jones is the fighter of the decade.

## 2000 AND BEYOND

Boxing goes on. Superstars come and go. It's too early to know who will deserve recognition as the next fighter of the decade. Bernard Hopkins is in the competition, but Floyd Mayweather Jr. is coming on strong. A dominant heavyweight champion could emerge or someone like Jermain Taylor could run the table. The only thing certain is that there will be considerable debate over who should receive the honor. Everyone is entitled to an opinion.❏

*Hanging around the fight game, one overhears bits and pieces of information, insights, and humor.*

# FISTIC NUGGETS

After a successful amateur career, junior-middleweight Sechew Powell won his first twelve pro fights without a hitch. But on June 17, 2004, the road got rocky. Powell was knocked down and hurt by a tough journeyman named Grady Brewer and barely escaped with a one-point split-decision win.

"That's the first time I was ever knocked down," Powell says. "What happened was, I lost focus for a second and got caught."

How does a boxer "lose focus" when someone is trying to knock his head off?

"It happens," Powell explains. "It's not like you're thinking about going to the movies or what you'll have for dinner after the fight. It can be something like, 'Am I winning this round?' or 'I wonder how the judges are scoring the fight.' Just for a moment, you're not concentrating one hundred percent on your opponent and what you're doing technically at that time. A split second is all it takes and—WHAM—you're caught."

●●●

Junior-welterweight Paulie Malignaggi was born and raised in Brooklyn and is a quintessential New Yorker. Thus, he considered it a hardship to leave the city for a two-month training camp in Tewksbury, Massachusetts, prior to fighting Jeremy Yelton.

"I had to go away because of distractions," Malignaggi explains. "In New York, everyone knows where I live and calls or drops in at all hours of the day and night. There's night life; there's club life. It made sense to go to training camp, but I can't put into words how much I missed New York."

"There's nothing in Tewksbury," Malignaggi continued. "I had to walk for ten minutes if I wanted some juice or a granola bar. I'm doing roadwork in this wooded area, and I'm saying, 'Yo, there's a chipmunk. Look out, I almost stepped on a frog.' Plus it takes extra effort to build killer instinct when you're homesick. No offense to Tewksbury; for training purposes, it did the job. But I love New York."

Malignaggi is a flashy dresser with a big mouth, who's basically a good guy. His Achilles heel as a pro has been a lack of punching power. But after an eight-month layoff occasioned by hand surgery in which three knuckles were fused together, Paulie has been punching with power in the gym.

"A lot of guys couldn't write with a hand like I had," says Malignaggi. "I had to fight with it. I broke my hand seven times in different places. Now I can whack."

● ● ●

Go to a club fight in New York City or Westchester, and there's a good chance that former heavyweight contender Renaldo Snipes will be there.

Snipes, a Yonkers resident, began his career with 22 straight wins. Then, on November 6, 1981, he entered the ring at the Pittsburgh Civic Arena to challenge heavyweight champion Larry Holmes.

In round seven, Snipes hit Holmes flush with an overhand right. The champion plummeted to the canvas, struggled to his feet, staggered sideways, and fell into the ropes. In today's world, the fight probably would have been stopped. But referee Rudy Ortega let the action continue. Holmes survived and went on to win on an eleventh-round knockout.

"I'm a happy man," Snipes says today. "I have no regrets. For twenty seconds, I was the heavyweight champion of the world."

● ● ●

On occasion, an unseen corner of the boxing world is illuminated for the unknowing. *Shadow Boxers*, a marvelously-produced coffee-table book featuring photographs by Jim Lommasson, does just that.

*Shadow Boxers* takes readers into the gyms where young fighters learn their trade. The photographs are accompanied a series of essays, the best of which are written by Katherine Dunn.

Dunn's words are telling. "Boxing gyms are more than training facilities," she writes. "They are sanctuaries in bad neighborhoods for troubled kids and shrines to the traditions of the sport. The gym is home. For many, it's the safest place they know." And Dunn is on target when she notes ironically, "A boxing gym is a place where men are allowed to be kind to one another."

● ● ●

Bill Cayton was one of boxing's best manager's ever. He was creative and smart and fought hard for his fighters. He also believed what he wanted to believe. Ergo, in early 2003, he said with great sincerity that Lenord Pierre (a novice middleweight he managed) would be ready to fight Oscar De La Hoya within a year.

"You misunderstood," Pierre's co-manager Steve Lott explained when advised of Bill's prediction. "Bill said Oscar De La Renta."

● ● ●

Promoter Sal Musumeci, who is trying to establish himself on the New York boxing scene, was asked recently how he felt about his 15-year-old son taking blows as an amateur fighter. "I feel good about my son boxing," Musumeci responded. "Knowing that he's properly conditioned and trained, I'm not concerned. Besides, if I can put someone else's son in the ring, I should be willing to do the same thing with my own son." ❑

*From time to time, I recount the memories of boxing personalities regarding the first professional fight they ever saw. The tradition continued with this article.*

# FIRST FIGHT

### PAULIE MALIGNAGGI

It was Naseem Hamed against Kevin Kelley at Madison Square Garden. I was sixteen years old and hadn't had any amateur fights yet. But I was a fan, and none of my friends wanted to go with me so I went by myself. I got to the ticket window, and the cheapest tickets they had were twenty-five dollars plus a two-dollar surcharge. All I had in my pocket was two subway tokens and twenty-five dollars. But the woman at the ticket window was nice. I was wearing an old sweatsuit, so she could see I wasn't made of money. She looked around to make sure no one was watching and then she slid me a ticket for twenty-five dollars. I sat up in the nosebleed section. Ricky Hatton was on the undercard in his second pro fight. So was Joan Guzman. Junior Jones fought Kennedy McKinney. There was some real talent that night. Then it was time for the main event. Hamed did this dance behind a screen and then he danced down a ramp into the ring. I saw what he was doing and I said to myself, "Wow! That's me." I was rooting for Kevin and Junior, and both of them lost. But I had a great time that night.

### JAMES "BUDDY" MCGIRT

I was fourteen years old and had been boxing in the amateurs for two years. Louie Anatra, who was my coach, took me. The fights were at the Long Island Arena in Commack [on April 29, 1978]. Two local guys— Paddy Dolan and Hubert Hilton—were on the card. Paddy knocked out Dave Bolden, and Hilton stopped some guy whose name I can't remember. I'd always wanted to be a professional fighter and I'd read about Dolan and Hilton in the local paper, so I was rooting for both of them. But what I remember most was, when I walked into the arena, I was quiet for a moment. I felt a rush of adrenaline and it was energizing, but I was in awe. Somehow, I hadn't expected it to be the way it was. It was like, even though I'd never been to a pro fight before, I'd found a home.

### JOE MESI

It was "Boom Boom" Mancini against Livingston Bramble in Buffalo. I was ten years old. My grandfather and uncle on my father's side of the family had been pretty good boxers. Both of them won Golden Gloves championships, and my grandfather had boxed a bit as a pro. I went to the fight with my father, my grandfather, and my older brother. "Boom Boom" Mancini was the only name I knew in boxing other than Muhammad Ali and Larry Holmes, so I was rooting for him. What I remember most about that night was the beating he took. I understood that I was watching something brutal. Bramble turned his face into a bloody mess, and the fight was stopped in the fourteenth round. Believe me, that night, I had no idea that boxing was something I'd ever choose to do in life.

### GEORGE KIMBALL

Joe Frazier against Terry Daniels in New Orleans [on January 15, 1972]. I was covering the Super Bowl between Dallas and Miami the next day and decided to go to the fight. There were smells and sounds in the arena that you just don't get on TV. Leather hitting bone doesn't sound the same on television. And at the time, I might not have even seen a fight on color-TV. Frazier had beaten Ali in his last fight, and Daniels wasn't much. He didn't belong in the ring with Joe, and Joe beat him up. What I remember most about the night is that, at one point, Frazier was pounding the shit out of him and stopped to look at the referee as if to say, "Come on, man. What's wrong with you? Stop the fight." But the referee let it go on, and Joe knocked him out. Afterward, on the way out of the arena, I ran into George Foreman. There's a lot of cynicism about George today. A lot of people think that his nice-guy persona is an act. But I've thought long and hard on it and I think that, if anything, it's the old George that was an act. Anyway, this was before George beat Joe for the title. George was in his surly unpleasant stage, which lasted a while. As we were leaving the arena, I mentioned to him that there was a point when Joe seemed to be asking the referee to stop the fight. George's eyes took on a questioning look and he said to me, "You saw that too?"

### HASIM RAHMAN

Vincent Pettway against Dan Sherry at the Baltimore Arena in 1993. I had just started boxing as an amateur, and Pettway was the biggest fighter in Baltimore. He was the franchise in the gym, and everybody from the gym got to go. I was feeling good about myself because, even though I hadn't had an amateur fight yet, Mack Lewis, who ran the gym, was saying that someday I could be heavyweight champion of the world. And Mack wasn't saying that about anyone else in the gym that I knew of. I remember walking into the arena and taking everything in. There was a lot of betting going on in the crowd. People were drinking and having a good time. There was a lot on the line because Pettway was close to a world title fight and, if he lost, the opportunity would be gone. It was an exciting fight. Pettway stopped him late and, the next year, he beat Gianfranco Rosi for the IBF junior-middleweight title. I look back on that, and now I'm on the opposite side of the spectrum. Back then, I was at the fights as a fan. Now, when I go, I'm part of the scene even if I'm not fighting.

### ROBERTO DURAN

It was in Panama. I was twelve years old, I think. There was a gym in the neighborhood I lived in that had fights. Each time, the kids would line up on the street before the fights to go inside and sell snow cones. Not everyone could sell snow cones to the people at the fights. You had to be chosen, and I got there too late. The kids had already been chosen, so I went up to the roof and looked down and saw the fights.

### SUGAR RAY LEONARD

I was boxing as an amateur. Dave Jacobs and Janks Morton, who were my trainers, took me. I'm pretty sure it was at the Washington Skating Rink. Johnny Gant was in the main event, and I remember thinking that the atmosphere was very different from the amateurs. Things were much more emotional and a lot of money was being bet. At the time, I didn't see myself becoming a professional fighter because I had bad hands. I was hoping to fight in the Olympics, and that would be it. But as you know, I did turn pro. And later on [in 1979], I fought Gant and knocked him out.

### JERRY IZENBERG

I'd boxed a little when I was fifteen and got the crap beaten out of me in my first two fights. Then, in my third fight, I got knocked unconscious. I remember thinking, "Oh, that's interesting. The floor is coming up to my face." The next thing I knew, there were three people standing over me. Then the three people became one. After that, the powers-that-be said they wouldn't let me fight anymore. But there was one guy in the group who was worse than me, and I told them, "I'll go quietly, but I want to fight him first." So they let me fight him. I beat the crap out of him, and then I retired as an active fighter with a record of one win and three losses. Anyway, now that I've told you about that, the first professional fight I saw was Freddie Archer, the Pride of Newark, against the Irvington Milkman, Charlie Fusari [on August 22, 1946] at Ruppert Stadium when I was sixteen years old. Freddie was my hero from the old neighborhood. I went to the fight alone and took two buses to get there. The crowd was blue-collar. Abner "Longie" Zwillman, who was a charter member of Murder Incorporated, was also in attendance. The promoter was a man from the Frankie Carbo era named Willie Gilzenberg, who needed to shave twice a day and was known as "The Beard." Gilzenberg put the main event on first because it looked like rain and he didn't want to have to give anyone their money back. The undercard fights were afterward. Fusari beat the crap out of Archer and knocked him out. But I loved it. I started going to the fights every week after that. That's where I went wrong in my life.

### RICHIE GIACHETTI

It was a fight in Cleveland. I was eighteen, maybe nineteen, years old and worked the corner for a guy my Uncle John was training. I was the bucket boy. I'd been to amateur fights before, but this was different. The dressing room was pretty much the same. The fighter gets his hands wrapped; you sit around. My uncle had rehearsed with me what I was supposed to do. Go up the stairs. Put the bucket between the fighter's legs so he can spit into it. Hand me the water bottle. Then we went to the ring. People were hollering. It was different from anything I'd experienced before. At first, I was blinded by the lights. Then my eyes adjusted and I could see the crowd. I felt important. It was a good feeling, like I was really somebody. I liked that feeling a lot, and I knew I wanted to stay in boxing so I could have that feeling again.

### DIEGO CORRALES

It was Tony Lopez against Rocky Lockridge in Sacramento. I think I was eleven. My dad took me. He loved boxing. He fought as a pro under the name Ray Woods until he was hurt in a car accident. Lopez was a Sacramento guy and my father talked about him a lot, so I knew who he was. I didn't know what to expect; and when we got to the arena, I thought it was the coolest thing in the world. I remember how happy everyone seemed to be there and how excited I was by what was going on in the ring. It was an action fight. Lopez was knocked stiff early. I still don't know how he got up, but he did and came back to win. At the time, I had no idea I'd ever be a fighter. That came later, when my father brought me to the gym. Then, early in my career, I got to spar with Tony Lopez.

## DON CHARGIN

My dad took me to see Jackie Jurich fight a Mexican kid named Donnie Maes [on April 15, 1941]. They were neighborhood rivals from my hometown of San Jose. In fact, Jurich was called "The Rose of San Jose." I was just a kid. The fight was in an old tin building called Foreman's Arena. It was a ramshackle place with a few rows of folding chairs at ringside and a lot of bleachers. But when I walked in, it looked like Madison Square Garden to me. My heart was pounding. 112-pound fighters seemed like giants. As far as I was concerned, every woman there looked like Betty Grable. It was a good fight [a ten-round draw], and from that moment on, I knew I wanted to be in boxing.

## OSCAR DE LA HOYA

I was six years old. It was at at the Olympic Auditorium. My father took me. The Olympic was famous for people throwing cups down from the balcony on the people below. The cups were filled with what looked like beer. If it was cold, it was beer. If it was warm, it was something else. I don't remember who fought. I do remember that Don King and Hector Camacho were walking through the crowd, and the whole place started booing. Then the cups started coming down and they started running.❑

*They're boxing's most essential equipment. But little is written about boxing gloves.*

# BOXING GLOVES

The Romans forced gladiatorial slaves into combat wearing cesti weighted with iron spikes on their fists. Getting hit with cesti must have hurt. Now boxers wear gloves, not to protect an opponent's face, but to safeguard their hands.

Modern gloves date to John Broughton, whose "Broughton's Rules" governed boxing from their promulgation in 1743 until 1838, when the London Prize Ring Rules were adopted. Broughton's "mufflers" were used for sparring and, unlike today's gloves, were designed primarily to protect the faces of his well-to-do students. Then the Marquess of Queensberry Rules came into play, mandating that matches be contested with "fair-sized boxing gloves of the best quality and new."

In the early years of the Queensberry Rules, gloves were often little more than skin-tight mittens weighing several ounces. John L. Sullivan is widely known as the last champion of the bare-knuckle era. However, "The Great John L." wore gloves for most of his fights. In 1892, when he lost to James Corbett in the first heavyweight championship fight contested under the Queensberry Rules, each man wore five-ounce gloves. Present-day regulations require 8-ounce gloves for fighters in weight divisions up to 147 pounds and 10-ounce gloves above that.

In recent decades, the color of gloves has changed from brown to red, which better enables fans to see the punches. Artist LeRoy Neiman, who calls himself "a product of the brown-glove era," says, "I suppose it's just a matter of time before some fighter comes into the ring wearing polka dots or stripes on his fists."

Regardless, boxing gloves aren't particularly fashionable; although promoter Don Elbaum opines, "If you put a pair of boxing gloves on a good-looking woman, she immediately looks sexier." There will be more from Elbaum later in this article.

The oldest major brand name in boxing is also the largest manufacturer of gloves. The "Everlast" logo is affixed to approximately one million pairs of gloves each year. Most of these are used for sparring, bag-work, and other gym activity. Training gloves are for learning and developing, not doing damage in the gym. They have more padding than fight gloves and weigh up to twenty ounces.

Only a small percentage of the gloves that Everlast makes are worn by professional fighters. These are hand-crafted at the Everlast plant in Moberly, Missouri. Much of the company's other glove manufacturing is outsourced to production facilities overseas.

Everlast offers a substantial discount on gloves sold to gyms, promoters, and others in the trade. It often gives away gloves for fights that will be seen on television. "We don't think about making a profit where gloves worn by professional fighters are concerned," says company CEO George Horowitz. "The fact that professional boxers wear our gloves is important to us as a marketing tool for all of our products."

Everlast's primary domestic competitor in the sale of gloves is Grant, which was founded by Grant Elvis Phillips in 1995. "I was 29 years old, managing fighters, and selling boxing equipment on the side," Phillips recalls. "I always felt that I could make a superior glove, but I didn't have the money to get started. Then Luis Santana, who was my fighter, fought Terry Norris and won on a disqualification. They fought again, and Luis won again on a disqualification. Norris knocked him out the third time they fought, but by then I'd made a half-million dollars. I put it all into starting the company, and things went from there."

Grant gloves are crafted in Mexico City. The other major manufacturers of boxing gloves are Reyes (headquartered in Mexico) and Winning (a Japanese company).

Reyes has a reputation as a "puncher's glove," which stirs a measure of debate. "Some people say this one is a puncher's glove and that one is something else," says Donald Turner, who has trained Evander Holyfield and Larry Holmes. "That's nonsense. Eight ounces is eight ounces. The gloves don't knock you out; the fighter does."

But trainer-commentator Teddy Atlas (who is an Everlast consultant) disagrees. "There's some truth to the idea that Reyes is a puncher's glove," Atlas notes. "A puncher's glove is in the construction. You can get ten ounces with soft spread-out padding or you can get ten ounces with tight-stitching and compressed padding. Everlast now makes a glove that feels comfortable and conforms to the hand and is more tightly-packed," Atlas continues. "But with Reyes, there's less cushion around the punching area and the leather is pulled tighter so the glove absorbs less of the impact. That leaves more impact for the opponents face."

However, by the same laws of physics, a puncher's glove also leaves more impact to be absorbed by the hand.

"Thomas Hearns loved Reyes gloves," recalls Emanual Steward, who trained and managed Hearns through most of the fighter's career. "But puncher's gloves are harder on the hands too. When Thomas started having hand problems, I insisted on a clause in all his fight contracts stipulating that the fighters wear Everlast gloves."

In virtually all jurisdictions, it's the responsibility of the promoter to supply gloves for each fight, subject to approval by the governing commission and the fighters' contracts. Many states (including New York and Nevada) require that new gloves be used in main events and any championship fight. Used gloves in good condition are acceptable for other contests.

In New York, for championship fights, four sets of new gloves are set out on a table at the rules meeting prior to the bout. The champion chooses his fight gloves first. The challenger has second pick. Then the champion chooses a back-up pair followed again by the challenger. Gloves for all non-title fights are given to the chief inspector. He then gives proper-weight gloves for each fight to the inspector assigned to that bout, who gives them to the fighters. A fighter can object to a particular pair, in which case he'll be given another pair chosen by the inspector.

Boxing connoisseur Charles Jay points out that, to his knowledge, no commission actually weighs the gloves, which opens the door to wrongdoing. Here, Don Elbaum admits, "There were times when I manipulated a situation so my guy wore six-ounce gloves and the opponent wore eights. I've done it with eights and tens too," Elbaum adds. "But I haven't done it in this century. Whatever I did, the statute of limitations has run on it."

On the lighter side, Elbaum was the architect of one of boxing's great glove stories. On October 1, 1965, Sugar Ray Robinson fought Peter Schmidt in Johnstown, Pennsylvania. The bout took place almost twenty-five years to the day after Robinson's first professional fight. To get some pre-fight publicity, Elbaum arranged for a dinner in Ray's honor. There was a 25th-anniversary cake. The media and assorted dignitaries were in attendance. The highlight of the affair came when Elbaum got up and said, "Ray, don't ask me how I got these. It took a lot for me to convince Harry Markson [president of Madison Square Garden Boxing] to part with them. But twenty-five years ago, you made your professional debut at the Garden, and these are the gloves you wore that night."

Robinson's eyes teared up. He was genuinely moved by the moment. He took the two battered gloves and cradled them in his arms like he was holding a newborn babe. Then someone suggested he put the gloves on for a photo op. That's when the world discovered that Don Elbaum had given Sugar Ray Robinson two left gloves.

But some glove stories have an ugly aura. In an earlier time, fighters were masters at causing damage with parts of the glove that weren't meant to be used that way. Rubbing the laces in an opponent's face and thumbing him in the eye were common. Fritzie Zivic, it was said, could beat an opponent without even punching by inserting his thumb in his opponent's eyes, biceps, and kidneys.

To counter those tactics, "thumbless" gloves became mandatory in the 1980s. Technically, the term "thumbless" is a misnomer. The glove has a thumb, but it's attached to the underside of the striking surface by a short piece of fabric woven into a seam at either end.

The most famous charge of wrongdoing related to gloves was leveled against Jack Dempsey by his one-time manager Doc Kearns. Kearns, who decades earlier had fallen out with the fighter, told writer Oscar Fraley that Dempsey's gloves were loaded with plaster of Paris when he brutalized Jess Willard to win the heavyweight championship on July 4, 1919. The allegation was published after Kearns's death in the January 13, 1964, issue of *Sports Illustrated*. Dempsey sued the magazine for libel, which led to a retraction and financial settlement.

An uglier incident occurred on June 16, 1983, when 21-year-old Billy Collins Jr. fought journeyman Luis Resto in a ten-round bout at Madison Square Garden. Collins was a fighter on the rise with 11 knockouts and a 14-0 record. In the dressing room before the fight, Panama Lewis (Resto's trainer) removed much of the padding from the punching area of his fighter's gloves. Resto battered Collins for ten rounds and won a lopsided decision. Both of Collins's eyes were horribly swollen. He suffered permanently-impaired vision, was unable to fight again, began drinking heavily and, nine months after the fight, was killed in a car accident. Resto was convicted of assault, conspiracy, and criminal possession of a deadly weapon, and served two-and-a-half years in prison. Lewis spent a year in prison and was permanently barred from working as a trainer in the United States.

Nor are glove stories confined to decades past. Before the first fight between Marco Antonio Barrera and Erik Morales, Barrera wanted to wear Reyes gloves while Morales voiced a preference for Winning. Nevada State Athletic Commission executive director Marc Ratner decreed that the issue would be resolved by a coin toss. Barrera said that was fine with him but, if he lost the toss, he wouldn't fight. The coin turned his way, so the issue became moot. Nevada now allows fighters to wear different-brand gloves as long as they're on the state's approved list (which includes Everlast, Grant, Winning, and Reyes).

One year later, Barrera found himself emeshed in another glove controversy when he fought Naseem Hamed. The contracts called for both boxers to wear Reyes gloves. The Nevada commission had agreed to requests that Hamed be allowed to wear green and Barrera yellow. Then, at the weigh-in, Barrera chose a pair of yellow gloves for himself. But Hamed had first choice under the contract and, changing his color preference, decided that the pair chosen by Barrera was the one he wanted. Thereafter, the situation degenerated into chaos. Two hours before the fight, the gloves still hadn't been chosen. Marc Ratner brought six pairs of red Reyes gloves to Hamed's dressing room. Naseem tried on each pair and pronounced them all unsatisfactory. Three more pairs were presented. Finally, after examining each glove, Hamed choose a pair. Then Ratner journeyed to Barrera's dressing room, where Marco Antonio's hands were being taped. Ratner set the remaining eight pairs of gloves on a table. One of Barrera's seconds walked over and, without looking twice, pointed to a pair at random.

And then there was the weigh-in for Roy Jones versus John Ruiz. Norman Stone (Ruiz's trainer) accused Alton Merkerson (his counterpart in the Jones camp) of tampering with Jones's gloves by removing them from their shrink-wrapping without a representative of the Ruiz camp being present. Actually, Ratner had done it. Regardless, one word led to another. Stone grabbed Merkerson by the shirt; Merkerson whacked him with a pretty good righthand; and the two men topped off the weigh-in platform into the crowd.

But the fighter with the most glove anecdotes to his credit is—drumroll, please—Muhammad Ali.

In his ninth pro fight, Cassius Clay fought Alex Miteff in Louisville. Teddy Brenner, who was affiliated with the promotion, later recalled, "A couple of hours before the fight, we realized that no one had brought boxing gloves. The stores were closed. It was too late to bring gloves in from someplace else. Finally, we found two pairs that were half-horsehair and half-foam-rubber. They'd been lying around in some gym for a long time and were hard as a rock. We thought it would help Miteff. He was a good puncher, and Clay couldn't punch. After five rounds, it was an even fight. Then, in the sixth, Clay hit him on the chin and knocked him out with one punch. In the dressing room afterward, Miteff kept asking what happened. He couldn't believe that Cassius Clay had knocked him out."

Ultimately, Ali would play a role in the elimination of horsehair from most gloves. According to George Horowitz, Ben Nadorf (then president of Everlast) attended Ali-Frazier III in Manila and was mortified by the fact that, as the fight wore on, the fighters' gloves (manufactured by

Everlast) began to lose their shape in the heat and high humidity. Thereafter, Nadorf decreed, horsehair would no longer be used in Everlast gloves. Everlast's padding now consists of a mixture of poly foam, latex foam and PVC foam.

Meanwhile, on June 18, 1963, Clay (18-and-0 by then) fought Henry Cooper in London. Marking time until he could make good on his prediction of a fifth-round knockout, Cassius got clocked with a left hook with five seconds left in the fourth round. He fell through the ropes, rolled back into the ring, and staggered to his feet, quite literally saved by the bell.

There are two kinds of being "hurt" in boxing. The first is when a fighter feels pain; most often from a body shot or blow to the ears, eyes, or nose. The second kind of hurt is when a fighter is dazed and loses control over his reflexes. At that point, Clay was feeling no pain.

"Cassius split his glove on the seam near the thumb," Angelo Dundee later explained. "Actually, it happened in the first round. I spotted the tear and told him, 'Keep your hand closed.' I didn't want anyone to see it because everything was going our way. Then, at the end of the fourth round, he got nailed. So when he came back to the corner, I helped the split a little, pulled it to the side, and made the referee aware that there was a torn glove."

No back-up gloves were available and, after a brief delay, the fight resumed. "I don't know how much time that got us," Dundee acknowledged. "Maybe a minute, but it was enough. If we hadn't gotten the extra time, I don't know what would have happened. I think Cassius would have made it through, but we don't have to answer that question."

Eight months later, in his next fight, Clay was in the ring against Sonny Liston. In one of boxing's most dramatic crises, he fought the entire fifth round with impaired vision believed to have been caused by an astringent that dripped into his eyes after having been rubbed onto Liston's gloves.

But the most endearing tale of Muhammad Ali and gloves dates to his 1975 encounter with Joe Bugner in Malaysia. That happening was notable for the pre-fight rules meeting. After going through the normal, interminably boring regulatory minutiae, the local commissioner announced that the fighters' gloves would be held in a local prison until the day of the fight. That got Ali's attention.

'Wait a minute," Muhammad interrupted. "You're putting my gloves in jail? This is awful. How can you do that? How can you put my gloves in jail? They ain't done nothing (pause) yet."❏

*Rocky Marciano evokes images of an era when boxing was a true national sport and whoever wore the heavyweight crown was one of the most famous men in the world.*

# REMEMBERING ROCKY MARCIANO

The heavyweight division is in wretched condition. There are four world sanctioning organizations, and each one has its own heavyweight champion. Athletes who would have been first-rate fighters decades ago now play middle-linebacker in the NFL or power forward in the NBA.

It wasn't always that way. Fifty years ago, Rocky Marciano was in the midst of a glorious championship reign at a time when the heavyweight championship was the most exalted title in sports.

Marciano was an idol in a simpler era, when professional athletes were heroes and sportswriters were complicit in building legends rather than exposing them. To the public, all that really mattered was that Rocky had 49 wins in 49 fights and retired in 1956 as the undefeated heavyweight champion of the world.

This is a time of year when Marciano's family and friends remember him. He was born on September 1, 1923, and died in a plane crash on August 31, 1969, one day shy of his 46th birthday. Thus, it seems appropriate to revisit The Brockton Blockbuster through own words and those of others who knew him well.

*Charlie Goldman* (Marciano's trainer): "I gotta guy who's short, stoop-shouldered, and balding with two left feet. They all look better than he does as far as the moves are concerned, but they don't look so good on the canvas. God, how he can punch."

*Al Weill* (Marciano's manager, as his fighter was moving toward a title shot): "Rocky is a poor Italian boy from a poor Italian family and he appreciates the buck more than almost anybody. He's only got two halfway decent purses so far, and it was like a tiger tasting blood."

*Rocky Marciano* (to a reporter who asked if he thought he'd win his upcoming fight against Joe Louis): "That was a fucking dumb question. If I didn't think I was gonna win, why the hell would I be fighting?"

*Ed Fitzgerald* (one of the premier sportswriters of the Marciano era): "Rocky is not in there to outpoint anybody with an exhibition of boxing skill. He is a primitive fighter who stalks his prey until he can belt him with that frightening right-hand crusher. He is one of the easiest fighters in the ring to hit. You can, as with an enraged grizzly bear, slow him down and make him shake his head if you hit him hard enough to wound him, but you can't make him back up. Slowly, relentlessy, ruthlessly, he moves in on you. Sooner or later, he clubs you down."

*Rex Layne* (after being knocked out by Marciano): "I was on my face. I heard the count from one to ten. I kept telling myself that I had to get up, but I couldn't move. I couldn't make myself move. It was the strangest feeling."

*Rocky Marciano* (after knocking out Jersey Joe Walcott to capture the heavyweight crown): "What could be better than walking down any street in any city and knowing you're the heavyweight champion of the world?"

*Archie Moore* (who was knocked out by Marciano): "Rocky didn't know enough boxing to know what a feint was. He never tried to outguess you. He just kept trying to knock your brains out. If he missed you with one punch, he just threw another. I had the braggadocio and the skill and the guts, but that wasn't enough. Marciano beat me down."

*Rocky Marciano*: "Why waltz with a guy for ten rounds if you can knock him out in one?"

*Al Weill*: "Rocky was great when he had to be great."

*Rocky Marciano* (explaining why he wouldn't come out of retirement for a big payday against heavyweight champion Ingemar Johansson): "I don't want to be remembered as a beaten champion."

*Jimmy Cannon*: "Rocky Marciano stood out in boxing like a rose in a garbage dump."❑

*On May 6, 2005, at the eightieth annual Boxing Writers Association of America awards banquet, I received the Nat Fleischer Award for Career Excellence in Boxing Journalism. My remarks in accepting the honor follow.*

# AFTERWORD: MAY 6, 2005

My involvement with boxing began two decades ago. I had just finished writing a novel about Beethoven and wanted to write a book about sports. You can't just walk into Yankee Stadium and talk with Derek Jeter. You can't walk into the American Airlines Arena and talk with Shaquille O'Neal. But boxing is an open sport. That's one of the many wonderful things about it. Anyone who wants to can walk into a gym and talk with the fighters who are training there.

Since then, in my writing, I've tried to paint a fair and accurate portrait of boxing:

Of its bare-knuckle days.

Of Muhammad Ali, who remains a transcendental towering figure.

And of the contemporary boxing scene.

I'm very grateful for this honor and hope it opens the way for recognition of other Internet writers and scribblers of books.

And the only other thought I want to leave you with comes from Mike Jones. I met Mike in 1984, when I began researching *The Black Lights*, which was my first book about boxing. Mike was a fight manager and a great boxing guy. He looked after his fighters in every way. His word was good. He never walked out on a deal.

Mike died of complications from multiple myeloma at age 55. He was taken from us much too soon. But the day we met, Mike said something that has always stayed with me. They're the words I used to start *The Black Lights*. And in closing, I'd like to share them with you now.

"To understand boxing, you have to understand tradition and what it takes to get inside a ring. You have to learn about promoters and television and what goes on inside a fighter's head from the time his career begins until the day it ends. You have to grasp the reality of smashed faces and pain, and understand how they can be part of something courageous, exciting, and beautiful.

Boxing is beautiful, the purest sport in the world. You can knock promoters, you can knock managers, trainers, even fighters. But don't knock boxing. It's the best sport there is; and anyone who's ever been involved will tell you, it's an honor to be associated with boxing."❏

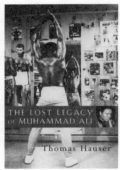
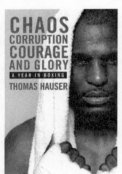